Rewriting the Rules

We live in a time of great uncertainty about relationships. We search for The One, but find ourselves staying single because nobody measures up. We long for a happily-ever-after, but break-up after break-up leaves us bruised and confused. We find a partner, but the reality of our relationships is not what we expected, and it becomes hard to balance them with all the other things that we want out of life. At the same time that marriage shows itself to be the one 'recession proof' industry, rates of separation and break-up soar ever higher.

Rewriting the Rules is a friendly guide through the complicated – often contradictory – rules of love: the advice that is given about attraction and sex, monogamy and conflict, gender and commitment. It asks questions, such as: Which to choose from all the rules on offer? Do we stick to the old rules we learnt growing up, or try something new and risk being out on our own? And what about the times when the rules we love by seem to make things worse, rather than better?

This book considers how the rules are being 'rewritten' in various ways, giving the power to the reader to find an approach which best fits their situation.

Meg Barker is a senior lecturer in psychology at the Open University, and a therapist specialising in sexual and relationship therapy. Meg has previously published books on sexuality and counselling and is co-editor of the journal Psychology & Sexuality. You can read Meg's blog to accompany this book at www.rewriting-the-rules.com.

Rewriting the Rules

An integrative guide to love,
sex and relationships

Meg Barker

Routledge
Taylor & Francis Group

LONDON AND NEW YORK

First published 2013
by Routledge
27 Church Road, Hove, East Sussex BN3 2FA

Simultaneously published in the USA and Canada
by Routledge
711 Third Avenue, New York, NY 10017

Routledge is an imprint of the Taylor & Francis Group, an informa business

British Library Cataloguing in Publication Data
A catalogue record for this book is available from the British Library

Library of Congress Cataloging in Publication Data
    Barker, Meg.
    Rewriting the rules: an integrative guide to love,
    sex and relationships / authored by Meg Barker.
    p. cm.
    Includes bibliographical references and index.
    ISBN 978–0–415–51762–1 (hbk.)—ISBN 978–0–415–51763–8 (pbk.)
    1. Interpersonal relations—Psychological aspects.
    2. Man-woman relationships—Psychological aspects.
    3. Love. 4. Sex (Psychology) I. Title.
    BF1045.I58B37 2012
    306.7—dc23
    2012006609

ISBN: 978–0–415–51762–1 (hbk)
ISBN: 978–0–415–51763–8 (pbk)
ISBN: 978–0–203–09766–3 (ebk)

Typeset in Times New Roman & Gill Sans
by Swales & Willis Ltd, Exeter, Devon, UK

MIX
Paper from
responsible sources
FSC
www.fsc.org   FSC® C004839

Printed and bound by CPI Group (UK) Ltd, Croydon, CR0 4YY

Contents

Illustrations

Figures

Tables

Acknowledgements

A book is never really the work of one person: rather the author named on the cover is a point of connection between the ideas of others and the reader. Many people have contributed to this book through their own work, through sharing reflections and conversation, and through being who they are. I'd like to acknowledge some of them here.

Primarily, my thanks go to the students, clients, and community members who have worked with me over the last decade, for being courageous enough to open up about themselves and to ask such difficult questions. It is mainly through classroom, therapy room, and workshop discussions that my own assumptions have been challenged and that I've been forced to keep asking how these ideas work in real life. I can't name you all, but hopefully you'll see how you have shaped this book.

Then I would like to thank the writers, colleagues and friends who have influenced my thoughts – both those I know personally and those I only know through their writings – particularly Rosalind Gill, Darren Langdridge, Feona Attwood, Lisa Downing, Jamie Heckert, Steven Stanley, Trevor Butt, Vivien Burr, Stephen Batchelor, Martine Batchelor, John Welwood, Pema Chödrön, Emmy Van Deurson, Ernesto Spinelli, Mick Cooper, Ken Plummer, Jeffrey Weeks, Kenneth Gergen, Alex Iantaffi, Ani Ritchie, Darren Oldridge, Peter Hegarty, Dossie Easton, Bjarne Holmes, Sandra Byers, Rachel O'Neill, David Gauntlett, Nash Popovic, Petra Boynton, Trish Oak, Gary Wood, and Estelle Noonan. Special thanks to Gayle Rubin for her inspirational work and for allowing me to use the charmed circle diagram in Chapter 4.

I am very grateful to the people who've read this book in various forms and encouraged me to keep going and get it out there, particularly Erich Schultz, Laura Harvey, Paolo Pizzolla, Phil Cooper, and Jess and Bee Barker. Many thanks to all at Routledge, especially my editor Joanne Forshaw, for believing in it and for helping me to get to this point. Also, much gratitude to the Open University and to all my colleagues there for their continued support of my work.

This book is dedicated to Christina Richards, who provided all of these things: challenges and questions, knowledge and insight, and support and encouragement. With so much love.

Introduction

Never buy drinks for a girl you fancy: Don't go Dutch. Get her talking: Speak about yourself. Be open about your feelings: Don't come on too heavy. Never waste an opportunity to say 'I love you': Don't be the first to use the L word. Always let him call the shots: Show the initiative. Don't use complete sentences during sex: Talk dirty. Act independent: Be easy to live with. Take him at face value: Figure out the hidden reason why he's upset. Avoid conflict: Schedule healthy arguments. Never forgive cheating: Infidelity can be the best thing for a couple. Work at your relationship: Be spontaneous . . .

Uncertainty and the rules

We are in a state of uncertainty about relationships.

Never before in our history has there been more advice on who and how to love. Online ads invite us to click for the top ten ways to find our perfect match. Agony aunts and uncles pass judgement on every celebrity break-up and make-up. Reality TV shows advise on how to fix our relationships. Pop songs tell us how to feel when falling in and out of love. Billboard advertisements confront us with images of happy couples who are somehow 'getting it right' as they eat their breakfast cereal, drive their car, and sit on their three piece suite. All day long we are bombarded by rules about relationships: who to be in order to get and keep one, what to want and expect from one, and how to know when it isn't working any more.

Also, never before have the rules we receive about relationships been more confusing and contradictory, as you can see from the selection at the start of this Introduction, which have been taken from various websites, magazines, newspapers and self-help books. At the same time that everything from official forms to social networking sites seem intent on defining us *by* our relationships, there is less and less clarity about what exactly we're talking about when we speak of relationships. If we were honest, perhaps we'd all tick the box which says 'it's complicated'.

So we are in a state of uncertainty, and it is all the more terrifying because it is in an arena which has the highest possible scope for pain and distress, as well as pleasure and fulfilment. Get it right – we are told – and we could achieve the ultimate happily-ever-after: the security of being seen as we are and loved for it, the safety of complete belonging, all of our needs and desires met. Get it wrong, however, and we risk being seen as we are and found wanting: the possibility of rejection after rejection. We could get badly hurt and, perhaps even worse, find that we are capable of badly hurting others. No wonder we look for rules to tell us how to get it right.

How did we get to this point? Historians and sociologists point to several changes which have altered the ways in which we perceive, and experience, love.[1]

Greater equality between the genders, and increased recognition that relationships can be between people of the same, as well as different, genders, has meant that couples today are generally composed of two independent people who have their own dreams and goals.[2] We have a strong sense of individual identity and desire for personal fulfilment.

At the same time, however, we look to relationships as our main source of validation, meaning and belonging, perhaps because of the decline of religion and community, and the insecurity and instability we now face in the world of work. Weddings are the one industry which seems to be unaffected by economic recession.[3]

This situation aggravates a tension which is already there whenever we are in a relationship with another person: the tension that we are *separate* people and also *together* in the relationship. People want fulfilling, rewarding relationships in which all their needs are met at the same time as wanting to be free to pursue their own goals and write their own life-story.[4] We see that tension played out in movies from *Knocked Up* to *The Devil Wears Prada*, as the main characters try to find ways to balance their own needs and desires with their relationship. Relationship therapists liken the tension between pursuing your own goals and managing your relationship to the notoriously difficult activity of simultaneously rubbing your belly and patting your head.[5]

Many writers argue that these shifts in society are the reason that relationships are in such a precarious place, with around half of marriages ending in divorce,[6] up to two thirds of married people having affairs at some point,[7] and one in three people living alone.[8] Things that used to be taken for granted now have to be figured out and negotiated between people: At what point does dating become a relationship? How much should our lives be entwined or separate? Do we live together? Sleep together? Have kids together? Whose job is prioritized: the one who makes the most money, the one who enjoys it most, or the one who is less interested in home or children? Should we stay friendly with our ex-partners? As the authors of the aptly titled book *The Normal Chaos of Love* put it, 'love is becoming a blank that lovers must fill in themselves'.[9]

Unfortunately, given the need for communication when filling in this blank, people are generally poorly educated about communicating with partners. It is assumed that relationships will come naturally to us and that if they don't there is something wrong with us. Perhaps this is why there is an increasing demand for books and TV programmes about how to manage relationships. But unfortunately, as we have seen, these often contribute to, rather than clarifying, the confusion. One of my main aims in this book is to demonstrate that it is understandable, normal, and, in fact, *sensible* to be confused about relationships, whether you are in one or not.

The overall idea of this book is that, when we are faced with such high levels of uncertainty, we tend to grab onto something for safety and to hold it tight.[10] In the case of relationships, what we grab onto is rules. Perhaps most of the time people turn back to old familiar rules, even if these didn't necessarily work very well in the past and may not apply to our current situation. At least we know them, and that is reassuring when things are so uncertain. As we'll see in Chapter 5, a lot of the existing relationship rules are about gender: what it means to be 'the man' or 'the woman' in a relationship, and how to relate to 'the opposite sex'. The alternative route that many people now take is to come up with new rules for their relationships, either in groups or communities, or on their own. However, there is a tendency to hold onto new rules just as tightly as other people do to old ones – sometimes even more so, because it is hard to be outside the mainstream.

Both of these paths (clinging onto the existing rules, or grasping for new ones) lead to more, rather than less, distress. Instead of making things better, they often make them worse.

Clinging onto existing rules has led to a culture which holds up being 'normal' as more important than almost anything else.[11] We have an image of a normal relationship in our heads in the same way that most people, when asked to draw a picture of a house, draw pretty much the same thing as one another.[12] Try it for yourself.

In the same way that hardly anyone lives in anything that looks remotely like this picture, so none of our relationships look much like our idea of 'normal'. We therefore desperately try to be *more* normal, fearing that people will notice if we stray at all outside of this, and beating ourselves up whenever we can't manage it. In sex therapy, counsellors see person after person who is more concerned with making sure that they're having a normal sex life (whatever that means) than with finding out what turns them on and how to do that. Similarly, a lot of us are far more concerned with getting and maintaining a normal-looking appearance than on whether our body feels good. And people are very concerned with having a normal relationship which ticks all the boxes of what is expected. The pressure to be normal constrains people and leaves them anxiously monitoring themselves and others for any sign that they might *not* be normal. This is perfectly illustrated in the episode of *Sex and the City* in which Carrie becomes convinced that every man she dates turns out to be abnormal in some way. She frantically searches her new boyfriend's apartment for signs of his secret freakishness, only to be caught in the act by him and thus revealed, herself, to be a freak.

But what of those of us who step outside the existing rules, whether through choice or because no other option is available? Often, we too feel the need to grab tightly onto the rules that we come up with. In part, this is because we are regularly excluded and treated with suspicion by those who find it threatening that there may be another way of doing things.

This situation creates an us and them: 'us' being the normal people striving to have normal relationships, and 'them' being the outsiders who are doing something freaky, unnatural, or wrong. In such situations 'they' are, at best, ridiculed, and, at worst, aggressively rejected. Think about how people have been treated over the years when they publicly step outside the accepted rules about whom it is appropriate to have sex with, and how: celebrities who have paid for sex, been unfaithful, or been outed as gay. Given this kind of treatment, it is tempting for 'them' to either try to prove how normal they are in every other respect, or to grab tightly onto their own rules and to dismiss the 'normals' in order to justify and defend what they are doing.

So all of us, 'normal' and 'outsider', end up grabbing hard onto the rules: comparing ourselves against others and judging them, fearing that we might be doing it wrong and desperately trying to prove that we aren't.

This book takes various key aspects of relationships and, for each one, explores what the existing rules are and why they might not always work so well. It then considers people and groups who have stepped outside those existing rules and what they are doing, exploring what we might learn from such alternatives. However, it also explores the limitations of any new rules and how they can become problematic themselves if held too rigidly. Finally, it explores a third alternative to either grabbing onto existing rules *or* desperately seeking new ones. This involves staying in the uncertainty of *not* having clear rules and finding a way to go on which doesn't require grabbing hold of anything. If that sounds a rather tall order, in reality it means that at least we try to notice when we are grasping onto rules and thus attempt to hold them more loosely.

Rewriting the rules

Of course, there usually aren't rules out there about how to do relationships in the sense of laws or policies that everyone agrees upon. There are no inscribed commandments of love or legal documents of dating, and new groups and communi-

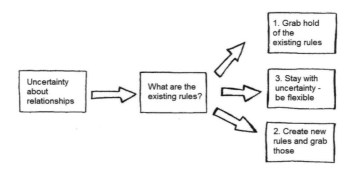

Figure 0.1 Rules options

ties rarely have a written manifesto either. I could have titled this book 'Retelling the Story', 'Rewriting the Script' or all kinds of titles that capture the same sense that there is *something* out there about how to do relationships which we might want to question. I chose the word 'rules' because it can often *feel* like there is a set of unwritten rules which everyone is trying to follow and which are unquestioned and taken for granted. They are just what everyone does.

I have also used the word 'rules' because, lately, people have been tempted to determine a set of rules of relationships which could be written down and followed in order to have a successful love life. There are several books and articles with titles like *The Rules*, *The Rules of Love*, *The Rules of the Game*, and so on. In this book I'm suggesting that we might want to be cautious about such rules. They may have something useful to offer, but they should stand up to questioning and shouldn't be grasped as the answer to everything. Perhaps the only rule of *this* book is that there isn't going to be one universal answer, but there *are* a lot of useful and interesting questions that are worth asking.

The rules I'm talking about are really 'ways of doing things' that we sense that we should follow. For example, a 'rule' might be that we should have a certain number of dates before we have sex with somebody, or that after a certain length of time together it isn't appropriate for us to still be dating anybody else. A lot of these are also linked to an idea that it is normal, natural, or morally better, to behave in some ways rather than others. For example, it is often thought to be natural for men to want sex as soon as possible, or normal to fall in love with one person at a time, or morally better to have some kinds of sex rather than other kinds.

Human beings are always searching for meaning: patterns and rules that make sense of what is going on around them. That's why you see a vase, or two people about to kiss, in the visual illusion (rather than just a bunch of lines and shadings). It is also why we develop our own system of rules about relationships from the messages that we pick up from the world around us. Some of these

Figure 0.2 Making meaning

come from our observations of others as we grow up (parents, siblings, teachers, friends), others from books, magazines, and films, and others from our own experience. For example, the character Rob Gordon in the book, and film, *High Fidelity* comes up with the rule that the women in his life will always reject him for somebody better. This rule is based on his 'top five all time worst break-up' experiences, plus exposure to a large quantity of heart-breaking pop songs. This is a good example of how our rules can be wrong and how they can trap us. Rob is reluctant to commit to his girlfriend at least partly because he fears the inevitable rejection. When he investigates those past break-ups, he discovers that, in at least one case, he was the one who did the rejecting, and in others he would certainly have ended things if the other person had not done so.

Whether it is our own personal system of rules, or the wider set of taken-for-granted rules to which we are exposed, a big problem with rules is the idea that there is one 'right' or 'best' way of doing things. The implication of this would, of course, be that any other ways of doing things is somehow wrong, inferior, or deviant. So, if we believe that the 'right' kind of relationship involves people who have a similar level of attractiveness, then those who don't fit into this category will have more of a struggle. If we believe there is one right way of having sex, or committing to someone, or raising a family, then, again, other ways will be frowned upon. I have friends who are constantly regarded with pity at parties when it is revealed that they are *still* single. I know couples who are pressured at every family event about when they are going to tie the knot. A colleague tells me of being taken to one side by well-meaning friends who worry that she is damaging her child by not finding a new partner to live with them.

The rules, whatever they are, are not only bad for people who fall outside them in some way. They can also be tough for those who are stuck inside the rule system struggling to stick to the 'right way' of doing things. There is the teenager trying to decide when to sleep with her boyfriend so as not to be labelled a slag or tight, rather than making a decision based on her own desires. There is the elderly couple who want to be sexual but find it hard to ask for advice about how to make it physically easier, because there is a taboo about having sex beyond the age of sixty. There is the person who loses the sympathy of friends when, six months on, he is not completely over a break-up. This book will question some of these ideas about the one true way of doing relationships and open up other options for consideration.

Over the rest of the book, we'll cover nine key aspects of relationships. Chapter 1 focuses on yourself because, as we have seen, it is that tension between who we are and the demands of being in a relationship which is a major element in the uncertainty we're all experiencing. We'll look in more detail at how we relate to ourselves, before considering how we relate to other people. Chapter 2 explores attraction, and particularly the role of physical appearance in relationships. A major source of anxiety today is how we look: whether we are attractive enough for a partner, and whether we are attracted to them.

Chapter 3 moves on to love itself. We'll spend more time on the happily-ever-after and what it is that people are looking for in The One. We'll also think about which relationships we prioritize in our lives. Chapter 4 then focuses on sex, a source of great anxiety and distress. We'll examine that idea of normal sex for which people are striving, what that looks like, and the impact of trying to force ourselves into a one-size-fits-all kind of sexuality. Chapter 5 explores gender, because so many of the existing rules about relationships are about what it means to be a man or a woman. We'll consider what is gained and lost by trying to match up to ideals of masculinity and femininity, and how this relates to love.

A major existing rule of relationships is that they should be monogamous, hence the pressure to find The One, and the fact that cheating and infidelity are seen as such a problem. Chapter 6 will examine the rules of monogamy and how these are being rewritten in various ways in modern relationships. Chapter 7 moves onto conflict in relationships, which often happens when people are seen as having broken the unwritten rules of monogamy. We'll think about the rules of conflict and how they help or hinder us in communicating about these, and other, problems. One possible outcome of conflict, of course, is relationship break-up. Chapter 8 explores the rules for breaking up with someone and the implications of these for relationships with ex, current, and potential, partners. Finally, one of the main existing rules about relationships is that successful relationships are those which last. Chapter 9 considers the rules that we commit to in long-term relationships, and what it means to have a successful relationship.

Chapter 10 then leaves you with some ideas about how to carry on with the journey you've started by reading this book: identifying the taken-for-granted rules, questioning them, and developing your own rules of relationships.

An anti-self-help book?

This book is a kind of anti-self-help book. For one thing, I don't want it to be another list of the conventional rules of relationships that are already out there. It isn't hard to pick up on how we are expected to manage our relationships: the rules are present everywhere from fairy tales and kids' cartoons through to women's and men's magazines and self-help books. Equally, I don't want to provide a list of alternative rules which I personally think are better than those already in existence. Self-help books are often sold on the promise that the author has figured it all out and is now going to provide you with answers which will enable you to have a better and happier life. I believe that human relationships are a complicated business of which we all try to make sense throughout our lives. There is no one true way of managing them, but rather we're all engaged in a process of finding out what works for us. This book thus aims to help you to explore *your* ways and to consider alternatives, rather than setting up another list of rules for you to follow and feel bad about when they don't necessarily work for you.

The other way that this is an anti-self-help book is that most such books implicitly blame you, the reader, for any problems you have, locating the cause of misery in your own faulty thinking, lack of understanding, or toxic emotions. If only you could follow the rules, or accept the gender differences, or find your true path, then it would all be better. As we'll see in Chapter 1, some philosophers have criticized the whole industry of self-help, counselling and psychotherapy for creating a society in which we all look into ourselves for the root of our problems.

There is a place for examining our ways of thinking and doing things. However, it is important to recognize outside forces as well as inner ones, to question the world around us and to see how wider messages and our own ways of seeing things are intrinsically bound up together. As I've mentioned, we all inhabit a culture which is saturated with stories, images and rules about relationships, some of which may be helpful, some less so, and some – I believe – potentially damaging. Our own personal rules don't come from nowhere, but are heavily dependent on the rules to which we are exposed. Where I do think we have some power (and responsibility) as individuals is in choosing which of these rules we want to take on board and which we don't. However, I will also talk in the final chapter of the book about how easy – or not – it might be to go against some of the entrenched and commonly accepted rules.

These are questions which face and tax us all, and we're all looking for answers that fit us and the people we are in relationships with. There is no one who has got it all 'right', however much some authors would like to say otherwise. Many people are invested in the rules and in ensuring that we follow them just like they do. If someone tries to prevent you from questioning the rules, or from coming up with your own rules, then you have to ask why what you do is so important to them, and why they prioritize maintaining the rules over your well-being. Going back to the only rules of this book:

There is no universal answer
&
It is okay to question the rules

What you do after you've questioned the rules is up to you, but please do, by all means, question them.

My aim for this book is for it to be a conversation, not a lecture. I would love it if you would *use* the book rather than simply reading it. The greatest compliment I can imagine as an author would be to see a scruffy, falling-apart, broken-spined, scrawled-upon version of something that I had written. In particular, before reading each chapter, you might find it useful to think about your answers to the main questions we'll be asking:

- What are the taken-for-granted rules about this issue? Think about the kinds of conversations you have, and overhear, and the messages we get in mainstream media (Hollywood movies, primetime TV, popular magazines and online)?
- Why might we question these rules? Are there any problems with them? Are they useful for people? What are the assumptions behind them?
- What alternatives are available to us? There usually isn't just one set of rules out there in the world. Think about the alternatives you hear considered in

conversations and in the media. Were there different ways that people thought about these things in the past? Are they done differently by different cultures or religions? Do you know of any groups or individuals who see things differently?

We ask ourselves questions all the time about how we should manage our relationships: what our rules should be. A businessman on his mobile irritably explains why he is upset that his partner is late for their date. Two teenage girls try to figure out why one of their boyfriends is angry that they kissed each other on the dancefloor last night. A couple of old friends spend dinner going through their mutual acquaintances: who is together, who is splitting up, who is having a baby. They judge each behaviour as good or bad, considering whether they expected it, and making predictions for the future.

The rules are around us in the babble of everyday conversation, and you already have your own expertise to bring to the questions raised in this book. You have your own relationships, your own conversations, and your own readings of the messages around you. While I'll try to draw on ideas from cultures and communities beyond my own, you'll also find that you have additional experiences to bring in about what the rules were in the area – and generation – in which you grew up, and what alternatives are considered acceptable, or possible, by your community or network of friends.

The other consequence of this book being a conversation is that it is open for you to come up with your own conclusions, and these are very likely to be different from mine. You might be perfectly happy with many of the rules which are out there, for example, and just value the opportunity to look at them a little more closely and think about why they work so well for you. Or you might already have questioned many of these rules and come up with your own alternatives, in which case the first parts of each chapter may feel like familiar ground.

Inevitably my own ideas – about the value of embracing uncertainty, for example – will come across in this book. It's impossible for them not to. But I hope that you will question and challenge these as much as the other ideas we're exploring. It is useful for us all to identify the rules that we are living by, to gently challenge them and to open up our options. But the choices about which rules to question and which to reject, which to accept and which to alter, has to be up to you.

Chapter 1

Rewriting the rules of yourself

What are the rules?

It might seem strange in a book about love that the first chapter is not about our relationships with other people, but rather our relationship with ourselves. Why are we starting here?

An early piece of advice that I remember hearing about relationships was 'you have to love yourself before you can love anyone else'. Or, sometimes, it was 'you have to love yourself before anyone else can love you'. Either way, the idea was that you need a foundation of loving yourself before good relationships with other people are possible.

On reflection, I think the situation is more complicated than this. I'm not sure whether it is possible to love yourself in your entirety. In fact we'll see in this chapter that this is a particularly big challenge these days. Also, like it or not, we are always in some form of relationships with other people. So, if the idea is that we have to get our relationship with ourselves to be really good before we relate to other people, that isn't going to be possible. As we'll see in Chapter 6, the notion of separating ourselves from others is tricky, because we are always entwined in relationships in one way or another. Also, we could get more philosophical and wonder, who is this self who is being loved, and who is the self doing the loving? But we'll come to that later. ...

What I'm suggesting for now is that, as with all such rules, the 'love yourself before loving anyone else' rule is only useful to a point. It will bend and eventually break if we try to stretch it too far. However, there is benefit in thinking about our relationships with ourselves as the foundation of our other relationships. We need to be somewhat okay with ourselves in order to be okay with other people, and in order to let them in close and to handle being loved by them. We need to know ourselves, at least to some degree, in order to know which relationships are likely to be good for us. We also need to know what buttons we have which other people might inadvertently push (something we'll explore more in Chapter 7, when we look at relationship conflict).

Sadly, having good relationships with ourselves is not given a high priority. When we are young, there is a lot of focus on what we need to improve about ourselves, rather than on being content with who we are. Education overwhelmingly concentrates on developing academic abilities, rather than emotional and social ones like how to deal with difficult feelings or how to communicate with other people. Most people spend little time by themselves and often become quite fearful of solitude. Instead, they keep busy with work, activities, watching TV or socializing. Their very selves have become unfamiliar to them, perhaps even scary, in terms of what they might find out if they spent time alone. Most people have unkind thoughts about themselves chattering away much of the time, so it is understandable that they're not too keen to be quiet enough to hear them.

So what are the taken-for-granted rules about our relationships with ourselves?

The first rule is that there is something called our self that we can point to and describe. We see this in the idea that we can 'find ourself', 'know ourself', 'love ourself' or 'be true to ourself'. These all imply that there is a clear self that we can identify in order to find, know, love, or to which we can be true. This rule is so taken for granted that it might seem peculiar indeed to question it. We think of ourselves as something that can be summarized in a few words in a personal ad (SWF, GSOH, etc.). We are fascinated by personality quizzes, in magazines and on social networking sites, which might reveal to us the truth about who we are. All of this suggests that there is a true self at the core of us that can be discovered, and also that it is something that is relatively fixed and stable over time.

At the same time, most people have a great fear that their self is somehow lacking and flawed.[1] Perhaps this is part of living in a consumer culture. Advertising has to tell us that there is something wrong with us in order to sell us a product that will fix it, so it invents new problems for people to be anxious about (from how white our sheets are, to how many friends we have) and then offers us the solution (a new stronger detergent, or a soft drink that will suddenly make us popular). This way of thinking has permeated far wider than the selling of domestic products, so that there are now more and more names for 'disorders' and 'dysfunctions' people might have, and proliferating drugs and therapies on offer to fix them for a price. Many magazines, reality TV programmes and self-help books also rely on us thinking that there is something wrong with ourselves that needs fixing: we're not having good enough sex, wearing the right clothes, being a good enough partner or parent, or feeling happy enough with our lives. And this author or TV presenter is going to set us right.

As well as fearing that we are lacking, the bar for what makes a successful self gets higher and higher.[2] The cult of celebrity suggests that the only way to be successful is to be famous and approved of by everyone. Reality TV programmes sell us the idea that we could get there overnight, if only we were good enough. Meanwhile, all the other contestants are fired week after week for not making the grade, fuelling the idea that most of us are lacking. Even celebrities themselves are constantly scrutinized for ways in which they are failing, as photo-journalists try to catch a picture of them behaving badly, or zoom in for a close up of some tiny bodily 'imperfection'. We are encouraged to compare ourselves against other people to judge how well we are doing on all kinds of measures, and the bar is set so high that we are bound to find ourselves wanting. The pressure is on to be perfect, or at least to make damn sure that we present ourselves as such and hide the ugly truth from everyone around us, including ourselves.

A great example of this self-monitoring, self-perfecting culture[3] can be seen in the novel *Bridget Jones's Diary*. Every day, at the start of her diary, Bridget lists her weight and alcohol intake, her cigarette and calorie consumption. She scrutinizes herself to see whether she has measured up, and beats herself up for her social faux pas and embarrassing mistakes. One reason for the huge popularity of the Bridget Jones books and movies was that so many people saw something of themselves in the character of Bridget. They, too, were convinced that happiness, a relationship, and a successful career, could be theirs if only they could somehow manage to make themselves better.

So, we could summarize the taken-for-granted rules of relating to ourselves like this:

- We are one fixed self that stays the same over time.
- This self is lacking in some way.
- We need to monitor it carefully in order to make sure we don't show this lack to anybody else.
- We need to work at perfecting ourselves and fixing all our faults.

Why question the rules?

These rules are problematic, because they have the potential to leave us in a painful state of oscillation between being hard and soft on ourselves.

When we're hard on ourselves, we think 'I'm rubbish compared to other people, and I must get better by eradicating all my flaws'. When we're soft on ourselves, we think 'I'm rubbish and may as well accept it because that's just who I am, and nothing I do can make it better'. In the hard state, we monitor ourselves closely, trying to maintain control over everything we do, always with the fear in the back of our mind that we're going to mess up and that will be the end of the world. In the soft state, we just give up and there doesn't seem much point to anything. We may as well stay under the duvet or distracted by whatever we find comforting.

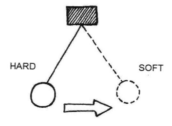

Figure 1.1 Hard and soft pendulum

At the extremes, we may find ourselves swinging from a state of high, sharp anxiety, to one of dull, grey depression and back again. Some of us end up getting stuck more at one end of the pendulum swing than the other. Perhaps because the hard end is just too frightening, we stick with soft, however rotten it feels. Or, perhaps because we are so tough on ourselves, we can't allow ourselves a moment of softness or comfort.[4]

Even if we manage not to go to such extremes, most of us pendulum swing between hard and soft in relating to ourselves in our daily lives. Our alarm goes off in the morning and we press snooze several times (soft) before dragging ourselves out of bed (hard). We jump on the bus (soft), berating ourselves for not walking because exercise would help us shed a few pounds (hard). At work we distract ourselves by clicking onto our social networking site (soft), all the time getting angry with ourselves for not knuckling down to the task for the day (hard). Then, when we do get work done, it is difficult to celebrate ourselves because we're too aware of how it could've been better, and don't want to be seen as blowing our own trumpet (hard). Instead, we reward ourselves with a gossip with colleagues (soft). We listen to them talking about their lives and wonder how we measure up to them in terms of how attractive we are, how successful we are, and whether we're in as good a relationship (hard). We go home shattered and collapse in front of the TV with a beer (soft). You might like to pause here and think about your typical day, or perhaps just the day you're having today. How have you been hard? How have you been soft?

Later on in this chapter, I'll propose an alternative to the hard and soft pendulum. For now, let's just think about some of the problems with it.

First of all, neither the hard or soft way of relating to ourselves really ever gets what it sets out to achieve. Being hard on ourselves never makes us better because nothing is ever enough for it. You never get the emotional pay-off for all that hard work. It is like climbing a hill where, when we reach what we thought was the summit, we realize that there is another, further, summit stretching up above us, and again above that, and above that.

In the same way, softness doesn't really get what it is aiming for. We swing into being soft because we've been so tough on ourselves that we are worn out and need a rest, but what we do when we're soft often makes us feel worse about ourselves, rather than better, and so we feel more exhausted. We don't really enjoy the beer, or the computer game, or losing ourselves in a book, because we're using it to try to drown out the hardness, rather than to really relax and be kind to ourselves.

Also, when we're in the soft place we're often so convinced of our lack that we have little to offer to other people around us. We might go from the hard place of trying desperately to do right by everyone and win their approval, to the soft place of giving up on that and not being there for other people at all. That isn't great for the people around us and can also feed the sense that we're rubbish and worthless when we see that people are disappointed in us.

Another problem with the hard and soft way of being is that it is strongly rooted in comparisons with other people which are based on incorrect assumptions. Think about it this way: if we are all trying to present this perfect mask to the world, a mask of someone who is fine and has got it all sorted out, then against whom are we comparing ourselves? Other people's masks – not how they really are.

So many times in my life, when things were rocky, somebody I haven't known well has commented on how great my life seems, and I've been struck by how all they must see of me is my politely smiling face with no idea of the turmoil going on underneath. One thing about being a counsellor is that you *do* get to see what people are like underneath their masks, when they are courageous enough to let you in. The most striking thing for me is that virtually every client has told me that they must be rubbish because 'everyone else' seems to manage. I made the cartoon below about the experience.

So the hard and soft way of being is bad for ourselves, and for other people. If we are hard enough to keep up this great public persona, and only allow ourselves to be soft in private, then we fuel the self-scrutinizing, self-perfecting culture, rather than changing it. I wonder if the best gift that we could give to other people would be to show them a little of our own anxiety and insecurity, so that they wouldn't have this fiction to compare themselves against.

Another way in which the hard and soft way of being is problematic is that, when we are hard, we often try to be perfect in every area of life. Hardness doesn't recognize that all of us have different capacities and abilities, some of which are stronger than others, and all of which change over time depending on how tired we are, what else is going on in our lives, and so on. Also, when we are hard we

Figure 1.2 Everybody else

often impose rules on ourselves which are contradictory, so we place ourselves in situations in which there is no way of succeeding. For example, we may try to please everyone in our lives, even when different people actually want different things from us. Being the perfect friend may actually conflict with being the perfect employee, the perfect parent, or the perfect lover. Working long hours may not be possible alongside being the popular party person. Even superhumans couldn't achieve some of the tasks we set ourselves. No wonder we crash back into softness and feel like giving up.

There is a final way in which hard and soft relating to ourselves is negative, and this goes back to the way we treat ourselves being related to the way that we treat others (the 'love yourself before you love others' idea we started with). If we treat ourselves in a hard and soft manner, we often find ourselves treating other people in the same way. Because we constantly compare ourselves against other people, and we are so scared that we might find that we are flawed compared to them, it is easy to become judgemental and hard on them instead. We find ourselves in endless gossipy conversations, or thinking about other people's behaviour and find them wanting. On the way into work we get irritated by the behaviour of other commuters pushing onto the train. Once there, we find ourselves dying for a break so that we can huddle with our friends to discuss a colleague who annoys us. Walking home, we realize that, for the past half hour, we've been rehearsing in our mind what we could say to reduce our friend to a quivering mass of apologies after she let us down at the weekend.

It cannot be underestimated just how tempting this judgemental attitude is. It soothes us wonderfully in the short term because, when we are focused on the ways in which everyone else is lacking, we don't have to think about the flaws that we are so scared we may have ourselves. We shore ourselves up by thinking about how everyone else is getting it wrong. Perhaps we even find ways of making our problems into something that is their fault. This risks us treating other people badly when we explode in a mass of self-righteous anger. Any benefit for us is short-lived because, rather than feeling better, we often end up feeling far more stressed and tangled up than when we started. We also lose the sense of having support and connection with others because we're so aware of how flawed they are.

We may then pendulum swing to the other extreme and become soft with other people: so desperate for their approval (to show us that we are *not* flawed) that we let everyone in, regardless of how well we connect with them or whether it is any kind of nourishing relationship. At this point, we have no barriers at all against cruel or thoughtless comments, and we can feel utterly overwhelmed by the demands of all of the different people around us, and by the possibility that they might view us negatively. Although we are open to others in one way when we are like this, in another way we don't really see them at all, because we are so concerned with how they see us.

We'll return to the implications of hard and soft behaviour on our relationships later in the book, particularly in Chapter 7. For now, let's think about whether there are any alternative rules of relating to ourselves that we might consider.

Alternative rules

Looking back to the list of rules we started with, we can see that the hard and soft way of treating ourselves is rooted in the idea that we are a fixed, singular self. For those rules to apply, there must be a self that we can monitor, judge against others, and perfect, or give up on and neglect. Like I said at the start, the idea that you *are* a singular self that remains pretty much the same over time may well seem so obvious that questioning it is an odd proposition indeed.

However, the singular, fixed self has been questioned in two important ways which point us towards an alternative way of relating to ourselves, and to others. This is the idea that we are:

- plural rather than singular; and
- in process rather than static.

Let's take these one at a time, with a couple of activities to explore them.

We are plural rather than singular

Write the names of five people in your life in the boxes along the top of the grid shown (for example, a close family member, a friend, a good colleague, someone you get on well with online). In each box, for each person, put 'X' if you mostly behave in the way described on the left of the grid with that person, put a '0' if you mostly behave in the way described on the right of the grid. Leave it blank if neither fits at all.

So, in the example row I have completed, I would be outgoing with person 1 and person 2, shy with person 3 and person 5, and neither term really applies to how I am with person 4. After you've completed the grid, reflect on the patterns of Xs and Os. Are you the same self in different relationships?

Table 1.1 Plural selves

X	Person 1:	Person 2:	Person 3:	Person 4:	Person 5:	0
Outgoing	X	X	0		0	Shy
Fun						Serious
Protective						Protected
of them						by them
They take						I take
control						control
Patient						Impatient
Emotional						Unemotional
Responsible						Free
I can really						I can't really
be myself						be myself

The psychologist Trevor Butt carried out a study using this kind of grid with lots of people,[5] only he got them to create their own opposites on the left and right hand sides, based on what was meaningful to them. For example, for some people the opposite of 'serious' would be 'fun', for others it might be 'silly', 'playful', 'laughing a lot', 'childlike', or 'immature'. For some people the opposite of 'emotional' would be 'rational', 'calm', or 'cold' rather than 'unemotional'. For some, seriousness and emotionality wouldn't be such important issues in their perceptions of themselves, but something else might be, such as how nurturing they got to be in that relationship, or how honest they felt, or how chatty they were. If you found the activity straightforward you might like to have another go, but creating your own table with opposites on the left and right that are meaningful to you.

Trevor and his colleagues were particularly interested in comparing how people experienced themselves in relationships where they felt they could 'really be themselves' (putting an X in the last row). He found that this was the most vital category for people: everyone thought it was important to have relationships where they could be themselves. However, what 'themselves' meant varied remarkably from relationship to relationship. People could feel that they were being themselves in relationships where they acted in seemingly completely opposite ways. For example, they might be playful and extrovert with one friend, serious and introvert with another, or they might be patient, deferential and protected with their father, and impatient, dominant, and protective with a partner.

We could do a similar activity for different situations, rather than different relationships, thinking about who we are in a work meeting, in bed at night, going to a party, walking with a friend, or in the midst of a crisis. Whichever version of the activity we do, it seems to reveal that our selves are more complex than we initially thought. Although all of the selves feel equally 'true' (we feel 'ourselves' when we are being them), quite different people seem to be drawn out of us by different relationships or situations.

This has led some authors to suggest that we are plural rather than singular.[6] A good metaphor might be that we are more like a community than an individual: perhaps like a gang, or the crew of a ship. The group generally has pretty shared goals, and is going in the same direction. Some characters in it are more dominant than others. But it is composed of different aspects, or selves, which have quite different qualities and capacities. In each relationship or situation, one aspect or self comes to the fore and others go more into the background. This can feel natural and comfortable with parts of ourselves which we are familiar and happy with, but it can also feel confusing and strange when we are used to thinking of ourself as a single, clear self. Think about times when you have got together with family or old schoolfriends and suddenly a part of yourself emerges that you'd almost forgotten about: the teasing older brother, or the gawky teenager. Similarly, we can feel stuck when others only see a certain aspect of us and we find ourselves playing along with it, for example if an auto-recovery person treats me as a damsel in distress, or if I bump into a business client out at the pub and find myself acting all professional in that social context.

We often try to limit ourself to one self, or at least only the selves that are comfortable to us. Self-monitoring involves attempting to police our selves so that only certain ones are revealed to others, and even to ourselves. When selves that we are highly uncomfortable with emerge, we may try to eradicate them. Or we may feel so horribly stuck in them, and in the realization that this is some-one that we can be, that we want to destroy ourselves completely. For example, we might find ourselves being the lecherous drunk or the scared little boy, the enraged bull or the callous manipulator. Particularly troubling are those selves against which we've received the strongest messages as we were growing up. For example, in some families it is not considered okay to express anger or sad-ness, or we might have been bullied for being wimpy, posh, or greedy, at school. An alternative to avoiding, or trying to battle, those sides of ourselves is to be open to all the different selves that we are: to cultivate awareness of them and good communication between them. This can be extremely difficult when it comes to the selves that we are scared of, or disgusted by. However, paradoxically, when we face them and listen to them, rather than trying to block them up on the other side of a high brick wall, we often find that they are less terrifying or overwhelm-ing than we feared. Perhaps rather than knowing ourself we should strive to know our selves.

We are in process rather than static

For this activity, imagine that your life was a book. What would the contents page look like? Write a list of the chapters of your life. You can start at any point in the past that feels right, and end in the present or the future. It is up to you.[7]

Spend some time reflecting on what you've written. Where did you start? Where did you end? You could also ask yourself questions like: What kind of book would your book be? What genre? Are there any major themes? Who is the primary author? What would it look like if someone else in your life wrote it? Is there any part of your life missing from it? How would it look if you focused on this instead? Who would be the most appreciative audience, or the most critical one? What would it be called?

Even the metaphor of a book isn't the best one for everyone. If you're not into books you might change it to the different acts or scenes in a movie, the different tracks on an album, or the levels of a computer game.

What this activity hopefully demonstrates is that, as well as being plural rather than singular, we are also a work in progress rather than something that it static and fixed[8]. In fact there are lots of different stories that we could tell through our lives. Again, we might get stuck on one particular narrative but it can be useful to open that up. Psychologist Kenneth Gergen[9] suggests that we tell stories to make sense of our lives, often starting from a particular endpoint: how I came to be X (where X could be anything from a doctor to a gambler, a dad to a divorcee, a liberal to a long-distance runner). We keep editing and repeating certain stories to ourselves over time so that they feel like the truth. Popular narratives include the tragedy (where we start in a successful place, but fall into failure), the comedy-romance (where a positive life is interrupted by calamity, but order is restored), the happily-ever-after (when things get gradually better and better), and the heroic narrative (where we struggle towards victory against a number of obstacles, but eventually win out). What would your story look like if you started from a different end point, or used a different narrative structure?

Sociologist Ken Plummer[10] points out that new stories, or at least variations on old ones, emerge in our culture over time, such as the 'coming out story' or the 'victim narrative'. Again, these stories might be very useful in terms of making sense of our lives, but it is also good not to get so stuck in them that they restrict our future. If you have a 'coming out' story, what might your life story look like if you focused on a different aspect of your identity? If you've been a victim, can you also tell stories through parts of your life as a rescuer, a hero, a survivor, or even a perpetrator?

As when we try to perfect and control ourselves, when we see ourself as something static that we could pin down and always be, we limit and constrain ourselves. Therapist Manu Bazzano says that it is like taking a bowl to the river, filling it with water, and then looking into that bowl to understand the river. Really we *are* the river, ever flowing and always in process.[11]

Another useful metaphor comes from the author Stephen Batchelor.[12] He suggests that we are like the pot spinning on the wheel, and the potter who spins it, drawing it up higher, pressing it low, always in motion and evolving. When we see ourselves as static, it is like putting the pot in a kiln and fixing it. When we fix ourselves, we become rigid, brittle, and fragile. Of course we want to fix ourselves, because we are under the illusion that we might be able to remain forever as the person we most like being at the best time in our life. Also, being fixed feels much more certain and controllable: this is who I am and this is how I do things. And if we can present a fixed, good, self to the rest of the world, hopefully they won't see how we are flawed. However, because we are not really fixed, our fluid life moves on. The self that we're trying desperately to cling to being doesn't fit it any more, or another aspect of ourselves breaks through and shatters the carefully fixed object.

Also, fixity is dangerous because we might feel fixed as the aspects of ourselves with which we are least comfortable, or see as most flawed. If we recognize our plurality and fluidity then those things aren't so threatening, because we know that they are only one part of us and that they will inevitably shift and change over time because we are always becoming something different. It is only when we fix ourselves that we feel paralysed and stuck in who we really don't want to be: that unbearable feeling that this it is all we've ever been, and all we will ever be. This is not about changing for change's sake, but rather being open to change and aware of ourselves as a process.

An alternative to that idea of learning to love yourself, with which we started this chapter, is that we might learn to love our unfolding stories. This would involve looking back on our lives and recognizing that they made us what we are today, as well as looking forward and recognizing our role as the author of what happens next. It is hard to love our self without fixing it, and it can be difficult to really embrace all the different selves that we are. However, we might reflect on our unfolding story in all its ups and downs, its triumphs and tragedies, and recognize that, at least, it makes a truly unique tale.

Beyond rules? Embracing uncertainty

So we've seen that our taken-for-granted rules about ourselves tend to regard us as one, fixed self. The rules suggest that this self should be scrutinized and policed to make sure that only certain aspects of it are revealed. It should be compared against other people, and perfected so that all flaws and uncomfortable aspects are eradicated. This leaves us oscillating disjointedly between hard and soft ways of being with ourselves. Instead of looking for definite rules about how we should be, we might acknowledge that this is an uncertain and uncontrollable area, that different parts of ourselves will emerge in different situations, and that we will shift and change over time.

If we question these rules by thinking of ourselves as plural rather than singular, in process rather than fixed, what happens to our hard and soft way of relating to ourselves?

Maybe we end up oscillating more smoothly between something like gentleness and firmness, rather than hardness and softness. When we are gentle, we are saying to ourselves, 'I'm okay and I need to go easy', and, when we are firm, we are saying, 'I'm okay and I can do it'.

You will notice that, with the hard and soft diagram, I put hardness first, followed by softness, whereas with this version I put gentleness first, followed by firmness. This is because I think that hardness is the foundation of the hard and soft way of being. We start off in hardness: harshly trying to force ourselves to be how we think we should be, and we either stay there, fall into softness because hardness is just *too* hard, or keep oscillating back and forth between them. On my alternative version, I put gentleness first (rather than firmness) because gentleness is the vital foundation. It is about treating ourselves kindly, recognizing that we can't do everything all of the time, and looking after ourselves so that we feel strong enough to face the world. Firmness follows as we recognize that we do want to strive for things in life, and to take responsibility for our actions. But

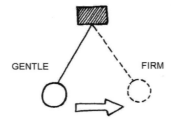

Figure 1.3 Gentle and firm pendulum

firmness is grounded in gentleness towards ourselves, so that we go for things in a way which recognizes what we are capable of, and gives us a break when we need it.

Firmness is different to hardness because, instead of pushing ourselves ever onwards and onwards and beating ourselves up each time we fail, it recognizes that there is no perfection to be reached. It celebrates our small triumphs along the way, and thinks carefully about failure. Is this a failure or a useful lesson about our (current) limitations? Or is it, perhaps, a helpful demonstration to those around us that nobody is perfect?

We can think of gentleness and firmness as ways of tuning into ourselves so that we know when we're energized and engaged enough to tackle something and when we're in need of relaxation and restoration: when to be out in the world, and when to retreat. Interestingly, when we treat ourselves this way, we may find that we achieve many of the things for which we were struggling when we were being hard, and that we enjoy the process a great deal more. We might also find ourselves reassessing what is important to us anyway.

I like this way of seeing things because, as we have found, the hard and soft way to relating to ourselves is deeply ingrained and easy to fall into, so we need another way to which it is possible to aspire, and into which it is possible to shift from being hard and soft. Perhaps each time we catch ourselves being hard or soft, we might understandingly acknowledge it and kindly shift ourselves sideways into a more gentle and firm way of being. I think a metaphor from Martine Batchelor is useful here. She says that our tendency in life is to grasp hard onto things that we want, and to hurl away from us things that we don't want. That is like oscillating from hard to soft: grabbing on so tight that it cramps our hand, or giving up and losing it entirely. Instead, she says, we should treat all things like a precious object. We want to hold a precious object firmly enough to protect it, but gently enough not to crush it, and so that we can see it and decide whether it is something to keep hold of or to put down.[13] This is a useful metaphor for much of what we'll cover in this book: how we treat ourselves, how we treat comments that are made about us by others, how we treat other people themselves, and how we treat the rules.

In writing this book, I've tried constantly to bring myself back from hard and soft to firm and gentle. It has been a good lesson in just how difficult that is. When I'm being hard I try to force myself to sit and write, even when I don't feel like it. I set myself tough deadlines and berate myself when I don't make it. I pick up on every cliché or bad turn of phrase that I use and make sarcastic comments to myself about them. The question 'who do you think you are?' yammers away in the background, never completely silent. In my mind, there is the academic critic telling me that I'm not rigorous or theoretical enough. Meanwhile another imagined reader – the person on the street – says that it's all far too complicated and abstract. Unable to please these two contradictory voices, I flounder into softness, giving up in disgust.

When this happens, I try to gradually shift from soft into gentle. Of course, not everyone will love this book, but even if it speaks to a few people who find it helpful then it is worthwhile. And yes, it isn't possible to please all of the potential readers, so I will just have to find my own balance point between being academic and accessible, as everyone does. Writing requires oscillating from gentle to firm as well: remembering that I do have something to offer, and sitting myself down to write.

Think back to the day that you remembered when, earlier in the chapter, you reflected on the ways in which you are hard and soft with yourself. What might it be like to live that day again, but being gentle and firm. How might you be gentle? How might you be firm? When you feel fixed by the way other people see you, might you remember that 'this is not all that I am or all that I'll ever be'?

An important part of the gentle and firm way of being is that it accepts that we are lacking, and therefore doesn't strive for perfection. The therapist Emmy Van Deurzen says:

> What a relief to admit that one is basically and totally lacking: what a discovery to recognize that this is the very thing that one is, and that far from being a handicap this is the very thing that makes human life possible at all . . . To come to terms with imperfection and incompleteness [is] one of the main tasks of life.[14]

In a way, perfection can only come at the very end of life when we close the final page of our book, or fade out of the final scene of our movie. Then what we have is perfect, because it is a complete story. In the meantime, we have to embrace the uncertainty of being lacking and imperfect, because it is impossible to be otherwise, because it has a beauty all of its own, and because wishing to fix all those lacks and imperfections is kind of like wishing for death, since that is the only time when everything stops moving and changing. This was brought home to me recently at my grandfather's memorial service. During the ceremony, my uncle told the story of my grandfather's life from birth to death, interspersed with recollections from the many people who had known and loved him at different stages. It was striking that a picture emerged which was fuller, richer, and more complete, than that which any of us had known before: for the first time we could see all the different selves my grandfather had been in all of his different relationships, as well as getting a sense of the full story from beginning to end.

Shifting from hard and soft to firm and gentle is no easy task. It is useful to keep reminding ourselves of it, but it is also important to give ourselves time to practice it, so that it becomes easier and more automatic. After all, we have had years and years of practising being hard and soft. We will keep falling back onto that deeply-worn path unless we create a different path and keep treading it until it is just as well eroded. In the final chapter of this book (Chapter 10), I consider various kinds of practice which might help us to be gentle and firm, rather than hard and soft, with ourselves and with others. If you want, you could skip ahead to that chapter now to get an idea of the kinds of things that might be helpful. Alternatively, reading the rest of the book first will help you see how foundational these ideas are in terms of our relationships: the way we treat people we're attracted to, how we relate to our bodies, the way we think about love, how we treat ourselves and our partners depending on our genders, the way we have sex, and how we conflict with others, communicate with them and commit to them. Hold on, too, to that idea that we are plural and in process. We'll see that accepting that in ourselves helps us to accept it in other people, which is key to all of these aspects of relationships.

So, returning to our first rule – 'love yourself before loving anyone else' – where does that stand, now that we've reached the end of this chapter? Cultivating a gentle and firm way of being with ourselves helps us to be gentle and firm with other people. But it works the other way around as well: cultivating a gentle and firm way of being with others helps us to be gentle and firm with ourselves. And, sometimes, it can be easier to be gentle and firm with other people, given the self-beating culture in which we live, so that can be a good place to start practising.

Being gentle and firm, rather than hard and soft, also means being open to the plurality of ourselves and others – all the different selves that we are – and to the shifting, changing process of being human. Instead of trying to fix ourselves and others, we can engage with how we are right now, knowing that we will alter again and again and again.

Chapter 2

Rewriting the rules of attraction

What are the rules?

Before starting this chapter, try drawing a picture of how you would ideally look, and also one of what you find most attractive in another person. Don't worry about your drawing ability, no-one else is going to look at this. You can always draw a stick figure with words and arrows pointing at the important bits, or cut out and stick in images of different body parts from magazines.

We'll come back to this activity later, but we're starting with it to highlight the fact that the usual rules of attraction are strongly rooted in physical appearance, and that this has a profound effect on how we view and treat our own, and other people's, bodies.

One of the rules which is so omnipresent that it can almost seem unquestionable, is that there is a body ideal to which we should all aspire and strive to match, and that we should be attracted to other people who come as close as possible to this ideal. Walking down the street, flicking through a magazine, switching on the television, we are confronted with image after image of this same ideal. Try it now. Watch a commercial break, pick up a magazine, or spend a city journey observing all the adverts that you see on the way. List the things you notice about the appearance of the people in the images. Also keep a list of things that you *never* see in these images, in terms of types of people or bodily features.

I think you'll find that there is a pretty clear ideal presented in all of these images. The ideal is young, it is slim, it is fit and able-bodied, it is unblemished, tanned and smooth-skinned with straight pearly teeth, and it is overwhelmingly white. For women, the ideal also usually involves long hair, long legs, flat stomach, firm buttocks and high pert breasts (whether these are larger or smaller depends on whether you're looking at high fashion or men's magazines). For men there is more emphasis on being toned and tall, usually with a six-pack and short hair.

Most years you can rely on at least one of the women's and men's magazines to produce a list of the 'sexiest' men or women.[1] Over the years, the 'sexiest women' have become even more similar to one another. It is almost the exact same body and face staring out at us from page after page. The sexiest men are usually a bit more diverse. Tall, dark and handsome still dominates, but it is not unusual to have an age range from twenty to sixty or even older, and for there to be a mixture of slimmer and heavier, hairier and more balding, men. However, before assuming that men have it a great deal easier in terms of body ideals, it must be remembered that all these men are hugely successful (usually a mixture of film and TV stars, sportsmen, musicians and comedians). The message is that if you are a rich and famous man you can deviate from the body ideal, but there may be lot less flexibility for the average guy on the street. Sexuality and race also come into it, as images in gay men's magazines are less diverse than those aimed at straight men, and black men, like black women, tend to be far less visible than white men in the magazines, and more sexualized when they are portrayed.

The promise of the 'perfect' appearance is used to sell all kinds of products, as well as drawing our attention to news stories and features, and encouraging us to watch movies and TV shows: most of which – from kid's cartoons to the latest rom com – are populated by actors who match these ideals. Indeed, when a supposedly 'ugly' character appears in a film or on a show that they tend to stray only very slightly from the ideal, often finding their way back to it by the happy ending.

There are ever more products available aimed at attaining and maintaining the ideal appearance, from face creams to cosmetic surgery to gym membership. Along with the fashion industry dictating that each season requires a new wardrobe, each season there is a new bodily feature to be insecure about, of which we had never heard before. In the last decade or two we've witnessed the invention of cellulite, the seven signs of ageing, muffin tops, bingo wings and, recently, increased attention on the genitals (promises of larger penises and designer vaginas). The body is fragmented down to every tiny part, all of which have associated beauty regimes and products which will ensure their appropriate appearance.

Often, the body ideal is explicitly linked to the promise of getting and keeping the perfect relationship (mentioned in the Introduction and explored more in Chapter 3). As a therapist, nearly every client I've seen has been deeply unhappy with some aspect their body, and their desire to improve it in some way has mostly been motivated either by a desire to attract a partner, or by a fear of losing the one that they have. The same has been true for most of the members of my classes when I've explored this topic with college students over the years. There is general agreement that we need to strive to meet the body ideal: from the girl who forces herself to go to the gym before work every day, to the guy who doesn't want the lights on during sex in case his partner notices his belly; from the people who decline to go on holiday with friends for fear of having to wear a bathing costume, to the giggling sharing of 'naughty' food and comparison of 'hideous' body parts ('My thighs!' 'But what about my nose', 'But at least you don't have my chin').

Psychologist Rosalind Gill analysed 'chick lit' fiction and romantic comedies.[2] She found that some groups of people simply aren't included in the range of those who are allowed a relationship: generally those whose bodies are regarded as too large, too old, or too different. Jokes in such fiction frequently rest on the possibility of ending up in bed with someone ugly after a drunken night out, or realizing that the man you've been chatting up is short when he stands up. Sex therapists frequently hear from people who've been told by other professionals that they should give up on the possibility of sex because of a disability or reaching a certain age.

Beauty is clearly highly valued: people who fit the body ideal are paid huge sums of money to be displayed. When someone is complemented on their appearance they generally feel flattered, as if it is something they did on purpose, when the vast majority of it is a case of a simple quirk of genetics matching the current social norms. The valuing of beauty can also be seen in the envy that is attached to people who have snagged a partner who is 'out of their league', or the approval given to a man who proves his ability to pick up 'hot babes' (see Chapter 5). Such ideas suggest that appearance is by far the most important attribute in a partner. This is echoed in the fact that physical attributes are often the qualities which take up much of the limited space in personal adverts (both what the person looks like and what they'd like their potential partner to look like). Online personal adverts increasingly focus on photographs, with burgeoning websites offering to evaluate people on how attractive they are. Also, think about the ways in which people expect to meet partners offline. Nightclubs pretty much ensure that getting together will only be based on physical appearance, given that they are probably too loud, and too alcohol-fuelled, for anything apart from visual and physical interaction.

Let's summarize the rules of attraction:

- Attractiveness of a partner is largely located in their physical appearance. It is important to have a physically attractive partner.
- Physical beauty is something to strive for, in order to ensure that we get a relationship. We need to stay attractive to ensure that we maintain that relationship.
- The appearance to which we should aspire is the body ideal that we see in the media.
- We must monitor ourselves and our partners carefully to make sure that we do not appear in any of the ways that are not allowed (the ones that get circled in red in the celebrity magazines).

Why question the rules?

So, why might we question these rules of appearance and attraction? The main reason has to be the utter misery that they result in. For those who manage to meet the body ideal, few actually feel attractive, and there is often huge anxiety about maintaining this beauty. For the much larger proportion of people who do *not* meet the ideal, vast amounts of time and energy can be put into striving towards it, and much pain associated when it is unattainable. Just think about the ridicule and rejection attached to being 'ugly' in our culture. Going back to that hard and soft way of thinking about ourselves which we covered in Chapter 1, we also treat our bodies in such ways: trying to force them to meet a restrictive ideal, or giving up and feeling like a failure.

You might think that this makes too big a deal of the situation. After all, night-clubs are fun, being told that we are attractive feels great, the fashion world is exciting and beautiful, and what's wrong with choosing to pamper our bodies or treating ourselves with the latest pair of shoes? As I'll say throughout this book, these things certainly are complex, and it is good if you can question what I'm putting forward as well as the rules themselves. We might wonder if it is even *possible* to step outside our culture, which values appearance so highly, and whether we would want to: isn't so much great art about displaying beautiful bodies?

However, we also need to be careful here. As Gill, and others, have pointed out, recent cultural changes can make it even harder to question our looks-obsessed culture.[3] This is the shift to the idea that being 'into looks' is fine because we are choosing it, and because it is fun and even empowering.

There has been a change, for example, in adverts for bras.[4] Back in the seventies and eighties, bras were often advertised with the message that women should look a certain way in order to be sexy and to keep their man happy. However, these days they are advertised with images of beautiful, strong women, looking straight into our eyes with captions like 'or are you just pleased to see me', 'I can't cook, who cares', and 'who said a woman can't get pleasure from something soft'. The message is that we should enjoy looking good for ourselves, not for a partner or potential partner. A related message is that we can be empowered by being attractive. A recent series of billboard adverts pictured a bar, a restaurant, or an escalator full of people, all of whom were turning to look at you – the viewer – in desire and envy. The implication was that this was reaction you would get if you wore their underwear. It is a potent fantasy, this prospect of being utterly wanted and of drawing everyone's gaze.

But these kinds of depictions still present us with a narrow definition of what is attractive. They still suggest that the be-all and end-all of existence is to be found desirable by other people. This message isn't great whatever your gender, as we'll see in Chapter 5. Also, by giving us the idea that striving for beauty is something fun that we are choosing to do, it makes it difficult for us to find a problem with it. If we complain, we may well be derided as humourless, or as denying people the freedom to choose to beautify themselves.

Again, we end up turned in upon ourselves: monitoring ourselves closely and comparing ourselves against impossible others, trying to make ourselves gorgeous *and* trying to give the impression that we are enjoying the process. We saw in Chapter 1 that we often compare ourselves against a mask that other people wear, which doesn't look much like the messy, complex, people that they are underneath. With physical appearance, it is even worse than this. The images we see on billboards and in magazines bear less and less resemblance to real people because they are the result of hours and hours of attention from hair, clothes, and make-up stylists, clever camera work, and then extensive alteration using computer programs to ensure that they fit the narrow ideal perfectly.[5] This means that fewer and fewer people will be able to fit the ideals, however hard they try, and however much money they spend. Even when we compare ourselves to other people on our journey to work, or out at night, there is the difference that we know what we look like first thing in the morning or when we are worn out, whereas we are comparing ourselves against the preened and perfected image that other people have put together before leaving their houses.

As with rules about ourselves and our relationships, the rules of attraction create problems both for those who fit within them and for those who are on the outside. We might be envious of people who seem to meet the ideals of attractiveness but, in many ways, their position is the most precarious and tragic. This is because, if you are 'beautiful', it is vastly tempting, in a culture which values beauty so highly, to define yourself in that way and to get all of your validation from it. Of course, this means defining yourself on the basis of something which will *inevitably* change. Even if people are lucky enough to avoid the kinds of accidents or illnesses that will suddenly alter their appearance, they will not be able to avoid the ageing process which happens to us all.

Current ideals of beauty are primarily about being young, being toned, and being slim, and these are all things which will change as we age. If our self-confidence is totally bound up in being physically desired by others, when we feel that slipping away we may either grab desperately onto it by trying to keep that desirability, or give up and feel loss and shame. It is easy, when you're young, to think that ageing is far away and to enjoy being attractive and desirable. But there is a danger, if we define ourselves in this way, that by the time things change it will be extremely hard to shift our habit of valuing attractiveness and desirability so highly. Also, if a relationship is strongly based on a physical attraction due to those involved having youthful, toned, and flawless bodies, then there are likely to be problems as we grow older. This often results in painful feelings of rejection, as well as some people trading their partners in for younger and younger models, with whom they may well have less in common, leaving them feeling isolated and alienated themselves. We need to think carefully if our sense of beauty and attractiveness is limited and inflexible – and it may be difficult for it to be otherwise, if that is all we have been exposed to.

What about the vast proportion of people who do not fit the beauty ideal and long to do so? Eating disorders are often put forward as the extreme, and life-threatening, end of the spectrum of misery in which body ideals are implicated, and there have been public panics about websites which advocate anorexia amongst teenagers and share ideas about how to stay dangerously thin. As usual, the situation is far more complex than the simplistic idea that restrictive beauty ideals *cause* eating disorders. There are many different reasons applicable at different times as to why people to take particular actions, and it is no different with those who starve themselves or purge themselves of what they've eaten. For example, these actions can help you to gain a sense of control over what seems a frighteningly uncontrollable life; they can be a way of punishing yourself if you feel you aren't good enough; and/or they might be a way of keeping a more child-like body when the adult world seems threatening. However, a culture which is obsessed with bodies, which promotes a narrow ideal of attractiveness, and encourages practices in order to change bodies, clearly underlies, to some extent, the kinds of bodies for which people are striving.[6] Global research certainly finds that rates of these kinds of starving and purging behaviours go up after 'Western' media has been introduced[7].

It is also problematic to separate out a group of people who are 'eating disordered' or have 'body image problems', when the truth is that you would be hard pushed to find anyone who didn't wish their body was different in some way, and who didn't engage in some behaviours to try to change it. A study of Australian teenagers[8] found that two thirds of them felt that they were too fat, the vast majority wanted the body ideal, and a third had used at least one extreme form of weight reduction in the previous month (crash dieting, fasting or smoking). Body-related distress in women is so common that it has been termed 'normative discontent'. Major surveys suggest that more and more people are experiencing such distress, and that it is affecting increasingly younger people, and men as well as women.[9] Studies have found that children are more prejudiced against fat people than any other group,[10] and fat remains one of the most acceptable prejudices overall, when we compare tolerance of fat jokes to those against people of certain racial or sexual groups, for example.

The paradoxes in this area make things even more difficult for us. The messages we receive are paradoxical because, at the same time as being encouraged to be slim and toned, we are also bombarded with images of delicious food inducing us to eat various products, as well as encouraging us to spend much of our leisure time in sedentary practices like watching TV and playing computer games. Similarly, dieting is generally promoted as the way to thinness, with a proliferation of dieting programmes, each promising to get you your perfect body for a fee. However, we know that most weight lost from dieting is put back on, and that dieting affects the metabolism in such a way that it will store *more* fat in future, making it easier to put on weight. In recent years, people have pointed out that obesity, as much as dangerous thinness, is related to the problematic messages about food and beauty that we receive, although there still seems to be far more anxiety about the health impact of obesity than there is about the, at least equal, danger of excessive dieting and thinness.[11]

Take a moment here to think about what food means to you. What messages did you receive about food growing up? Was food related, for example, to pampering and feeling cared for, being 'spoilt', getting a reward for something (sweets if you were good), feeling guilty (starving children elsewhere in the world), danger (getting fat), or being well-behaved (clearing your plate, or eating your greens)? What about now? What are the main rules around you in the world and in your home about food? How does this impact what you eat, how much, and how often?

As well as the paradox about being encouraged to both eat and diet, body dissatisfaction has also been related to some paradoxes around gender that we face at the moment. The focus on bodies can be a reaction by some women to the 'superwoman' ideal: the pressure to be successful in career *and* relationships, to be nurturers *and* independent, mothers *and* sex-goddesses. Food and bodies can be one area over which women can have control in a world of chaos and excessive, contradictory, demands. Men increasingly face similar contradictions. As traditional male work and father roles become more tenuous, men are increasingly likely to locate their identity in what they look like, rather than in what they do, so they are likely to be more image-conscious and body-focused too.[12]

How do these things apply to you? Think back to what you drew at the start of the chapter. Are you satisfied with your body? What things would you have to change to have your ideal appearance? What do you already do in order to look different?

One way of simplifying things is to see all these ways of treating our bodies – dieting, dragging ourselves out for a run when we don't enjoy it, binging and starving, wishing we looked differently, and the makeover culture – as rooted in us treating our bodies as *objects*. In Chapter 1, we saw that the rules encourage us to fix ourselves, and treat ourselves as things to be monitored and perfected. In the same way, the rules of attraction encourage us to fix and perfect our bodies. When we break our bodies down into different fragments to be toned, buffed and polished, and when we gaze in the mirror and judge what we see there, we are treating our bodies as objects: as something separate to ourselves. This risks alienating us from our bodies: forgetting that they *are* what we are, not something separate to ourselves. We experience the world only through our senses: our eyes, noses, ears, fingertips, skin, etc. The selves which we explored in Chapter 1 are only the combination of these perceptions and sensations – the firing of nerve cells throughout our bodies and brains – and the interactions we have with the world and people around us, which all happen through our bodies. We have taken a problematic turn when we start treating our bodies, and those of other people, as objects to be judged, desired, rejected, or altered, rather than as an intrinsic part of who we are.

Ironically, treating our bodies as objects often takes us further away from what we wanted in the first place (the body ideal), rather than closer to it. Refusing to eat when we are hungry or avoiding certain foods can leave us out of tune with what our body needs and less able to know when we do, and do not, need to eat, such that we end up eating too much, or too little, or food that isn't good for us. Forcing ourselves to do a particular kind of exercise, in order to lose weight or gain muscle, can deny us the pleasure of finding forms of activity that we might really enjoy (and thus find much easier to keep up). As we become more alienated from our bodies, it can be difficult to tune in to when we are tired and need rest, or when we are active and need exercise. Similarly, it is harder to tune in to emotions and sexual desires (as we'll see in Chapter 4).

Also, as we saw in Chapter 1, the way we treat others and the way we treat ourselves are often intertwined. So, if we judge other people on scales of one to ten of attractiveness, or point out their bodily flaws, we may find ourselves increasingly dissatisfied with our own bodies.

Alternative rules

Occasionally in life there is a moment which cuts through all the rules and leaves them exposed in their absurdity, opening us up to something different. This happened on the UK television show *Britain's Got Talent* in 2009: one of the national talent shows that have become popular in so many countries. This episode of the show became a YouTube phenomenon, viewed by millions of people around the world.[13] In the clip, a short, thickset 47-year-old Scottish woman with frizzy hair, little make-up and an unfashionable dress, walks out onto the stage. She stumbles over her answers to the questions from an increasingly bemused panel of judges. The audience begins to laugh at this person, who has so clearly failed to grasp the rules for success on such a show: struggling to conform to even the basics of appropriate body, clothes, or manner for a wannabe celebrity. As the music starts to play for her number, we see harshness and judgement on the faces of audience and panel alike. And then she starts to sing, and it is beautiful.

What was marvellous about this moment was that it broke through the rules of attraction to reveal, in an instant, how utterly flawed they are. We saw in Chapter 1 that people's judgements of others are frequently rooted in their sense of their own flaws. When Susan Boyle came on stage, the audience were ready to deride her and to enjoy the sense of relief that here was somebody who was doing a worse job than them at wearing the mask and following the rules. But when she began to sing, it seemed that, in recognizing the beauty in her, they could also see the beauty in themselves instead of having to hide behind such a façade. It is sad that an astonishing voice is required to shatter the brittle rules and rituals of body and attraction – and it is a shame that the rules popped back into place so quickly afterwards, as Susan was hounded by the press and encouraged into makeovers and all the pressures of celebrity. But such moments should still be cherished for offering a brief insight into the possibility of something different. Even the presenters recognized this as they asked the camera, 'you weren't expecting that were you?' We can linger on this question for some time, wondering 'why not? What do our looks have to do with our voice, or the person behind it?'

When we have a sense that the rules might be unquestionable or unchangeable, it is always useful to look to the past and across cultures to check whether there is a possibility of something different. In the case of attractiveness, we only have to glance at various cultures around the world, or back in time in our own cultures, to see that what is considered attractive varies widely from time to time and place to place. Even just picking one aspect – women's size – we can see the shift from the Rubenesque ideals of the 1800s to the early twentieth century flapper, to the buxom Marilyn Monroe, to today's extremely thin supermodel. Similarly, largeness rather than slenderness is valued more highly in many countries around the world today, although, as we have seen, the increasing proliferation of 'Western' norms seems to endanger this variety.

We could also point to times and places where age has been more or less revered, where darker or lighter skin has been the ideal, or where vastly different forms of

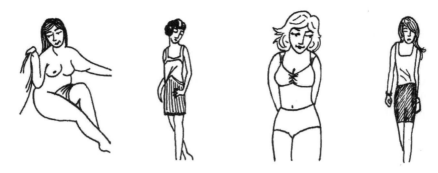

Figure 2.1 Changing body types over time

hairstyle, body adornments, and clothes were fashionable. Even within a single culture, we know that there is massive diversity in what physical aspects people find to be the absolute pinnacle of attraction. While a steady diet of billboard adverts and mainstream mags might leave many hankering after taut bottoms, six-packs or pert breasts, there are also many who adore a slender ankle, a rotund belly or a large bosom. Bring in historical and cultural diversity, and we can add tiny feet, long necks, and thin eyebrows to the list of specific appearances that have been seen as the height of beauty. We only have to look at the changing fashions for clothing to recognize that what we find attractive in ourselves and others *can* alter in a matter of years, or even months, rather than requiring whole generations. Think about the shifts in just one item of clothing: jeans. What once seemed attractive may now seem ridiculous, and vice versa.

Despite our attraction to 'looks', the development of the internet has shown just how unimportant physical appearance can be in dictating our feelings of desire and love. More and more people of all ages and social groups now meet romantic partners online, whether through specific dating sites, through social networking, or through virtual worlds such as Second Life or World of Warcraft. And many

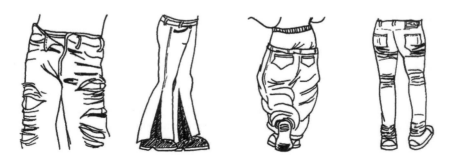

Figure 2.2 Changing fashions for jeans

people now have the experience of love burgeoning for somebody who they have never even met, to the extent that some exchange vows online or have marriage ceremonies as their avatars in online environments. It is interesting that all the feelings that we associate with falling in love are possible with somebody whose appearance we may have no clue about. People report butterflies in their stomach each time they receive an email from that person, or rising arousal when seeing their unrelated user-pic. Intimacy can build quickly, as the anonymity in online forums enables us to reveal more about ourselves, and more quickly. Meeting in person can be a strange experience but, for many, the feelings they had online quickly catch up and map onto the body and face that they now see in front of them.[14]

So, we now know that it is perfectly *possible* to find diverse things attractive in others and in ourselves. However, we might still find our own attractions quite limited due to being saturated by limited body ideals for so long. The online romance phenomenon suggests that we *are* able to open up our notions of what is beautiful and attractive, but how might we do this in practice? Just as we opened up our notion of ourselves and who we were in Chapter 1 as plural rather than singular, in process rather than static, can we open up our ideas of attraction and find that they are less fixed than we assumed them to be?

One interesting activity is to spend some time in a busy place, such as a railway station or city street, paying attention to people's appearance in a different way to the way that you ordinarily do. Instead of using some inner template to judge the conventional attractiveness of passers-by, try relaxing your gaze and finding the beauty in other aspects of appearance. Can you enjoy the grandeur or quirkiness of that Roman nose? The vulnerability or nobility of that bald patch? The seductive softness of those broad hips? The cuteness of that man's short legs? The complexity of wrinkles when that woman smiles? The cheekiness of an exposed scattering of moles? Maybe your notions of attractiveness can expand to enjoy a diversity of different appearances, rather than getting stuck on sameness and symmetry. People who go to naturist resorts often report feeling differently about their own, and other people's bodies after seeing the real diversity of human forms that exist under the clothing and make-up.

From enjoying a range of appearances in others, we can move on to the – often much harder – task of finding beauty in ourselves as we are, rather than constantly wishing that we were otherwise. Shortly, we will consider some less obvious ways of learning to love our bodies but, sticking with the visual for now, perhaps you can begin to apply that same valuing of diverse and interesting appearances, rather than sameness and 'flawlessness'. Sometimes, it can help to look in the mirror and to expand our attention right out to take in the beauty of the whole, rather than zeroing in on the bits we find most problematic, as we often tend to do.

Another tactic, which might be more challenging, is to focus directly on the parts we find difficult, and explore ways to view them differently. In the film *Shirley Valentine*, the lead character is perhaps rightly suspicious when her holiday lover pronounces her stretch marks to be beautiful. But, let's think about it for a moment. Can we zoom in and see the beauty in those spider-thread silver or red patterns weaving their way across our skin? Can we maybe trace a finger along them, enjoying the satiny-smoothness that we find there? Move away from the purely visual and try to access your other senses to richly describe aspects of your own, and others', appearance. We sometimes find that this happens of its own accord with lovers, as we learn to delight in the feel of our cheek against their chest, the unmistakable sound of their feet on the stair, the scent of their hair, or the taste of their skin.

I love this quote from the book *Tongue First* by Emily Jackson, which is all about experiencing our bodies in different ways. It speaks to ways in which our body, just like ourself, is plural and ever-changing.

> Some days my body is matronly, shelter to a housewife in slacks who spends her afternoons making Jell-O molds in Far Rockaway. My belly rounds out in expectation of childbirth and my shoulders curve forward with years of scrubbing. Other days it is frail: I can see the bones in my hands and feet; my shins are sharp; my back aches; blue veins ooze across my skin like a grandmother's. Still others find me feeling like a superhero: thighs bulging with muscles, shoulders spread broad, the swollen veins becoming part of my athlete's physique.[15]

So we can open up to a fascination with our day-to-day shifts in bodily perception, as well as being intrigued, rather than unnerved, by the way our bodies change over the years. Why should finding a grey hair or wrinkle be such a bad thing?

If you do struggle to feel anything but negative about your body and appearance, it can be useful to try activities like this in order to encourage a different way of seeing and experiencing yourself. Remember, also, that it is understandable to find this tough in a looks-obsessed culture which has such an incredibly narrow definition of beauty. Different things work for different people. Some people find it useful to list what they are happy with about their bodies, and to try to keep adding to this. Some find it good to be photographed, or to have their picture drawn, to get an outsider perspective on their appearance. Others experiment with alternative forms of body art such a body painting, hair dye, fingernail polish, tattoos and piercings, to redefine for themselves what is attractive and to experience the surface of the body in different ways: as a canvas, a map, or a place to store memories.

Another thing you might find useful is to focus anger outwards rather the inwards on your own body, on the social messages which leave so many of us feeling so bad so much of the time. Books like Naomi Wolf's *The Beauty Myth*,[16] Kaz Cooke's *Real Gorgeous*,[17] or Susie Orbach's *Bodies*[18] can help with this. My friend Trish engaged in a bit of daily body-positive activism by putting stickers around the place to counter all the adverts for diets and cosmetic surgery. They said things like 'Eating food brings good luck' and:

Worried about your weight?

Tempted to phone people whom you've never met and who don't know about your health and let them sell you a food substitute so they can make a profit?

There is hope.
Get a bit of exercise.
Eat some fruit and veg every day.
Don't worry about it.

You are a wonderful person.
You are vastly more important than what you weigh. Hundreds of people are making the same realization every day.

Finding a role model like Trish can also be helpful when you are struggling to feel positive about your body. A useful idea, for many difficulties, is to ask how would you treat a friend in your situation: would you be so hard on a friend if they had these same aspects of appearance of which you are so critical in yourself? Another useful thought experiment is to consider what it would it be like if we spent the time and energy we spend on trying to alter our appearance (or on keeping it a certain way) on coming to peace with it as it is (and the inevitable changes it will undergo)?

If learning to love your visual appearance seems too big a challenge, you might focus on other bodily sensations. What things make your body feel good? Is it taking a hot bath? Stroking an animal? Eating a square of chocolate? Smelling the flowers in a florist's shop? Having a long stretch? Getting a shoulder massage from a friend? Make a list of simple things like this and try to do one per day, really focusing on the experience and letting yourself enjoy it. In the last section of this chapter, I'll say more about the ways in which we can alter the whole way we relate to our bodies, and why this is important.

Beyond rules? Embracing uncertainty

The previous section focused on alternative ways of viewing our body and the bodies of others. Here we'll consider going beyond these, to question the whole idea of having an 'image' of our body which we can evaluate. Earlier on, I pointed out that all of the looks-obsession, beauty-cruelty, daily self-criticism, and appearance hang ups could be boiled down to one thing: treating bodies as *objects* when, in fact, our bodies *are* what we are. The act of judging someone else on their outward appearance, or scrutinizing ourself in the mirror, is, in a way, an act of violence as we wrench ourself in two: the body being judged, and the self that is doing the judging. We turn the body into a surface on which to create a certain appearance, rather than recognizing that we *are* our flesh through and through, and that all sorts of flesh may be beautiful.

Writers such as the French philosopher Maurice Merleau-Ponty[19] have pointed out that we have a cultural tendency to split our minds off from our bodies, but that this is a false separation. In actuality we are 'embodied' beings. Everything happens through our bodies as we sense things, feel an emotional response and communicate it to others: this all occurs through our sense organs, our brain processes, and our vocal chords. Right now, as I write this book, I am engaging in the embodied practice of writing. I get my words down with little deliberation or checking as to whether I am striking the correct keys of the computer. However, if somebody asked me to write out the layout of the letters on the keyboard I couldn't manage it. It's my body that knows. We can also see how inseparable our bodies and selves are, when we realize how physical our emotional experiences are (hollowed out with sadness, bubbling over with glee), and how much our body perceptions are impacted by the way we feel in ourselves (our levels of confidence and self-esteem).

The psychologist Helen Malson demonstrated the violence and alienation of treating bodies as objects in her interviews with young women who had been diagnosed with anorexia nervosa.[20] Her participants talked of a sense of failure in not being able to control their weight and talked of 'fat' as alien to their bodies: 'a hated enemy to be got rid of'. My clients in counselling often use similar terms, as they speak of their hatred of genitals which don't look as they wish them to, or consider plastic surgery to rid their body of the enemy of flabbiness or sagginess. The author Susan Bordo says that we mostly see 'the body as an alien attacker, threatening to erupt in an unsightly display of bulging flesh . . . To achieve results (often envisioned as the absolute eradication of the body: e.g. 'no tummy') a violent assault on the enemy is usually required'.[21]

So how might we shift this view, coming to see our body as friend, rather than enemy; as our very selves, rather than as a separate object to be beautified, controlled, or even eradicated? An answer comes in those times when we experience our bodies differently: when we feel *in* our bodies, rather than separated and split. Lilliana Del Busso and Paula Reavey studied times when people felt like this.[22] They found that people were most split from their bodies when they were aware of other people treating them as objects, for example, when somebody in the street whistled at them, or when they felt themselves being evaluated in a nightclub. At those times, people felt limited and boxed in. Much more positive and free were the stories people told of being at one with their bodies. Often, these were times when they were active and in motion, and/or times when they were alone, so they knew they were not being monitored by anyone and that they could 'lose themselves in the drama' of whatever they were doing, as Merleau-Ponty puts it.

Think about it for yourself for a moment. When do you feel most free from the sense of being monitored by others? When do you feel most embodied and able to lose yourself in the drama?

The people in del Busso and Reavey's research told stories of swimming in the sea or running, for example. We might also think about times we have lost ourselves in the rhythm and darkness of a dancefloor, surrounded by people who are equally caught up in the music. Or perhaps you are someone who has such moments when walking in the countryside, gardening, playing a game of football, or enjoying a moment of stillness in a busy city park. One of the reasons that I question the kind of exercise that people do to stay fit and attractive is that these often prevent us from finding forms of activity which offer so much more.

Try writing a vivid memory of the last time that you felt this kind of feeling of attunement or embodiment. You might like to write in the present tense ('I am doing this', 'I feel like that') to get a vivid sense of what it was like in the moment, making sure that you attend to all the different senses and feelings involved. It may well be a moment of body in motion, or of solitude, but those are not the only times when such feelings can occur. Think about the moments when this happens for you. Might it be possible to cultivate them further, and to expand out those feelings to the rest of life, so that you treat your body as a separate object less and less? If we do this, we may well find that we become more tuned in: aware of when we are hungry, tired, energized, or shaky. We are less likely to try to force ourselves to eat when we aren't hungry, to work when we are tired, to go out on the town when we need to be looked after at home, or to have sex when we aren't turned on.

It is ironic that many of the unfriendly, objectifying ways of treating our bodies are done in the name of health. Dieting, forcing exercise, and trying to make ourselves thin or muscled, are often done under the veneer of trying to be fit and healthy, when actually they are much more about fitting a certain body ideal, and frequently involve practices which are bad for our bodies (starvation, pushing joints and muscles too far, taking steroids or diet drugs, smoking, etc.) The alternative – of tuning into our bodies – can be healthier, as we learn better how much rest our body needs, what foods are good for us at what times, what activities we enjoy, and how to be comfortable in our body shape rather than wishing it otherwise.

Being embodied does not mean trying to conform to what our culture expects of certain bodies, but rather coming to a friendly relationship with the body that we have and moving forward with it, rather than against it. For example, there are cultural expectations that women will be childbearers because of the bodies that they have, or that men will be constantly ready and willing for sex because of their bodies (see Chapters 4 and 5). Trying to match such expectations if they don't work for us is not a kind way of treating ourselves.

Being embodied also doesn't mean that our bodies won't change over time. Tuning into our bodies might reveal that we feel better when we are fitter, or have more strength, or when we wear certain clothing, or make bodily alterations. By tuning into our whole selves, instead of imposing splits between body and self, we can better understand how we want to be in our bodies, rather than altering our bodies to match some external ideal. We might understand how our bodies can change to better match how we feel about ourselves, and also what the limits are on these changes, and how we might treat our bodies kindly during the process.

When we learn not to hurt ourselves by imposing some false split between body and self, perhaps we will be less likely to hurt others by simply judging them on appearance. We can avoid responding only to the outer surfaces of people, or separating the physical aspects out from other parts of their being. Instead of focusing on breasts and six-packs, we can learn to love the stocky way that person carries themselves which reflects their solidity as a friend, or the lopsided smile that echoes that person's quirky sense of humour, or the slight shaking of the hand that reminds us of that person's fragile beauty.

Chapter 3

Rewriting the rules of love

What are the rules?

The whole of this book is, of course, about the rules of love. We started exploring these in the Introduction, when we looked at the current state of relationships. In Chapter 1 we considered how our rules of relating to ourselves were important in our capacity to love, and be loved by, other people. In the last chapter, we focused on one aspect of the rules of love: the importance of physical attraction. The rest of this book will consider several aspects of the ideal love relationship for which we are encouraged to strive: rules about the kind of sex we should be having, the gender roles we should follow, monogamy, commitment, and how to deal with conflict and break-up. Before looking at those specific aspects, however, we need to consider the general rules of love: what are we looking for from love, and how do we imagine that it happens?

Before going any further, have a think about your own idea of the perfect love relationship. Who would it be with? How would it start? How would you feel about them? How would they feel about you? How would it develop? What type of time and space would you share together? What kind of future would you imagine?

You might also think about where these ideas of the perfect relationship come from. How did you learn what a relationship should be like, or how love should feel? How would you know when it happened and what course it should follow? This isn't some kind of trick to point out that you've been mindlessly following 'the rules'. All of us will have ideas about how relationships should be, and all of these will come from somewhere. It is helpful to explore what they are and where they come from, rather than accepting them without consideration. If we understand the rules more fully, we are better able to decide which of them are more or less useful to us.

Probably the most pervasive rule of love today is the rule of The One: the idea that we are all half-people wandering the world in search of a perfect match who, in the words of *Jerry Maguire*, will 'complete us'. In the movie *I Love You, Man*, the character Sydney challenges his best mate Peter on his upcoming marriage. 'Is she the next one, or The One?' he asks. We all understand the question, because the rule of The One is so deeply ingrained. We may go through several 'next ones' in our search, but eventually we must all meet, and settle down with, The One.

This perception lies behind many of the other rules covered in this book. The One should be immediately and overpoweringly attractive to us. If we haven't found them then we should invest a lot of time and energy in searching for them and making ourselves as desirable as possible to them. Sex with The One should be out-of-this-world: our bodies meeting from the first time as if they were designed for each other. Our love for The One should be so all-consuming that we should never want to look elsewhere. We should understand them on an almost telepathic level so there is never any need for conflict. We should be completely committed to them and live amicably alongside them for the rest of our days. This is the happily-ever-after that we are promised by everything from children's stories to Hollywood movies.

In her book *Fantasies of Femininity*,[1] Jane Ussher writes that children are taught, from an early age, to look for a special someone. Stories and cartoons tell them that there is a prince out there for every princess and that the princess's aim in life should be to make him hers. Only, she shouldn't be too active about it: Cinderella, Rapunzel, Sleeping Beauty and Snow White all got their man by waiting patiently and passively for him to turn up and rescue them, and by behaving kindly and self-lessly in the meantime. Princes, on the other hand, should be actively searching for their princess, and willing to go through any hardship to make them theirs and to rescue them from the perils of life alone. If a partner turns out to be less than desirable in a fairy tale (for example, a beast or a frog), then it is possible to change them into a handsome prince or perfect princess through love.

On reaching adulthood, of course, we move on to media like women's and men's magazines, romantic comedies and action movies, and the omnipresent billboards and television ads which bombard us with images of perfect couples. Women's magazines and romantic comedies in particular are almost exclusively focused on the rules for getting and keeping the perfect partner. Looking at the cover of the first women's magazine I come across, I see headlines about how to dress and apply make-up in order to be 'super-sexy' (presumably in order to attract men), what things to avoid because they are a 'turn offs' to men, what women 'need to know' about how men think during sex, 'naughty sex tricks' to keep sex exciting in relationships, 'relationship truths' that every woman should understand, how long women should wait to sleep with a guy so that he doesn't get bored or disappear afterwards, and 'fun things' to try with 'your man' in a long term relationship (presumably to keep it going).

We might think that there are more messages about relationships in media aimed at women than there are in media aimed at men. However, it is worth remembering that men often read women's magazines and watch romantic comedies too, despite them being generally aimed at a female audience. Also, much media containing the rules of love is not so gendered (adverts and pop songs for example). Finally, even though men's mags spend less time on relationships than women's magazines, researchers such as David Gauntlett[2] have found that, alongside all the gadgets and stories of macho adventure, they contain clear messages about relationships, particularly the idea that men should be attracted to women and should enjoy looking at them. Certainly, page after page of images of women of a certain appearance gives a pretty clear message about the kind of partner for which men should be striving (see Chapter 2). Also, there are strong messages that men need a lot of help and advice in order to find out how to relate to women, how to have sex with them, and how to succeed in relationships. As with women's magazines, men's magazines spend a lot of time decoding and deciphering female behaviour so that men can understand women (see Chapter 5), and there is, again, assistance on how to answer the big question: 'Is she The One?'

We also don't have to look too far into action movies to find similar messages to those of fairy tales. With the exception of a few *Tomb Raider* style films with tough heroines, women mostly require rescuing by men, and part of men's reward for stoic strength and courage is to ride off into the sunset with a woman, James Bond style. Finally, the surge in popularity of 'lads' flicks' or 'bromance movies' suggests that men are interested in watching films about other men trying to figure out their relationships with women. The key plot of most of these movies is about the man meeting, having sex with, and committing to, a woman, and the end of the film is most frequently a wedding or other form of long-term commitment between the male character and his love interest.

We'll examine some of the more gender-specific rules of love in Chapter 5, including the fact that they nearly all assume that relationships will be hetero-sexual, meaning that the rules of gay, lesbian and bisexual relationships are rather less available to us, or have to be inferred from the rules of heterosexual relation-ships. For now, we can simply conclude that most people, whatever their gender, are exposed to these rules of love on a daily basis.

The ideal of The One is not only sold to us by eager advertisers, directors, and magazine editors, it is also embedded in the words we speak. Our language of rela-tionships is one of couples, partners, and soulmates. People refer to their spouses as their other, or even better, half. The lack of available words can make it difficult for people to talk about intimate relationships in any other way. The 'other half' implies that people are not enough on their own. The soulmate suggests that find-ing this person is essential, and that nobody else could possibly provide the com-panionship that someone who was a mate to our very soul would do. The notion of The One implies there is only one such person out there in the world for us, so we must strive to find them (second best is not enough), and keep hold of them once we have them (because there won't be another One). The perfect match, or the idea of Mr/Ms Right, implies that this person, when we find them, will be right and perfect for us in all ways. Finally, the language of love creates hierarchies between romantic relationships and other kinds of relationship. Our partner should also be our *best* friend, the *most* important person in our life. They will be *everything* to us. *True* love is romantic and sexual love, bonding for life with a partner. All other kinds of love (brotherly or sisterly love, platonic love, friendship love, casually sexual love, etc.) are rendered pale and lifeless in comparison.

Some of the main love rules are so pernicious that they require chapters all to themselves. We'll consider the rule that love is so encompassing that we couldn't possibly look elsewhere in the chapter on monogamy (Chapter 6), and the idea of happily-ever-after in Chapter 9. Also, the idea of the perfect partner will come up in Chapters 7 and 8, when we explore the potential for conflict in this way of thinking, and the role of striving for perfection in relationship break-up. For the rest of this chapter we'll focus mostly on the following, connected, rules:

- You must find and keep The One.
- They must be everything for you, and you for them.
- You are not enough alone.
- Love conquers all.

Before we go on, think about this for yourself. What might be problematic about the notion that we should be searching for one person to fulfil all our needs, or the idea that love will conquer all problems in that relationship? Are there alternative ways of doing things that we might consider?

Why question the rules?

The musician Frank Zappa said that bad mental health in the United States was caused by the fact that 'people had been raised on love lyrics'.[3] When you listen to a few such songs you have to wonder whether he was onto something. Time after time, we hear how the singer can't live without their loved one, how they were lost until they found them, how they think about them every moment of the day, and how they long to spend forever in their arms (regardless of the hellish cramp that would inevitably result). There have indeed been joking suggestions that romantic love should be placed on the psychiatric lists of 'mental disorders', given that it has all the hallmarks of an obsessive state which interferes drastically with a person's social and occupational functioning.

Psychologist Bjarne M. Holmes went further than Zappa and conducted research into whether romantic comedies were bad for our health.[4] He found that those who enjoyed rom coms certainly had more unrealistic expectations of relationships: they believed in pre-destined love, for example, and expected partners to be able to read their minds.[5] Other research has found that these ways of thinking are linked to lower relationship satisfaction and more distress, as well as unconstructive approaches to dealing with problems.[6] Ironically, the kind of love we are encouraged to seek is precisely the kind that is most likely to ensure its own demise.

I should be clear here that the point of all this, indeed the point of this book, is not to be anti-love. Being loved, and loving other people, are wonderful things indeed. Some of the best moments in our lives may well be those times when we discover a connection with somebody new, or when we sit up late talking or enjoying each other's bodies, or when we spend a slow weekend with a person with whom we've found an easy intimacy. And love can be the motivating force behind the very best of what humans are capable of: moments of great altruism and self-sacrifice. But these things don't necessarily require the specific kind of romantic love we've examined here in order to happen. In fact, sometimes that version of love may even get in the way. What I'm questioning is the idea that there is only one way of doing love, and the burden that puts upon us and on our relationships.

Before we go any further, let's do a quick exercise to knock romantic love off its perch as the *ultimate* experience in life. I asked a class of students to list the things in their lives that felt as good as the feeling of falling in love (or at least in the same ballpark). These are some of the things they came up with. You can add your own.

- Dancing to my favourite music in a room full of people.
- Holding my newborn baby for the first time.
- My team winning the cup.
- Having something that I wrote published.
- Making it to the finish line.

Of course, it doesn't take long for most of us to become aware that there are a few problems with the romantic love ideal: real life love generally doesn't quite match up to the fairly tale. Even the girls in *Sex and the City*, a programme all about the rules of love, are fairly cynical about the idealized version. Miranda points out the tragedy in going around feeling that you are not enough by yourself, Samantha says that The One is an unattainable ideal which sets people up to fail, and Carrie asks whether soulmates are 'reality or torture device'. Only Charlotte clings to the myth in its entirety, in her statement: 'I believe that there's that one perfect person out there to complete you'. Despite their scepticism, it should be remembered that all of the *Sex and the City* girls meet and commit to their Mr Right by the end of the final series, implying, perhaps, that Charlotte knew best all along. The *Sex and the City* films are a bit more interesting, in at least partially asking the question 'what happens after happily-ever-after?'

Sometimes we forget that mainstream films and TV shows have a certain narrative structure which they follow, with specific plot points and character arcs. Books on scriptwriting state, almost to the second, when each act of a film should start and end, when we should have the turning point, the darkest hour before the dawn, and so on.[7] When we really enjoy a film, it is often because it has hit these moments at just the right times. The problem is that viewing film after film, despite the pleasures involved, can leave us imagining that life should work like this too. As I said in Chapter 1, we are tuned in to stories and narratives. The complexity and messiness of our own love stories can seem wrong when compared against the movie narrative that has become so familiar. But real life doesn't follow a straightforward script. If we're not careful, we end up chasing an elusive once-and-for-all happily-ever-after, either in one relationship, or from relationship to relationship, rather than recognizing that all relationships, and emotional states, will inevitably ebb and flow.

Let's think about a few further reasons for questioning the idealized version of romantic love. Perhaps the most obvious problem with The One is the magical thinking that it involves to believe that there is really only one person out there in the whole world who will be *right* for us, and that we are somehow *meant* to be together. We would need to believe in some powerful force of fate or destiny to bring us into contact with that person. What are the chances that it will just so happen that we grow up in the same neighbourhood, attend the same college, or end up in the same club on a Saturday night?

Psychologists have analysed thousands of relationships to find out what it is that draws people together. They've found that three less-than-mystical forces lie behind most relationship formation: familiarity, similarity and physical attraction (see Chapter 2).[8] We buy products that are familiar and safe (the washing up liquid that was used in our home when we were kids) and we tend to like people more if they are a familiar face as well. We are attracted to people who are similar to us because it's easy to interact with them, because we feel safe that they will probably like us back, and because they give us a good sense of validation about our own values and interests. Familiarity and similarity feed into each other because we're more likely to interact with people who are similar to us (working with us or going to the same classes), and more likely to find similarities with people we see frequently. So we could replace the concepts of Mr and Ms Right with Ms Convenient and Mr A-bit-like-me.

Moving from psychology to sociology, we also know that cross-culturally and historically people 'do' relationships in all kinds of ways. The concept of romantic love we have now is different to the understandings of relationships there have been at other points in time, and concepts of love also vary around the globe today. Just think about the four rules we laid out at the start of the chapter:

- *We must find The One.* There are many times and places in which people have had more than one husband or wife over their life, or at the same time (see Chapter 6).
- *They must be everything to us.* Historically and globally, it is actually quite rare for a spouse to be a person's main confidante or the most intimate person in his or her life. Friends, siblings and colleagues see much more of each other than spouses do in many cultures and communities.
- *We are not enough alone.* There are groups and religions which advocate and value solitude over relationships and/or communal living over coupledom (think about Christian and Buddhist monks and nuns, for example).
- *Love conquers all.* Romantic love is not, and has not always been, the driving force behind unions. Far more often, marriages and similar commitments have been about bringing families together, child-rearing, business arrangements, and meeting financial needs.

Historian Stephanie Coontz reports that the idea of marrying for love and personal choice only became dominant in the eighteenth century, and it was really only in the 1950s that the *majority* of people in Western Europe and North America could afford to marry for those reasons.[9] So the 1950s marriage (and the related nuclear family of two parents and a couple of kids), which is often seen as 'traditional', has, in reality, only been a very recent phenomenon. It was also quite short-lived because, by the 1970s, people had taken the 'love and personal choice' idea to its logical conclusions. They saw that, if marriage was based on personal choice, then both genders would have to have it – so the 1950s breadwinner husband and homemaker wife were out. And, if marriage was based on love, it would have to end if the love was no longer there, hence the rising divorce rate. We see the instability of the 1950s notions of love in the television series *Mad Men* where, even by the early 1960s, marriages are all beginning to fray at the edges and show signs of strain. Coontz concludes that 'people have always loved a love story. But for most of the past our ancestors didn't try to live in one'.[10]

Another problem with The One is that many people find more than one One in their lifetime. Of course. in cases where previous relationships have broken up, we can tell ourselves that our previous One wasn't really right in the same way the current One is (see Chapter 8). The manner in which memories become indistinct and vague, losing their intense heat of emotion over the years, helps with this rewriting of the story of our past. But it is hard to deny that there are people who love once, lose a partner to break-up, death or relocation, and then love again, establishing just as powerful and passionate a relationship with the second (or third, or fourth) person. Also, presumably if they had had a different life they would have met different people with whom they would have formed such relationships. People who are trying to sell us their dating website or magazine might want us to believe in the scarcity of potential partners, but perhaps we could take the pressure off by realizing that it is more likely that there are many people with whom we could connect.

Perhaps the main problem with the pressure to meet and keep The One is the pain and suffering it can result in, both for those who are not in a relationship, and for those who are. It can easily make people feel that they are not enough by themselves. This can result in people who are single, or who leave a relationship, feeling as if they are failures, and that there is something wrong with them. At the same time, people in relationships may stay in them even if they are very unhappy.

Rosalind Gill analysed chick lit fiction and found that singledom was presented as the ultimate horror in these novels.[11] In *Jemima J*, for example, the main character asks 'what could be worse than being single?' She says that it is entirely understandable that 'women stay in relationships, miserable, horrible, destructive relationships, because the alternative is far too horrendous to even consider: Being on their own.' Lack of a partner is equated in these books with loneliness, and finding one is seen as something that gets harder and harder as time goes on. Similar themes occur in films like *Sleepless in Seattle*, when the characters speculate over made-up statistics that a woman over forty is more likely to be killed by a terrorist than to get married.[12] The scarcity idea suggests that people should stay coupled, just in case the person they are with is The One.

There is a similar sense, in lads' movies, that being alone is highly problem-atic.[13] In films like *The 40-Year-Old Virgin* and *Knocked Up* the main character is rather pathetic, often with an unfulfilling job, unrealized dreams, slacker friends, and geeky hobbies. His relationship with a woman rescues him from this state into a more grown-up world where he can be fulfilled at home and at work, and leave childish things behind him. In movies like *Ghosts of Girlfriends Past*, *Shallow Hal* , and *Wedding Crashers*, the main character is a seemingly happy and care-free bachelor at the beginning. Perhaps he is even a successful celebrity, rich and having sex with lots of women (as in many of Will Ferrell's movies). However, the emptiness of this way of life becomes apparent, and the happy ending is some form of commitment to The One. Clearly being alone is not acceptable long-term. It means that you will miss out on the important stuff of life, and perhaps remain stuck in an increasingly isolated form of childhood.

Following from this, it is easy to think that people in relationships have it easy compared to 'singletons'. However, as with so many of the rules, things are hard both for people who don't match up to them *and* for people who do. Many people who desperately want a relationship find that, when they finally get one, it is ter-ribly difficult because of the rules they feel they should be following. Either they spend a lot of time panicking about whether this person is *really* right for them, or they assume that this must be The One and that prevents them from acknowledg-ing things that aren't good about the relationship. The cultural insistence that there is only one One, and the horror that we'll never find anybody else, can keep us in a relationship which is doing nobody any good any more, or may even be destruc-tive. We'll return to this idea when we consider break-ups in Chapter 8.

The romantic ideal can also mean that we neglect the other people in our lives when we embark upon a relationship.[14] How many friends and colleagues do you know who just seem to disappear the moment that they are in a new relationship? If we're honest, how many time have we been the person doing the disappearing? The important bond that we have with friends is steadily weakened because one of us is now putting all their time and energy into their One. Of course, if we isolate ourselves from our friends, we may become even more stuck in a relationship because our partner really does become the only person we can rely upon. The pressure of expectations can land us in a relationship with which we are unhappy (because our partner is not perfect in the ways we'd hoped), but which we are scared to leave (because we have isolated ourselves, so there is nobody to support us through a break-up).

Alternative rules

Of course, all this means that when we do find a Mr or Ms Right, the pressure is on for them to be completely *right*: to be *everything*. This Mr/Ms Right idea is linked to a more general notion we tend to have, that there is always a right and a wrong path when we are faced with a decision in life (in this case whether to have a relationship with a particular person or not). This can leave us feeling terrified of choosing the wrong path. Also, once we have chosen a path we can become highly invested in proving to ourselves, and to others, that it is indeed the right path – so much so, that we might deny any negative points and feel that we are stuck on that path and unable to change.

Actually, decisions are more like the image on the right in Figure 3.1: all the different possible paths (and there may well be more than two) will probably have some negatives and positives attached to them. To complicate it more, some of the things that we initially see as positives might become negatives and vice versa. In the same way, if we decide to form a relationship with a particular person, some gifts and gains will come of it and there will also be some drawbacks and losses involved, just as there would be both good and bad if we decided not to pursue that relationship, or for it to be a different kind of relationship, such as a friendship, or to wait and pursue it later.

If you prefer a story to a diagram, try this version of an old Buddhist tale which I have updated from the original into a bromance formula.[15]

A wise young man's car broke down on the day that he had an important job interview. He took the train but it was heavily delayed. A woman he met on the train drove him in her car at speed through heavy traffic from the station to the offices where the interview was held, but even so he arrived too late and was turned away.

When his buddy came to console him for not getting the job, the young man said, 'Who knows what's good or bad?'

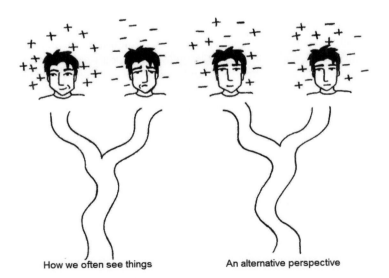

How we often see things   An alternative perspective

Figure 3.1 Right and wrong paths

The next day, the gorgeous woman who had driven him to the interview called him up and asked him out on a date. The foolish buddy came to congratulate him on his good fortune.

'Who knows what's good or bad?' said the young man.

After dating for a while, the woman moved in with the man. All was fine initially, but then they started to have arguments and get on each other's nerves. She was clingy and needy, and the young man needed his own space. Eventually they broke up and she moved out, taking several of his favourite DVDs and his best jacket. The buddy came around to sympathize, bringing a six-pack of beer.

'Who knows what's good or bad?' said the young man.

The young man came up with a bright idea to help other men who'd been through painful break-ups like this. He set up an online company offering advice and a place to chat. Soon he was giving talks around the country. He was a big success and was invited onto TV talk shows. His buddy came around to congratulate him.

'Who knows what's good or bad?' the young man responded.

When do we expect the story to end?

You might have felt sorry for the guy when he missed his interview, and pleased for him when he met the woman, sorry for him when she turned out to be difficult, and happy for him when she left. But if he hadn't missed the interview he wouldn't have met her, if she hadn't helped him they wouldn't have got together, if he hadn't had that relationship at all he wouldn't have learnt many of the things he used to set up his online company (or at least wouldn't have learnt them then, or in the same way), and if she hadn't left him he wouldn't have experienced all the other triumphs and tragedies, loves and losses, that would mark the rest of his life after that point. Perhaps we could see all relationships, and relationship endings, as having potential positives and negatives to them (something we'll explore more in Chapter 8).

The other problem with the idea of meeting the *right* person is the massively high expectations that it places on people. Once we've found Mr or Ms Right, presumably they should be right in *every* way, completing us and fulfilling each of our needs. Such expectations can cause many problems. Given the extreme improbability of somebody matching up to our ideal of perfection in every way, it could mean that we never take a risk on a relationship because we can always spot one thing about the person that we don't like. This could lead to the kind of high turnover dating we see in sitcoms, where each week the characters find somebody who seems absolutely perfect until we discover that they have an overbearing mother, a strange sexual kink, or the habit of leaving the toilet door open.

Such pressure could also mean that all our relationships are doomed to failure. One alternative to assuming that our partner *is* The One (and thus ignoring any problems in the relationship), is assuming that a person is only The One if there are no problems in the relationship at all: an extremely unlikely situation, as we'll see in Chapter 7. Putting that kind of pressure on our partners seems a pretty sure way of chasing them away. When I first heard the Bob Dylan song *It Ain't Me, Babe*, I thought the singer was a callous person who didn't love his partner enough. I now see it as being about someone whose partner wants an impossible level of perfection. They want someone who is always strong, always there, who makes their decisions for them, looks after them, and stands up for them no matter what they do: someone who would die for them if called upon to do so. It is this romantic dream that wrecks any possibility of a relationship. Nobody could ever be enough.

So what are some alternatives to these rules of love? One alternative to The One who is everything to us might be to recognize the different things that we get from the different relationships in our lives.

Try writing a list of the things that you would like from an important relationship, and then noting the people in your life from whom you might also get these things. They might be people you already know, or people you could find in future. Below is an example to give you the idea.

This activity links back to that one we did in Chapter 1. It reminds us that we are plural, and that different sides of ourselves emerge in different relationships and situations. Perhaps it is a good idea to cultivate a variety of relationships to remind us of all the selves that we are.

An alternative to the idea that we are not enough alone is to recognize the importance of solitude as well as relationships. We've considered how too much focus on one relationship might take away from the importance of other people in our lives. The other thing that we can give up when we commit to a major relationship is our time alone. As we saw in Chapter 1, some time alone is probably vital in order to find some peace with ourselves, which is an important foundation to our relationships with others. We'll return to this idea in Chapter 10. Solitude can help us to cultivate our imaginations, to keep track of our own goals and dreams rather than getting completely bound up in someone else's, to remember what we are capable of rather than always allowing the other person to do certain tasks, and to aid recovery and processing of the situation when times get difficult.[16]

Table 3.1 What I want and who I can get it from

What I want	Who I can get it from
Someone I feel really at ease with – like I can be myself.	My partner, my close friend, my sister. I feel this way when I go running alone.
Someone who understands what my job means to me.	My work colleagues are the only ones who completely get it.
Someone to watch old movies with.	My old friend. I could join a group who go to the art cinema once a month.

When we are in relationships where we live and sleep 24/7 with somebody else, we can get so entwined that we rather lose track of ourselves, and we can get used to having somebody else's eyes on us much of the time. As we saw in Chapter 1, we easily slip into constantly monitoring ourselves through the imagined gaze of this other person. This is another good reason for getting some solitude or space. Of course, today solitude might require more than just being alone physically. We are not really in solitude if we are always available to emails, phone calls and text messages.

So an alternative to seeing ourselves as incomplete people searching for one person to make us whole, is to see ourselves as people who need both time alone *and* connections with many people in our lives. What about the final rule that love will conquer all? The Beatles sang that 'all you need is love', and it may well be that caring for other people – and getting cared for – is a pretty good recipe for happiness. However, if what we mean by 'love' is romantic love, then it is risky to imagine that it will cure every ill.

The first part of the idea that love conquers all is that love is enough when problems come along. People often imagine that by loving their partners they will show them how loveable they are, and thus cure all their problems. Of course, it's not that love is unimportant in this way: support and love are important in enabling people to feel good about themselves. But they are not enough to make all problems disappear, because problems are an inherent part of life. It is also unlikely that one person's love will eradicate all the negative messages their partner received before they were together (see Chapter 1).

Beyond this, the desire to 'cure someone' with your love can actually be damaging rather than beneficial. This has been found in many studies of those who try to help and heal others.[17] Going back to Jane Ussher's analysis of fairy tales, it can be just as tempting to be the knight on the white charger whom everybody applauds, as it is to be the princess in the tower who doesn't have to be responsible for anything and can just wait to be rescued (and these things are not necessarily tied to gender: see Chapter 5).

It is a fantastic feeling when somebody says that you've made their life better. However, there are risks in taking on somebody else's troubles and trying to fix them. For one thing, most people, as we've seen, need some solitude in order to deal with their problems and to come to a sense that they are an okay person. If we try to come along and fix everything, it can be hard for them to get that time alone, and easy for them to focus their whole life around the relationship with us instead. Also, it might well be that we offer the person a great deal, only to realize, later on, that we can't actually give that much, or that they want even more from us. We have to let them down, leaving them feeling resentful and us feeling guilty.

Additionally, trying to rescue somebody gives a clear message that we don't think they are capable of helping themselves, which will likely further damage their confidence. We may deny them the chance to address their problems and to learn from sorting things out themselves. The philosopher Jean-Paul Sartre fell, several times, for young, vulnerable women who didn't really know where they were in the world yet. Each time he set them up, finding courses for them to attend or jobs for them to do, deciding that they should become an actress, a writer, or an artist, and often buying them flats to live in. Most of the women became more and more unhappy. By 'rescuing' them, Sartre denied them the chance to find their own ways forward.[18] It is ironic that what seem like the kindest acts can be the most cruel. These problems are worth remembering, whether we are the knight rushing to the rescue without a second thought, or the princess who is ready and willing to give up all their own power and responsibility in order to be saved.

The other myth which is linked to the idea of love conquering all is that love will combat any differences between us in relationships. From fairly tales, through Shakespeare and Jane Austen to romance novels and Hollywood movies, we've been taught that it is possible to change people into what we want them to be: beasts can be domesticated and shrews can be tamed. When we find that The One isn't the ideal of perfection we'd hoped they would be, instead of getting rid of them and continuing our quest, or convincing ourselves that they really are The One and putting up with it, we might decide to embark on a project to mold them into the perfect partner. This is fraught with problems. Again, we are giving the other person the message that they aren't good enough as they are. They might respond by changing but then resent us for it. They might take on board this message and become despondent, wondering what it was about them that ever appealed to us in the first place, given that we seem to find them so unacceptable now. We end up feeling like a nag who is always on their case and the whole thing can spiral downhill from there.

Rather than trying to change somebody into being the same as us in their behaviour, attitudes, and values, it might be better to realize that differences between people are inevitable, and to think about how we manage those differences when they come up without trying to change the other person into a clone of ourselves. We will consider some of these issues in more depth in the last section of the chapter.

Beyond rules? Embracing uncertainty

There's one final rule of romantic love which we haven't addressed yet, and that is the rule about how it happens. The metaphors we have for love give us some clues to this: love is something we fall into, it hits us like a thunderbolt, it drives us wild and crazy, we go head-over-heels for it, and we burn with passion as we feel the electricity or chemistry between us.

People rarely pay attention to the metaphors that they speak all the time: they are such a mundane and ubiquitous part of our language. But metaphors are vital in giving voice to our experience and in shaping it.[19] The metaphors of love describe an uncontrollable force which hits us, knocks us over, or drives us into a volatile state which is red hot and potentially explosive.

What does it mean that we describe, and experience, love in this way? Well, one thing it does is to absolve us of any responsibility for our actions. If we are bowled over by love, or consumed by its fire, then surely there's nothing much we can do other than give in to it. As we saw in Chapter 1, we have a tendency to view our world through opposites, and romantic love is clearly placed on the side of passion, emotion, and heat, rather than the side of reason, rationality, and coolness. But these opposites are problematic.[20] The brain does not work in such a way that logic, reason, and rationality happen in one place, and emotion, passion, and feelings happen somewhere quite different. We are always and inevitably both thinking *and* feeling. The two things are not extricable. It can help, with love, to question our metaphors and to consider this 'passion and reason' perspective. This brings an element of choice to the matter: perhaps we can choose whether to be overwhelmed by love or to surf it like a wave, to close off from it or to open up to it. Rather than viewing love as a thunderbolt or fire, we might view it as a beast that we have the power to ride or tame, or as an invitation which we might refuse or accept.

This ties back to the work of Bjarne M. Holmes, which we considered earlier. He explored the rom com version where love is predestined and partners are tele-pathic. Holmes and his colleagues have found that there is more relationship satis-faction to be gained in the view that love is something that is cultivated, rather than something that is mysteriously there or not there. Here, we have a metaphor like a farmer's field which needs tending year on year to continue to yield a crop. A problem in some of the psychological writing on this topic, though, is a tendency to compare the emotional version of love in the rom coms to a more sensible rational version which doesn't actually sound very exciting. This set of opposites is also worth challenging: perhaps we can have controllable thunderbolts and reasonable chemistry, as well as passionate invitations and fields of feeling to cultivate.

Looking back to Chapter 1, we can see now how interlinked our ideas of love are with our ideas about our selves. A lot of what romantic love offers is somebody to prove that we are okay in ourselves and not lacking in any way. Indeed, one of the intoxicating things about falling in love is this very possibility of finding that we are not lacking after all. At first, we present all the best sides of ourselves, and we have them reflected back in the eyes of somebody who finds us amazing, and this makes us feel wonderful. Understandably, we want to get as much of that feel-ing as possible. Perhaps we really *are* okay? As love deepens, it may be that our partner sees some of the parts of ourselves that we are less comfortable with. Per-haps, in the flush of love, they are positive about those too, finding them endearing rather than irritating, and we are reassured again that we are not lacking. The thing we most fear may not be true.

But our fear that we are lacking is so intrinsic that it is bound to sneak back in.[21] As we saw in Chapter 1, we simply *are* all imperfect, complex, ever-chang-ing people, so there is no way that it couldn't. This is the big horror of intimate relationships: the person we wanted so desperately to prove to us that we were not flawed is the very person who is *bound* to see our flaws. It is impossible to monitor ourselves all the time. And it is at home, with those with whom we live, that the mask is most likely to drop and we will show the vulnerable sides of ourselves. It can feel unbearable when our partner sees those parts of ourselves that we least want to acknowledge.

There are many ways in which lack sneaks back in. Perhaps we discover that this person was actually in love with the *idea* of us, rather than who we really are. They loved the outgoing party-person, not the homebody we are the other six days of the week; or the high-flying success story, not the vulnerable little child we can become in the middle of the night. Alternatively, our partner might genuinely love us warts-and-all, but we are so invested in seeing that look of total adoration in their eyes which seems to prove that we are completely un-warty that we seek it more and more desperately, and end up seeing it less and less often. Finally, it might be that we become irritated with the puppy dog gaze of our partner because we know for a fact that we aren't that perfect. Because of our own deep down belief that we are lacking, we start to see our partner as stupid for not recognizing this, and we brush off all their compliments. Maybe we place them in a double-bind: yearning and needy for their love and approval, but struggling to accept it when it is given.

Of course, at the same time, the situation is working in reverse and we may feel betrayed to discover that our lover is not just the shiny version that we saw when we first laid eyes on them, or irritated that they become needy and clingy when we stop gazing at them in wonderment during every mundane moment that we share. Sometimes one, or both, people in the relationship then try subtly, or not so subtly, to change the other person into what they would rather they were (the person they thought they were initially, or their idealized perfect partner). Judging, nagging, tweaking, and comparing can result, leaving them feeling even more lacking and imperfect, and increasingly defensive because they don't want to be seen in this way.

We'll consider this conflict spiral more in Chapter 7. For now, let's remind ourselves of the alternative to seeing ourselves as fixed things which are lacking: that is to see ourselves as both plural and in process (see Chapter 1). If we can remember that this is true of ourselves, then we have no need to be defensive when a partner sees a different side of ourselves to that which they have seen before. We can accept that that is part of us too. Also, we understand that it is not *all* that we are, nor is it who we are *all* of the time, so we don't have to feel trapped by the fact that they have seen it.

Of course, this works the other way too. If we accept that anyone we are with is inevitably plural and in process then we are more able to accept the different aspects of them that we see. Perhaps we can enjoy the intimacy of being let in to the selves to which few others have access. Also, we are unlikely to try to change them, because we recognize that fixing someone is impossible anyway, and that they will inevitably change over time. There is a moment which encapsulates this in the film *Inception*. Leonardo DiCaprio's character, Cobb, needs to find out whether he is in reality or stuck in his own dream state. His moment of realization comes when he sees that his wife is too much like his ideal version of her: not the real person with all her flaws, intricacies, and complexities. Importantly, Cobb chooses not to remain with this fantasy version, however perfect she might be, and however much he has longed for her since her death, because he preferred the real multifaceted and ever-changing human being that he knew. We are in danger of harming the other person, and ourselves, if we try to make them into a too-perfect ideal.

Understanding that we, and others, are plural and in process links back to another of the pervasive ideas about love that we hear repeated in love songs and romance fiction: the idea that people *belong* to each other in relationships, that they are our *possession*. Accepting that someone is plural (and that we may, or may not, see all sides of them), and that they are constantly changing (rather than being something that we can fix and control), means embracing not only uncertainty, but also the freedom of the other person: recognising that they do not, and cannot, really belong to us. That is a difficult thing to do when so much is invested in our romantic relationships and when we so want the world to be controllable and to give us the happily-ever-after for which we long.

These themes will crop up again and again over the rest of the book, particularly when we think about freedom and belonging in Chapters 6, 7, and 8. In chapter 9, we will ask ourselves what we can commit to in love, if it isn't to belonging to someone.

Before we go on, let's summarize the alternatives to the rules that we have considered here:

- *You must find and keep The One.* There is no One but many people in our lives who will be close and important to us.
- *They must be everything for you, and you for them.* Nobody can be everything to us, because there are many sides to us and to them, and we are all constantly changing. Trying to keep someone as The One we met at aged 20 denies them the inevitable changes they will go through in life.
- *You are not enough alone.* You are okay and don't require another person to prove that to you. Some amount of solitude is vital and you will inevitably relate to many different people in your life.
- *Love conquers all.* Loving someone can be a powerful force in self-confidence and support, but possessive love which insists on fixing people and holding them back can be bad for both relationships and for individuals.

Chapter 4

Rewriting the rules of sex

What are the rules?

When we talk about relationships (as in, 'are you in a relationship?', 'who was your last relationship with?', or 'are they having a relationship?') what we almost invariably mean is a *sexual* relationship. Sex and love have become intertwined and we generally assume that they come, and go, together. We even use the word 'lover' synonymously with 'sexual partner'. It is taken for granted that partners will have sex together, and that stopping having sex is a sign of problems in a relationship. To be attracted to someone (see Chapter 2) means to want to have sex with them.

Sexual compatibility is seen as vital in demonstrating whether a relationship is 'right' or not. In the film *The 40-Year-Old-Virgin*, the virgin of the title, Andy, is encouraged by his mates to have sex with someone other than the woman he is falling for, because sex is so important that he needs to get it right before being sexual with a potential life partner. How many potential *Sex and the City* relationships failed because the characters liked different things sexually? We can see just how significant this is when we compare sex to religion. Charlotte and Trey struggle because they can't have sex, but Charlotte and Harry do fine despite being Episcopalian and Jewish respectively.

Also, going back to Chapter 1, our own self-identities have also become increasingly sexualized. Sex is seen as being such a huge part of who we are that our sexual 'orientation' is one of the things we list about ourselves, along with gender, age, and occupation. We increasingly tell sexual stories about who we are and how we came to be that way (such as coming out stories, stories about having been the victim of sexual assault, or the proliferation of blogs in which people write about their sex lives).[1] We hear these stories on talk shows and documentaries; contestants on reality TV shows are chosen for their spicy sexual identity or history; and there are now whole sections of bookshops devoted to biographies and autobiographies of people who have been sex workers, or who have histories of childhood sexual abuse. Sexual fantasies and desires are often assumed to provide some kind of insight into who we *really* are (see Chapter 1), perhaps due to the impact of Sigmund Freud's theories on our culture. Society has become more sexualized, such that many people's self-confidence and sense of themselves is tied up with how sexually desirable they think they are, whether they are sexually fulfilled, and how open they are able to be about their sexuality.

So sex is extremely significant in our relationships and in our personal identities. What are the taken-for-granted rules about sex? This is easy for me to answer having worked as a sex therapist. Virtually every client, of whatever age, gender, or cultural background, who came into the clinic, wanted one thing above all others. That was to be

Normal.

People were happy to have sex that wasn't particularly pleasurable, as long as it meant that they were normal. Some people would even have sex that was painful if it would show that they were normal. Plenty of people came along to sex therapy, despite being hugely embarrassed by the process, in the hope that it could make them normal. Some had put themselves through all kinds of drugs and medical procedures in an attempt to become more normal. People who had all kinds of anxieties and discomforts around sex still made themselves do it regularly in order to prove that they were – you guessed it – normal.[2]

So, what is this normal sexual relationship that everyone is trying to have? Think about it for a moment. You might want to consider questions such as: Who is involved in this sexual relationship? What kind of relationship do they have? How often are they sexual? When and where are they sexual? What kind of sex are they having? What is the purpose of the sex? When does sex start and finish? What are the vital elements of the sexual encounter? How long does it last?

The sociologist Gayle Rubin writes that a key aspect of the way that we view sex is that it is on a hierarchy.[3] The kind of proper, normal, sex which you considered goes at the top of the hierarchy, and everything else goes underneath. She visualizes it like a pyramid. Somewhere on the pyramid each culture, religion, government, or medical profession draws a line which separates the sexual relationships which are seen as normal, healthy, and good, from those which are seen as abnormal, unhealthy, and bad. You might have a go at drawing for yourself where different kinds of sexual relationships are on our current sex pyramid. Your 'normal sexual relationship' (from before) goes at the top, and then you can work your way down the pyramid (writing on the sexual relationships which are next most acceptable, then next, then next). Alternatively, you might start at the bottom of the pyramid with the least acceptable forms of sexual relationship you can imagine and work your way back up. Think about where your own society or community would draw the line between acceptable and unacceptable sex. We'll come back to the variations in the hierarchy of different groups within society later in the chapter. Right now, we're focusing on the mainstream perspective. Your pyramid might look something like the following (obviously I haven't included all possible kinds of relationships here, and this is likely to vary across groups, cultures and communities).

Rubin herself drew the diagram on page 58 to illustrate how sex was viewed. In the inside circle of the diagram we have what she called the 'charmed circle' of

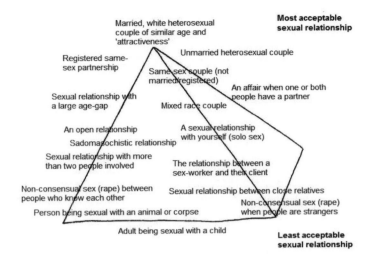

Figure 4.1 The sex hierarchy pyramid

sexuality. The more that people's sexual relationships fall into this circle, the more acceptable, good, normal, and natural they are seen as being. Your earlier definition of normal sex probably included many of these ideas. In the outside circle of the diagram we have the 'outer limits' of sexuality. The more people's sexual relationships fall into this circle, the more unacceptable, bad, abnormal, and unnatural they are viewed as being. You can see how it is a matter of degrees. For example, if a heterosexual woman has casual sex, rather than sex in a long-term relationship, she is generally not too frowned upon, but if she starts taking payment for sex, or filming it, then she becomes increasingly unacceptable. Similarly, sex between women and between men has become increasingly acceptable, but much more acceptable if they are a couple in a marriage or civil partnership who do it in private, than if they are in an open relationship and go out to kinky clubs.

So, linked to the idea of a hierarchy of acceptable sex, is the fear that a person might fall into unacceptable sex. Rubin says that people see it as a slippery slope: if they stray outside of the charmed circle a little bit they might get sucked all the way out of it. She says we fear that if we step outside, 'the barrier against scary sex will crumble and something unspeakable will skitter across'.[4]

However, in recent years, the situation has become more muddled. You might already have found yourself thinking 'hang on, I thought that everyone today was meant to be adventurous about sex and to do some of those things that are in the outer limits, or lower down the pyramid'. Particularly amongst younger people, it has been increasingly expected that they will have had several sexual partners, and perhaps be bi-curious, and to try out things like anal sex, light bondage, or threesomes. Certainly, clubbing clothes for young women have become more

The charmed circle:
Good, Normal, Natural,
Blessed Sexuality

Heterosexual
Married
Monogamous
Procreative
Non-commercial
In pairs
In a relationship
Same generation
In private
No pornography
Bodies only
Vanilla

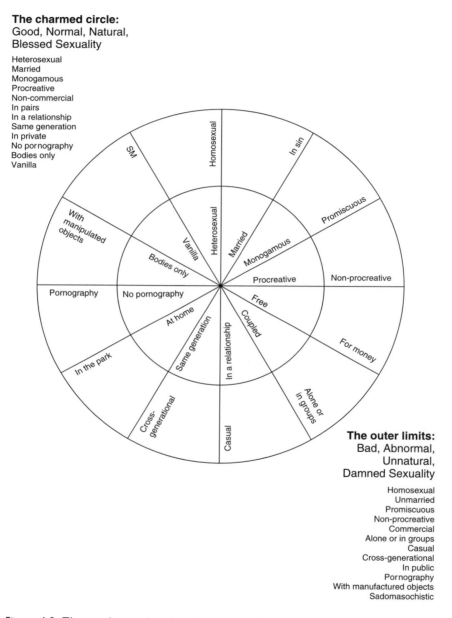

The outer limits:
Bad, Abnormal,
Unnatural,
Damned Sexuality

Homosexual
Unmarried
Promiscuous
Non-procreative
Commercial
Alone or in groups
Casual
Cross-generational
In public
Pornography
With manufactured objects
Sadomasochistic

Figure 4.2 The sex hierarchy: the charmed circle vs. the outer limits

sexualized, and sex-related activities like pole-dancing have become fashionable as leisure pursuits.[5] These days it can be seen as boring not to have a history of sexual experimentation.

I would say that the sex hierarchy remains, although certainly the line is drawn somewhat lower down the pyramid than it used to be. It is clear that we still do have a strong idea about what 'normal' sex should be like in relationships but, in addition to that, we also have the idea that we should be having 'great sex' in relationships. This might involve being more adventurous and open to trying some of the spicy activities that used to be strictly in the outer limits. Because sex and love are so bound up together, we feel that relationships must stay sexually exciting over time in order to prove that they still loving and, therefore, still working. This leaves people in a new kind of tension whereby they are constantly policing the boundaries between great sex and dangerous sex.

The researcher Merl Storr found this when she studied women who attended parties to buy sex toys (an event in people's homes which has become increasingly popular in recent decades).[6] She found that women now buy products like fluffy handcuffs, fancy-dress outfits for role-playing, and sparkly riding crops, but that they work hard to distinguish these things from 'properly' kinky activities which are still viewed as deviant and dangerous. You can see this in the way the products are marketed. Everything is pink, studded with gemstones, or soft, to make it safe and non-scary. Similarly, there may be implicit rules about how far it is okay to go with bi-curiosity: kissing and dancing with a friend in a nightclub might be okay, but having a more ongoing sexual relationship might be viewed as going too far. Also, what is known as the double standard of female sexuality remains: the idea that women who have lots of sexual partners are whores or slags, while men are considered studs or lads for doing the same things. It is, just now, rather harder for women to find the balance point whereby they are considered experienced enough not to be boring, but not so experienced that they are labelled a slut.

So two of the main rules about sex – to have normal sex and to have great sex – may often be in conflict, and there is anxiety and discomfort about this which remains unspoken because, despite all the increasing sex talk, people still find it difficult to open up about their personal thoughts and feelings about sex. Canadian psychologist Sandra Byers has studied communication about sex in many contexts.[7] She found that people who had been in relationships for over a decade still hadn't told their partners all of their sexual likes and dislikes. Also, they understood about 60 percent of what their partner liked sexually but only around 20 percent of what they didn't like, so both communication and understanding about sex in relationships isn't great.[8]

To summarize, the rules of sex at the moment seem to be:

- sex is very important, and a defining feature of our relationships and identities;
- we should have *normal* sex in our relationships;
- we must not stray into abnormal sex; but

- it should be *great* sex; and
- we mustn't communicate openly about what we really want sexually.

Why question the rules?

We need to question these rules about sex because, when we bring them all together, what they add up to is a good deal of suffering. We saw in Chapter 1 that people generally walk around with a mask on, pretending they are fine when underneath they actually share similar anxieties and worries about themselves. This is particularly the case in relation to sex. The billboards, internet porn sites, Hollywood movies and boastful blokey conversations tell a story of easy, exciting, explosive sex where everyone is always up for it, while the agony columns, sex therapy consultations, and spam emails promising longer, bigger, and better sex tell quite a different story of fear, self-doubt and even desperation.

For most people, sex is not simply a matter of falling into bed with someone at the drop of a hat, and easily finding their way to a mind-blowing orgasm. Rather, it frequently involves concerns over how to know whether they should have sex or not; whether their body is going to do what it needs to for sex to occur; whether their partner will be turned off by their naked body (particularly their genitals); how they will make sure that sex is safe without ruining the moment; whether they will orgasm too quickly or slowly or not at all; and how they will know what to do to turn the other person on, amongst many other anxieties.

The sexual 'dysfunctions' listed in medical and psychiatric manuals are, according to a lot of surveys, so common that it is wrong to think of them as abnormalities at all.[9] You could say that, actually, it is most normal *to* have a problem with sex. That doesn't mean that we are somehow all suffering from medical disorders which we need drugs and operations to fix (although clearly some sexual matters are related to health issues like heart disease and diabetes). Rather, it means that we are all striving to meet this ideal of normal sex which often does not look anything like what we really find exciting, if, indeed, we even have a clear idea of what that is.

We saw in the Introduction that rigid rules are generally bad both for those who fall outside of them, *and* for those who fit within them. This is sometimes a difficult concept to grasp. We can see how it must be tough for those in the outer limits who are regarded as bad, dangerous, or crazy, for their sexual proclivities, but surely it is easy enough for those who occupy the charmed circle of sexuality. Don't they have an easy time, totally accepted by the society in which they live?

The pyramid sex hierarchy gives a useful clue to how the rules are bad for those at the top, as well as lower down. Think about that tiny point at the top of a pyramid. What a precarious place to be standing. How easy it would be to fall off. That can be what it is like for those who do manage to fit within 'normal' sex. There are so many possible ways to fall. They have to constantly police the boundaries against scary sex, whilst making sure they are still having exciting enough sex to show that they are desired and that their relationship is good. Also, they have to be wary of all these possible sexual problems (and it seems like a new one is invented every year) because it would be so shameful to fall into being 'dysfunctional'. This is another way of feeding that fear that we spoke of in Chapter 1 – that we are somehow a flawed or failing human being. People on the inside of the charmed circle have to do a lot of work to *stay* on the inside, by constantly monitoring themselves.

Also, people within the charmed circle may often be those who enjoy sex the least, because they are much more concerned with fitting what is normal than with finding out what is pleasurable to them. As I've said, a lot of clients in sex therapy have little idea what they might enjoy sexually, because the desires to be seen as normal and to keep their relationship going overwhelm any curiosity they may have about how their own unique sexualities might work. Often, they are so tuned in to what society wants, and what they assume their partner must want, that they have given little thought to what might turn them on[10] or – if they have – they keep this purely in the realm of private fantasy, feeling guilty and ashamed about it.

People in the outer limits may communicate fairly well with each other about sex because there are fewer assumptions there about what sex *should* be like. But, as we have seen, people in the charmed circle often communicate badly about sex, perhaps because they assume that their partners will want them to have 'normal' sex and that everybody shares the same rules about what this means.

A concrete example of how the rules may lead to less enjoyable sex is the assumptions many people have about what normal sex involves: some 'foreplay', followed by a penis penetrating a vagina, both parties becoming more and more excited and then having orgasms. We can see that this is the norm because all of the 'dysfunctions' listed in medical manuals, and many of the sex aids which are advertised, are about something going wrong with this process: vaginas being too tight for penetration, penises not being erect, men orgasming 'too soon' to penetrate, or people not reaching orgasm.[11]

Bizarrely, there is still relatively little awareness that this version of sex is actually unlikely to result in orgasm for women. One consistent finding in sex research is that most women require clitoral stimulation in order to have an orgasm, which means that 70 percent of women cannot orgasm from penetration alone.[12] This is because it is quite difficult for penetration to stimulate the clitoris: most women need to use their hand, their partner's hand, a vibrator, their legs squeezed together, or some other means. For some women it can be easier for this to happen if they are *not* being penetrated, and some prefer certain positions which make it easier to do this as the same time as penetration.[13]

There is also an assumption here that men will want penis-in-vagina sex. Not all of them do: some prefer oral sex, manual sex, and other varieties. And, of course, this is clearly a heterosexual model because it involves one penis and one vagina. It has also been argued that the focus is mostly on male orgasms (as the end point of sex) and that the wording we use to describe it puts the focus on men, rather than women: why do we call it 'penetrative' sex, rather than 'enveloping' sex?

This norm of sex actually *causes* people to have sexual problems which they wouldn't have if the kind of sex that they found most pleasurable was considered just as normal as penis-in-vagina intercourse.

We also know that many of those who appear to be in the charmed circle, or at the top of the pyramid, really aren't. We live in a time when perhaps the most newsworthy story after terrorism is the story that somebody strayed into the sexual outer limits. How many times do we hear about the politician who had an affair, the sportsman who is rumoured to be gay, the celebrity who filmed themselves having sex and is now all over the internet, or the public figure who has been discovered to have some kind of fetish? We know that rates of secret infidelity in marriage go as high as 50 or 60 percent (see Chapter 6). If we added that up with all the people who are keeping other aspects of current, or past, sexual desires and activities from their partners, friends, and families, then the proportion of people who are really on top of the pyramid would get pretty small. How many people have a hidden folder of porn on their computer, for example, or some sexy clothing that they enjoy wearing when nobody else is around, or a sexual encounter they had when younger which they hope nobody will ever find out about?

Of course, the sex hierarchy *is* also very bad for those who are lower down the pyramid. They might be freer to explore their sexuality and to find out what they enjoy, but they also live with the great burden of being seen as less than normal, less than acceptable, by the rest of the world around them. And that is the best case scenario. At the worst, in many cultures, they are demonized, criminalized and pathologized: seen as evil, bad and mad.

Think about the people who come just under the top of the pyramid. None of those groups has a completely easy ride. Families and friends still put pressure on unmarried couples to tie the knot or to raise children in a certain way. Bisexual people in relationships are frequently not recognized at all, because they are assumed to be straight or gay (depending on the gender of their partner), and people often expect them to be promiscuous and to go off with someone else.[14] While homophobia may have decreased, it is certainly not a thing of the past.[15] The word 'gay' remains amongst the most common playground and bar-room insults. Generally speaking, in our culture, heterosexuality is assumed unless proven otherwise. All of the billboard and magazine images of couples that we see every day are heterosexual. All of the anniversary cards are for heterosexual couples. Nobody ever asks a heterosexual person when they realized they were heterosexual, or what they think caused their heterosexuality.[16] A lot more everyday work has to go into mundane things like phone conversations (a woman having to correct the cold-caller that actually there is more than one 'lady of the house', or a man having to tell the plumber that no, my wife will not be in on Tuesday, but my husband will).[17]

As I mentioned in the Introduction, another feature of the rules, for those who are just slightly outside them, is the pressure to show that they are, in every other respect, just like those on the top of the pyramid. The line of acceptability remains, and those who can't prove themselves similar enough to the norm stay underneath it. This means that the rules for those just outside the charmed circle may be just as constraining as for those completely inside. For example, lots of lesbians, bisexuals, and gay men have just as restrictive ideas about what normal sex should involve as heterosexuals do: how often they should be having it, and with whom, and how their bodies should work. There might be an idea that sex between women should be very mutual with both people orgasming simultaneously, which doesn't work for those who need to focus on either giving or getting an orgasm, or for whom orgasm is less important. There might be an idea that sex between women should involve toys and gadgets, which isn't what everyone wants. There may be rules that sex between men should, or should not, involve penetration in order to be 'proper' or 'normal' sex, or that sex should always be edgy and new, when a regular sexual script is just as acceptable.

As we've seen in the previous chapters, one thing which alerts us to the fact that the rules are not set in stone is the fact that they vary over time and across cultures. Certainly this applies to the rules of sex. For men in positions of power in Ancient Greece, it was acceptable to have sex with anyone of a lower status than yourself (which included women, servants, and younger men). Before the nineteenth century there was no conceptualization of people who were heterosexual or homosexual, rather there were just some sexual acts which were, or weren't, acceptable. Masturbation was frowned upon for many years and considered to cause all kinds of medical problems, while, now, many sex therapists prescribe it to their clients. When 'heterosexuality' and 'homosexuality' were invented as terms they were both regarded as perversions, since they involved sex which was not for the purpose of procreation. In the last century, homosexuality was seen as a sin, then a crime, then a mental disorder, and then a sexuality alongside (if not quite equal to) heterosexuality.[18]

We don't even need to cross continents or centuries to see how sexual acceptability can change. Even in one person's lifetime, fashionable sex can alter such that an activity like oral or anal sex has gone from being totally beyond the bounds of acceptability to something in which many, or even most, people engage.

These shifts alert us to the possibility that some of the things currently in the outer limits, or lower down the pyramid, may be problematically located there. Perhaps the inside/outside, or hierarchical, way of viewing sex that we have at the moment is not the most useful way of understanding things.

Another problem with our current way of viewing sex and sexuality is that it involves a lot of problematic conflation. Think back to the inner and outer circles. There is often an assumption that:

natural = normal = healthy = good
and
unnatural = abnormal = unhealthy = bad

There are problems with every one of those '=' signs.

There has been a great concern, in recent years, to find evidence that sexualities can be explained by biology – in order to prove their legitimacy. This is based on the assumption that things that are natural are more acceptable or good. However, it is worth questioning this link. First, it is highly likely that something as complex as sexuality is intricately constructed rather than being simply *either* biological *or* social. Rubin likens sex to food. People certainly have biological impulses to eat, but the ways in which these manifest themselves in our lives (the specific foods we eat, when and how we eat them) is massively shaped by our experiences growing up, the cultures we live in, and the choices we make through life. Second, even if we could simplistically say that one particular sexuality was biologically caused, one was a result of someone's childhood experience, and one was something they had chosen as an adult – which we *can't* – would that mean that we should treat those people differently from one another? Why is something being 'natural' assumed to be somehow better? We certainly don't apply this reasoning when we come up out of the subway talking on our mobile phone and looking for a place to buy a latte.

Another point about purely biological explanations of sexual behaviours is that it is generally assumed that something being biological means that we were born that way. For example, if people of a certain sexuality turn out to have a certain map of brain functioning, or hormonal make-up, it is often assumed that biology *caused* their sexuality. However, our choices in life, and social pressures upon us, also shape our biology. That is how learning works: when we teach ourselves a new skill, our brain connects up in new ways such that the skill comes increasingly easily to us. A good example is the impact that long-term meditating has on brain functioning, hormonal levels, breathing and heart-rate.[19] So, when researchers make claims that certain sexualities are inborn, we might question whether that really follows from finding a neurological, or other physiological, difference.[20]

As we saw, in the case of love, in Chapter 3, we need to be cautious with metaphors. Sex therapist Leonore Tiefer suggests that we often use physiological metaphors, like digestion, for sex. When we view it it in this way we tend to see sex as something evolved and inbuilt which stays consistent over our lifetime, which is the same across people and cultures, and over which we have no choice. If we have any problems with it we should seek medical help to fix it. If, instead, we used a metaphor like dancing we would view sex as something we learn from the culture around us, which has many different styles, which changes over our lives and varies across cultures, and about which we have choice (the kind of dancing we do, or whether we enjoy dancing at all). If we have any problems with dancing, we might take lessons, learn from others, or try a different kind of dancing.[21]

Turning to the idea that normal = good, we can ask ourselves whether the fact that lots of people do something is necessarily grounds to think that that thing is somehow better, or more healthy, than something that fewer people do. Lots of people eat junk food and watch over 20 hours of television every week, for example.

The notion that some forms of sex are more or less psychologically healthy is also problematic. For example, as previously mentioned, homosexuality was included in lists of psychiatric disorders until the 1970s (and only completely removed in the 1980s and 90s). Sadism and masochism are still listed in these manuals at the time of writing, despite many studies finding that people who are into kinky sex are as psychologically healthy as the rest of the population.[22]

What the rules distinguishing different types of sex are *really* all about is what somebody *thinks* is good or bad. Most of these arguments about natural/unnatural, normal/abnormal, and healthy/unhealthy types of sex are ways of justifying moral decisions which have already been made, for problematic reasons, about what is and is not acceptable. The most tenacious idea about sex is that there is one right way to do it and that everyone should do it that way. Rubin says:

> Most people find it difficult to grasp that whatever they like to do sexually will be thoroughly repulsive to someone else, and that whatever repels them sexually will be the most treasured delight of someone, somewhere. Most people mistake their sexual preferences for a universal system that will or should work for everyone.[23]

You might want to reflect on this for a minute. How do you feel morally about the sexual practices that you yourself most enjoy, and are most disgusted by? On what basis do you judge what is and isn't okay sexually? We can see how problematic universal assumptions are when we imagine that somebody different to ourselves was creating the rules. For example, imagine that you were a straight, married woman who enjoyed sex in the missionary position only, and the norm of sexuality was based on radical feminist notions that women should only have sex with other women because heterosexual relationships are inevitably patriarchal and oppressive. Or, imagine that you weren't particularly bothered about sex, but that the norm was a free-love idea that good sex is swinging from the chandeliers, twenty different positions a night with different people, breaking all the taboos. Any kind of insistence that everyone has sex in the way that we want them to is problematic.

Alternative rules

So do we need *no* line distinguishing acceptable and unacceptable sex or *no* rules about what is and isn't okay? That isn't what Rubin and co are proposing. Rather, we might question the grounds on which such lines are drawn and such rules are made, recognising that, whenever we do draw a line, we are imposing our own values. Here, I'll cover two alternative suggestions which have been made about where such lines might be drawn.

The psychiatrist Chess Denman says that the way we currently distinguish sexual activities is on the basis of whether they are *transgressive* or not. Those which transgress current societal norms are the ones we often ridicule, consider to be psychologically unhealthy, or even have criminal laws against. What she suggests instead is that we could distinguish activities on the basis of whether they are *coercive* or not.[24] Does the activity involve anybody forcing anyone to do anything against their will, or to which they are not able to consent (for example in the case of children, or adults who are drugged)? If so, then it should be disallowed.[25] If not, then it is really up to the people concerned.

This is a useful distinction when we worry about the things that turn us on and whether to act on them. Often, people find it difficult to decide what it is okay to look at online, for example, or whether it would be acceptable to suggest doing a particular activity with a partner. The transgressive/coercive distinction is a helpful way through this murkiness. If there is coercion involved then the activity isn't something that should be done for real or encouraged. However, that does not mean that the fantasy should be locked away behind a mental brick wall (which is often what is done with such taboo ideas). When we do that, the thoughts become even bigger and scarier behind the wall. Instead, it is worth looking at them head on, with curiosity, saying 'I'm not going to act on you, but I am interested in what you have to tell me', perhaps (if it is something that you find very uncomfortable) with a trusted counsellor.

One of the real dangers about the way in which we demonize certain sexualities in our culture is that it means that people don't look at their scary sexual thoughts in this open, curious, way. Avoiding them often makes the thoughts feel more powerful and overwhelming, perhaps even making it more likely that people *will* act on them. If you read any of Nancy Friday's collections of people's sexual fantasies, you will see that fantasies involving some kind of coercion are really quite common (both of being forced and of forcing others),[26] so it is important that people find a way of admitting and accepting that they have these thoughts, without acting on them in ways which would be actually damaging.[27]

This links back to the rule about communication mentioned previously. Psychologist Sandra Byers links our difficulties communicating about sex to people feeling coerced and having sex that they don't want to have.[28] When we don't communicate clearly with ourselves, or others, about sex it is far more easy for things to go wrong. Also, when there is encouragement to dip a toe into spicy sex (as with the sex toy parties mentioned earlier), but fear about going 'too far', people often end up doing things without good knowledge or education about how they work physically, or what they might be like emotionally. For example, they might use a riding crop without realizing that it is dangerous to hit someone near their kidneys, or they might blindfold someone without properly checking whether this is a turn on for them or something they find alarming. There is a danger in keeping kinky sexualities in the outer limits when they are actually rather common: around two thirds of people have bondage fantasies[29] and consider the huge popularity of the book *50 Shades of Grey*.[30] Keeping such things in the outer limits prevents people from becoming informed so that they can do them as safely as possible. Avoidance of coercion actually *requires* open communication.

So, we could draw a line between consensual and non-consensual sex. But is this enough? Researchers have found that over a third of people regularly have consensual sex that they don't really want to have.[31] Historian Hugo Schwyzer says:

> The opposite of rape is not consent. The opposite of rape is enthusiasm . . . My goal is to . . . offer shy and uncertain young people tools to prevent them from

having bad sex characterized by obligation, confusion, and detached resignation. I always argue that anything short of an authentic, honest, uncoerced, aroused and sober 'Hell, yes!' is, in the end, just a 'no' in another form.[32]

Rubin echoes this, concluding that, as well as considering consent, we should judge sexual practices by the ways in which people involved treat one another and the quantity and quality of pleasure they offer. So, if activities involve mutual consideration and enjoyment on all sides then we should view them positively, whereas, if people don't care for themselves and each other, or don't experience much enjoyment, then we might question them.

When we look openly at the variety of sexual feelings, expressions, activities, and relationships that exist in our own cultures, around the world, and over time, *diversity* is actually the rule, not any one specific kind of sexual practice or partnership. If we can stop feeling threatened that other people may do things that we find difficult to understand, then we might let go of the need for everyone to be like us to shore up our sense that we are okay. We may see that there is something fascinating and beautiful about the range of different ways of expressing sexuality which are out there. This is what Alfred Kinsey discovered when he conducted in-depth interviews with Americans, about their sex lives, back in the 1930s and 1940s.[33] More recently, blogger Franklin Veaux designed a map of human sexuality based on online sexual communities.[34] This includes zones such as anonymous sex; group sex; role-play; sex games; erotic massage; enjoying watching others being sexual or being watched; dressing up; having sex in certain locations (such as outdoors or on a plane); writing or reading sexy stories; and being into certain body types, professions, or uniforms. This is an interesting counterpoint to the medical manual definition of sex that we explored before. On Veaux's map that kind of sex just occupies a tiny island compared to all the possible sensations, dynamics, activities, roles, and objects that people can be into.

So what alternatives are there to the sex rules which we outlined at the start? A good way to answer this is to step outside the charmed circle and ask what kinds of things people in the 'outer limits' are doing. What can this tell us about what is possible sexually?

Interestingly, perhaps the one thing that is common to many of these groups is an emphasis on communication about sex, the very thing that we saw, from Sandra Byers' research, is still lacking in most relationships (both long-term and dating couples). Communication with others about sexual interest is emphasised by many sexual communities, for example in the guidelines that are given for how to behave appropriately at events. These particularly focus on how to negotiate consent. We may, therefore, turn to the outer limits for suggestions about how to communicate and negotiate, something we will come back to towards the end of the chapter.

Perhaps the defining feature of charmed circle sexual relationships is that they are all about the gender of the people involved. For a start they are heterosexual, and – as we've seen – the definition of 'real', 'proper', sex is requiring one penis and one vagina. We saw that lesbian and gay sexual relationships have become increasingly accepted, but they are also about the gender of the people involved. Indeed, when we use the word 'sexuality', what we mostly mean is to which gender we are attracted, i.e. whether we are heterosexual, gay or lesbian, or bisexual.

We will look in more detail at some issues around gender in the next chapter but, for now, let's just pause on that idea that the defining feature of our sexuality is the gender to which we are attracted. If you think back to Kinsey's research, or Franklin's map, or Nancy Friday's collections of sexual fantasies, you'll see that sexuality encompasses a whole lot more than whether we fancy men or women or both. One group who have challenged the conflation of sexuality with gender-of-attraction are the bisexual communities. On the face of it, you might think that bisexuality is still about gender: it's just about being attracted to *both* genders, rather than one or the other. However, many bisexual people don't define themselves as attracted to 'both'. Rather, they say that their attraction to people is 'regardless of gender'. Gender is perhaps just *one* aspect of attraction, like preferring people of a particular eye or hair colour. Also. there is a recognition that there are many kinds of ways of expressing, or not expressing, gender, all of which might be more, or less, attractive to different people. The 'bi' in bisexual can mean being attracted to both people of a similar gender and to people of different genders to ourselves.[35]

So, from bisexual communities we might learn that our sexuality is not *all* about the gender to which we are attracted. Think about the types of things people find attractive: a good sense of humour, kindness, confidence. None of these things are necessarily related to gender. Gender might, of course, be one aspect of our attraction, but perhaps we need to widen our definitions to encompass other things, too.

People who are into kink help to broaden the idea of what might be sexual yet further, to give us some ideas of the realms we might consider if we are not just fixing sexuality to gender-of-attraction. The stereotype of kink, based on representations in the media, is pretty limited: perhaps a leather-clad dominatrix, wearing high-heeled shoes, standing over a hooded man and holding a whip. However, there is a vast array of activities, identities, relationships, and practices which come under the broad category of kink. Kink encompasses sensations such as dripping candle wax, pinches, or stroking with feathers. It includes role-play, such as medical or school scenarios, as well as tying people up, whether in ropes or ribbons. People may dominate or serve each other. They may bring in elements of humiliation and discipline, or being pampered and looked after. Also, people do kink for many different reasons. Even one activity, such as spanking, can mean very different things to different people. For some, it can be a way of giving up control and letting go; for others it is a fun, playful, activity. It can mean taking on a different role and being somebody else for a while, it can be a form of relaxation, or it can be a way of showing strength and how much you are capable of enduring. It can help some to explore something that scares them (pain, or corporal punishment), it can be a way of building intimacy with another person, or it can provide a reason for being looked after, and cared for, afterwards. It could means many of these things even for the same person, or on different occasions.

One important aspect of 'normal' sex that kink challenges is the idea that sex must always be about genitals and orgasms. Many people do have penetration or orgasms as part of kinky activities, but others focus instead on sensations to other parts of the body, perhaps parts we don't usually think of as sexual. They might build up to a climax of emotion or physical stimulation instead of orgasm, or there might be no particular climax at all. Kink begins to question some of the lines that we draw between sex and other activities such as play, leisure, spirituality, art, and relaxation.

Another group of interest are people who write erotic fiction online. Over the last couple of decades, more and more people have used the internet as a place to share their fantasies and sexual stories. One common type of story is erotica about fictional characters from TV programmes, books, and movies. One kind of writing within this genre is called 'slash' fiction because of the punctuation mark used. For example if people write about a sexual relationship between Captain Kirk and Mr Spock from Star Trek, it is called Kirk/Spock, or if they write about Buffy the Vampire Slayer and her friend from the show it is Buffy/Willow. An interesting thing about this fiction is that, in the early days before the internet, it was mostly written by middle-aged heterosexual women, and they generally told erotic stories about male characters with other male characters. This questions some of our common rules about gender and sexuality. These women were not fantasizing about 'normal' penis-in-vagina sex, nor were they imagining themselves having sex with a man. When you think about it, a lot of fantasy involves people enjoying the idea of people of a different gender to themselves having sex (think about all the 'lesbians' in male pornography). Clearly, even 'normal' heterosexual sexuality has some interesting twists when it comes to gender and attraction.

Nowadays, slash fiction is written by a diverse range of people for all kinds of different reasons (rather like kink). For many people, writing and reading slash is a useful way of exploring their own sexualities safely: things they might want to try, or to think through. Another fascinating thing about the popularity of slash fiction is that it questions the idea that people who are sexual together need to be in the same place, or even in the same *time* as each other. Writing and reading slash online involves one person giving another person stimulation, quite often to the point of orgasm (a fairly standard definition of sex), but their bodies never physically meet and the person who wrote it may not even ever know the impact that it had on the other person.[36]

Finally, perhaps the latest sexuality to become more widely spoken about is asexuality.[37] Asexual (or 'ace') people have similar emotional and relationship needs to everyone else, but don't experience sexual attraction. This questions the number one rule that we currently have about sex: that it is a vitally important defining feature of relationships. It also challenges the idea that people who don't experience sexual desire are somehow dysfunctional. Clearly there are many people out there who don't experience themselves as particularly sexual and are quite content with that. Asexuality and celibacy are useful counter-examples to the excessive significance that sex is given. Perhaps we could all consider other ways of defining what makes a relationship (see Chapter 9), rather than building it on the potentially shaky foundation of needing to share this particular kind of physical interaction.

Of course, considering these different sexualities does not, in any way, mean that everyone should try them, or take on board their ways of understanding and experiencing sex. As mentioned before, there is a danger, in each of these groups, that they will put their version of sex at the top of a new hierarchy, judging everyone else in relation to it, and restricting their own sexuality in the process. Being aware of the multiplicity of different sexualities helps all of us to think about ways in which our concepts of sex and sexuality *might* be able to expand and diversify.

Beyond rules? Embracing uncertainty

Going back to Chapter 1, you will remember that we challenged the idea that our self is something singular and fixed. Rather, we realized that we are plural and that we inevitably change over time. It is useful to come to a similar understanding about our sexuality or sexual selves.

As we've seen, the taken-for-granted rules state that we have a singular sexuality which is just about the gender of the people we find attractive: whether we are bisexual, heterosexual, gay or lesbian. The rules also state that this sexuality is fixed: it is who we are for our whole life. What I'm suggesting here is that we shift towards a view of sexuality as both plural and in process.

Think about the labels that you use when asked to define your sexual identity. Are they sufficient to sum up your sexuality?

- To what kinds of people are you attracted, in terms of physical appearance, age, gender, personality, clothing, etc.?
- What kinds of situations, images, roles, activities, or fantasies, if any, excite you physically and/or mentally?
- Does any of this vary over time? Do you always see yourself as having this identity?

Perhaps we can shift our view from singular sexuality to plural, so that sex involves far more than gender-of-attraction, but also things like the roles we enjoy playing in sex, the positions we enjoy, the activities that most turn us on, the sensations we find pleasurable, the sounds we make, the places or times of day we want to have sex, whether we like physical, and/or visual, and/or narrative, forms of stimulation, and so on.

Another aspect of this plurality is recognizing that sex can have different meanings to different people,[38] and to the same people at different times. For example, sex therapist Marny Hall suggests that we map our sexual territory, giving ourselves permission to move between different zones at different times. We could have zones, for example, for 'earthmoving sex, silly sex, mood-elevating sex or sorrowful sex . . . sex for intimacy and sex for distance . . . sex-free zones . . .

mechanical sex . . . only-if-I-don't-have-to-lift-a-finger sex . . . and . . . maybe I'll feel like it after we start sex'.[39]

Also, every different aspect of sex (such as mouth-to-mouth kissing, having one's genitals licked, penetrating someone's vagina, or cuddling) has different possible meanings between different people, and even for the same person at different times. An orgasm, for example, can be experienced as all of the following things and more:

> a mechanical release, a demonstration of one's masculine or feminine sexuality, a relief of stress, a loss of control, allowing someone to see you at your most vulnerable, a display of intimacy, the height of physical pleasure, a transcendent spiritual experience, a performance demonstrating prowess, a giving of power to another, an exerting of power over another, a form of creative self-expression, a humorous display of our rather-ridiculous humanity, an unleashing of something wild and animalistic, a deeply embodied experience, an escape from bodily sensations and pain, and/or a moment of complete alive-ness or freedom . . .[40]

Given this, it is understandable that, for some people, orgasms are the most amazing feeling imaginable, for some they are utterly terrifying, and for some they are quite mundane – and that this can vary across people's lives as well. Having an orgasm after going through a painful bereavement feels different to an everyday orgasm and to the first orgasm you ever had. As well as meaning different things to us at different times, an orgasm – or any other activity – can mean two or more of these things simultaneously.

As well as being plural, there is increasing evidence that people's sexualities are changeable and fluid over their lifetimes.[41] We know that even the identity labels of lesbian, bisexual, heterosexual and gay do not capture people's behaviour over time. Many women who have sex with women, and men who have sex with men, define themselves as straight; and many gay- and lesbian-defined people have had sexual relationships with people of the other gender, even quite recently. Of course, we've always known that the extent of sexual desire varies across the lifespan, with common peaks around adolescence, at the start of new relationships, and perhaps during a 'mid-life crisis'.

What if we stopped trying so hard to fix our sexualities by defining to whom we are attracted and trying to maintain a consistent type and amount of sex throughout our life and relationships? Instead, we could simply be with our sexuality as it is in the present, allowing it to ebb and flow, enjoying ourselves if a new crush or fantasy bubbles up, and not worrying if we have a fallow period where sex becomes less important than other things, or even not important at all. Instead of trying to force ourselves to fit what we perceive as the norm, perhaps we could put that energy into letting go of our preconceptions about sex and discovering our sexualities anew.

Here, it is also important to think back to the issue of coercion which we mentioned before. These days we are alert to the dangers and traumas possible when people are forced to have sex against their will. We are shocked and appalled when we hear of children being sexually abused. Rape is rightly considered a serious crime which can have a devastating impact on the victim. When we hear about someone having sex with another person who didn't want it, we see that as rape. However, most people frequently make *themselves* have sex that they don't really want, and try to force their own sexuality in the directions that they think it should go. Perhaps we should be just as condemning of that kind of coercion as violence against our selves. Going back to Chapter 2, we might consider befriending our body, such that when it tells us it doesn't want to do something (e.g. by not allowing orifices to be penetrated, or by not getting erect) we listen to it instead of carrying on regardless.

And, just as we link the way we treat ourselves with the way we treat other people (see Chapter 1), we could do the same with our sexualities. As we learn to respect and embrace our own shifting and diverse sexualities, so we can open to the fact that other people's sexualities are as okay, for them, as ours are for us. We have a despicable history of judging and condemning people on the basis of their sexuality. We have also frequently denied some groups any sexuality at all: disabled people and elderly people, for example, and those we don't regard as sufficiently physically attractive (see Chapter 2). Regarding sex as plural and fluid involves opening up to the diversity of possible sexual expressions and stopping ourselves from telling other people, including our partners, what it is and isn't appropriate for them to find sexual, and what kind of sex they should, or should not, be having.

For those who are not in touch with what they might or might not enjoy sexually (perhaps because of worries about being normal or meeting their partner's approval), sex therapists often suggest starting by taking sex off the menu completely, so that you can 'reboot' your sexuality, gradually bringing in things you really *want* to try. You might find the collections of fantasies mentioned previously useful for thinking through what might turn you on. Similarly, you can build up different physical sensations alone or with partners.[42]

A useful activity for figuring out what you want to do sexually is to create a yes/no/maybe list. Start by spending some time thinking up every single remotely sexual activity that you have ever heard of or can imagine. Write a long list of these down one side of a piece of paper. Then privately go through the list writing 'yes', 'no', or 'maybe' for whether you would like to do each item. You can elaborate on this if you want and make a 1-10 scale of how much you'd like to try it, or include signs for whether you've already done it, or whether it's something you would like to try but are embarrassed to admit.[43]

Completing a checklist like this is a good starting point for better communication with *yourself* about sex. One common myth is that solo sex is somehow less 'proper' than sex with someone else, whereas actually it can be the most satisfying sexual situation (because you may well know how you work better than anybody else). Of course, the list can also be used as the basis of communication with sexual partners. You might exchange lists, talk about them, or even draw up a longer piece of writing or 'user's manual' to give to potential partners. At the very least it is worth putting together a list of the things that you absolutely *must* have for sex to work for you, and also one of the things that are completely off limits, so that you can communicate those to others before having sex. When such conversations become commonplace it is also much easier to negotiate safer sex with partners, something that is notoriously difficult when there is a certain sexual script that everyone is expected to automatically know and follow, without communicating about it.

Of course, it is completely okay to say that the forms of physical or emotional intimacy that you like with other people are not sexual at all, whether that is for a period of your life or for the foreseeable future, so long as you explain clearly what 'sexual' means for you. While sex can be a wonderful way for people to play, to relax, to learn about how they work, and to experience intimacy with others, it certainly is not the only way of doing these things (think about sports, for example, or creative arts, cooking, or spirituality). Sex has been given excessive significance in our culture, as has its role in our identities. As Rubin suggests, maybe we could bring sex down to the significance of food: people have all different kinds of tastes and preferences about what they eat, but we don't base our relationships on this, or throw people out of families or into prison for liking spicy food.

To conclude the chapter, let's think about how we might revisit the rules of sex, given what we have explored.

- *Sex is very important, and a defining feature of our relationships.* Sex can be wonderful but it doesn't need to define us or our relationships. It is something that ebbs and flows throughout our lives.
- *We should have normal sex in our relationships.* There is a wide diversity of ways of expressing sex and sexuality.
- *We must not stray into abnormal sex.* It is fine to be sexual in whatever ways feel right to you, so long as it is consensual for all involved.
- *But it should be great sex.* Sex can be all kinds of things at different times, just like food. Expecting it to be great every single time is a lot of pressure to put on it.
- *And we mustn't communicate openly about what we really want sexually.* We *must* communicate openly about what we do and don't want sexually (with ourselves and with the people with whom we are sexual).

Chapter 5

Rewriting the rules of gender

What are the rules?

We saw in the last chapter how deeply gender is embedded in our concept of relationships. The overwhelming image of a relationship – the one in billboard ads, magazines and movies – is of a heterosexual relationship with one man and one woman. Try searching online for images of 'relationship' and the majority of the pictures which come up look something like the one below.

As we saw in the last chapter, this is echoed in our notion of what constitutes normal sex. An image search for 'sex' throws up a lot of pictures like the one on the next page.

Such images are omnipresent in our lives. Just the other day I received a clothing catalogue in the mail and it was full of photographs of a rugged man and a slim, long-haired, woman holding hands and kissing on the beach, curling up by the fire, and getting ready for bed. It is hard to estimate just how many times on a daily basis we are exposed to this same happy, young, usually white, heterosexual couple.

Figure 5.1 Search image for 'relationship'

Figure 5.2 Search image for 'sex'

We can't explore the rules of love and relationships without exploring the rules of gender, because those rules are with us all the way. Men and women are expected to be different kinds of people (or selves, see Chapter 1), who are attracted to different things (Chapter 2), who take on different roles in relationships (Chapter 3), and who have different parts to play in sex (Chapter 4).

Drawing on the gender theorist Judith Butler, David Gauntlett summarizes this understanding in Figure 5.3.[1] This demonstrates how everything we have considered so far in the book is interlinked. The current rules say that we are born into a body which looks a certain way (Chapter 2). This body defines us as male or female. This means that we regard ourselves as either masculine (if we are male) or feminine (if we are female) (this chapter) and we try to fit in with what our culture expects of these opposite genders in terms of our self identity (Chapter 1). Our gender then also defines our desire (towards the 'same' or 'opposite' sex, Chapter 4) and the love relationships we will form (Chapter 3).

So, perhaps the main rule underlying love today is that it involves the coming together of two opposites (the opposite sexes) to form a complete unit. The idea of opposite sexes is linked to that of being complete in a couple (and incomplete out of one) which we explored in Chapter 3. However, gender roles have changed dramatically in the last few decades, with much focus on reaching equality between women and men. As we saw in the Introduction, this leads to uncertainty: now we have two people in heterosexual relationships who know how they are *meant* to be as men and women, but they are *also* expected to be equal partners and to both pursue their own individual goals in life.

One outcome of this uncertainty has been a return to the idea that men and women are rightly, normally, and naturally different. It has been proposed, in

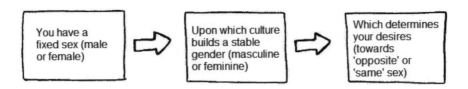

Figure 5.3 Sex, gender, and sexuality I

countless best-selling books, that it is our failure to recognize this that is the cause of problems in relationships. Women and men now pretend to be similar when actually we are different and need to accept these inevitable, unchangeable, gender differences.

So we have books, articles, and documentaries proposing that men and women are from different planets, speak different languages, have different qualities, and require different rules to function in relationships. Headlines on the cover of every men's or women's magazine promise insights into the mind of the opposite sex, along the lines of 'Top ten secrets he doesn't want you to know' or 'How to tell what she's thinking'. Hollywood movies often take up this idea in romantic comedies where men and women switch bodies and learn what it's like from the other perspective. The oppositeness of gender is a staple of comedy – how impossible it is for men and women to understand each other, and how ridiculous it is if men try to be like women, or vice versa (think how many humorous moments in films and television rely on men having to pretend to be women, from *Some like it Hot* to *Mrs Doubtfire* to *White Chicks*).

The same is true in everyday conversation. Think how many chats between friends over coffee, or around the photocopier at work, end with an exasperated 'men!' or 'women!' We enjoy scrutinizing the psyche of the other gender together and finding ourselves anything from fondly baffled to highly enraged. As we'll see in Chapters 7 and 8, in times of conflict or relationship breakdown people are keen to find something to blame that *isn't* themselves: the vagaries of the other gender are a handy scapegoat in such moments. Of *course* a relationship is hard when you have to deal with a woman who is nagging and suffocating and who bursts into tears at nothing. Of *course* the relationship broke down when he couldn't stop looking at other women and never lifted a finger around the house. It's *because* she was a woman, it's *because* he was a man and, as we all know, they are *all* the same.

A prime example of the idea of totally opposite genders was an advert for a UK newspaper in 2007. We saw the 'battle of the sexes' recreated for real to the soundtrack of *Two Tribes* by Frankie Goes to Hollywood.[2] Crowds of men lined up on one side of the battlefield, hurling sports equipment and technical gadgets at women who responded with make-up, handbags, and small dogs. The battle only stopped (albeit briefly) on Sunday, when this newspaper brought out separate magazines for men and for women. So heterosexual relationships are portrayed as warfare which can only be peaceful when the genders are treated as rightly and properly different.

Adverts can be a useful barometer for 'where we are at' as a society with gender, because they are frequently aimed either at men or at women, and therefore demonstrate what each gender is thought to be like and what it is imagined will appeal to them. Every year there are collections of 'best ads' on YouTube which you can watch to see what current representations are like. Try searching YouTube for 'best ads' and 2010, 2011, 2012, etc. to view these. Watch the adverts, paying attention to the ways in which women and men are portrayed. Write down, under two columns, what it means to be feminine and masculine in our culture (covering all aspects, including behaviour, roles, emotions, and appearance).

Even if you don't watch the adverts, you will probably find it easy to write a list of masculine and feminine features. The oppositeness of gender is so pervasive that almost every trait, preference and behaviour is seen in a gendered way. If women are X, then men are Y. We'll return to this list of masculine and feminine attributes later in the chapter.

Coming back to relationships in particular, in the last few decades the battle of the sexes has had two key moments: those of the Rules girls and Game boys.

First, in the late 1990s, came the publication of the book *The Rules*, by Ellen Fein and Sherrie Schneider.[3] This was aimed at heterosexual women and has resulted in many spin-offs, articles and documentaries. *The Rules* promised to teach women how to make the perfect guy fall in love with them, marry them, and treat them wonderfully forever: a real happily-ever-after. The rules offered were based on the idea that women and men were rightly and properly different, and encouraged women to return to a more 'old-fashioned' femininity. Fein and Schneider argued that active, initiating, strong women threaten the male ego, and that women need, instead, to 'play hard-to-get' in order to be seen, by men, as precious, sexy, and exciting. Rules included 'ladylike' behaviour (not talking too much, not making jokes or complaining); not initiating anything (dates, drinks, or phonecalls); not having sex too soon (the assumption being that men will want it and women should withhold it); being mysterious; and letting the man take the lead.

Almost as a direct response to this version of hard-to-get femininity was the emergence, in the years leading up to the new millennium, of 'seduction communities' for heterosexual men. First carried out in secretive groups online, these came into the open with the publication of *The Game* by Neil Strauss, in 2005,[4] and a number of articles and documentaries which followed. Strauss' book reveals the world of the pick up artist (or PUA) and the rules they learn in order to develop the kind of masculinity which will successfully seduce 'hot babes'. The seduction communities draw on a range of skills from magician's tricks, neurolinguistic programming, and body language psychology. For example, the skill of 'negging' involves making negative comments to the woman you are trying to pick up so that she will be less secure and more keen for your approval. Negs include asking whether her nails are real, or saying that you saw someone else wearing her skirt. Men use tricks like this to persuade women that they aren't really interested in them, or in having sex, so that the women will feel safe and will come on to them. There are also tricks to make men appear interesting and 'alpha male', and to make it seem that they have some special insight into women. Techniques are handed down through workshops and also militaristic 'field reports' about their conquests, which PUAs write up online.

The rules and games of the Rules girls and Game boys are echoed in pretty much every women's and men's magazine published today, all of which present the 'opposite sex' as mysterious and in need of figuring out. A common article is the one which promises to reveal to the reader how their partner thinks. For example, *FHM* magazine's website includes an article entitled 'Relationships: how the honeys think', which compares trying to figure out what is going on inside women's minds to being 'asked to rebuild the CERN Supercollider using Lego'.[5] *Cosmopolitan* magazine promises to tell us 'What he's really thinking the first time you have sex', claiming that 'you may assume you know what's running through the male brain, but believe us, you have no idea'.[6]

With the Rules girls and Game boys, women's magazines and lad's mags, we see a perpetuation of the idea that the other gender is totally different: they want different things in life and are an alien species in how they think, feel, and act. In order to make them want what *we* want (marriage for women, or quick sex for men) we need to figure out how they work and *play* them. Luckily, the other gender is pretty simple and we can quite easily trap them by the application of a few basic rules.

Once women and men are in relationships, there is a wealth of literature about how they are different *within* these relationships, and how these differences are the root of all conflict. To summarize just a few rules from some of the best-selling books of the last couple of decades, women want to be understood whilst men try to problem-solve; men want to feel capable and women offer advice which undermines this; men like to be alone to think through what bothers them, while women pressure them to talk; women want to be adored, while men want to feel needed; women's moods ebb and flow, which confuses men; men need to pull away from intimacy, which confuses women; men are direct and act as if they are always right, and women are indirect and send out subtle messages of approval and disapproval; women need communication, men need sex; women multi-task and men need to focus on one thing; men lie about things like finding other women attractive, but women can see through these lies; women nag men, and men do annoying things like leaving the toilet seat up, making disgusting jokes, flicking through the TV channels and moaning about going shopping.[7]

Most of these books propose that such differences are natural, unchangeable, and need to be understood and accepted in order for relationships to work.

So, to summarize the rules of gender:

- There are two genders, men and women, and they are normally and naturally different and opposite.

- Relationship problems are down to these inevitable gender differences, which we need to accept.
- Women want to get men to marry them. In order to do this, they should play hard-to-get, be ladylike, pretty, submissive, passive, and withholding of sex. In relationships women like to talk about their feelings, they want to feel loved and cherished, and they like to nurture and care for others.
- Men want to get women to have sex with them. In order to do this, they should be dominant and confident, and play the game of seduction. In relationships, men need time alone; they like to feel capable, needed, and successful.

Why question the rules?

You might have thought of a few reasons already why these rules are questionable. However, like me, and most of my students over the years, you may well also be thinking 'but some of these things seem really familiar: men and women really *are* different like that'. Of course, all those books about gender differences wouldn't be best-sellers if they didn't tap into something that resonated with people.

If we look at the most common words which online search engines automatically use to complete the phrase 'how can I get my girlfriend/boyfriend to . . .', we see the same differences reproduced. At the time of writing, the girlfriend phrase was completed with 'shut up', 'sleep with me', 'lose weight', 'let me go down on her', 'forgive me', and 'take me back', whereas the boyfriend phrase was completed with 'propose', 'love me', 'kiss me', 'trust me', and 'break-up with me'. The gender differences in self-help books are recognizable because they echo real conversations that happen in couples. Often women *do* nag men to change, and men *do* retreat in front of the TV when they get home from work. So what are we to make of this?

Such differences *do* come up in relationships because they are about the tensions which are always present when people are intimate. However, these are more about the roles people have in relationships than they are about whether a person is male or female.

The evidence for this?

If all problems in relationships were down to gender differences, then relationships between men, or between women, would be perfect.

Clearly, women who are in relationships with women, and men who are in relationships with men, do not have perfectly sunny and happy relationships with no problems whatsoever. In fact, when you work with bisexual, gay, and lesbian people in therapy, you find that they have similar difficulties to anybody else in an intimate relationship. They argue, sulk, and break-up just as much as heterosexual couples do, and the problem of abusive relationships certainly isn't absent in lesbian, gay, and bisexual communities. Similarity in gender is no buffer against relationship problems.

The kinds of differences spoken about in relationship self-help books *do* frequently map onto gender because, in our society, men and women have conventionally taken on particular roles and have been encouraged to act in particular ways. However, these things are not *always* tied to gender, and it is problematic to propose (as most relationships self-help books do) that they are unchangeable and should just be accepted.

An example which illustrates this point occurs in season 2 of the TV series *The Wire*. Following the dangerous situation the police team faced in season 1, two of them were moved to desk jobs, much to the relief of their romantic partners. However, in season 2 they get the opportunity to go back undercover and they jump at the chance. We see both Cedric and Kima sitting over dinner with their increasingly irate partners as they tell them what they are planning to do. This is a classic gender-difference type of dispute: the man prioritizes his job ahead of his relationship and family, and the woman is enraged about this. However, in this case one of the characters in the situation, Kima, is a woman with a female partner. The programme cleverly demonstrates just how similar the dynamics are in the two relationships. The problem is about one person prioritizing the relationship, and the other prioritizing their own goals – not about gender.

This is not at all to say that, in relationships between women (or men), one person is *really* the man and one is *really* the woman. The vast majority of lesbian, bisexual, and gay relationships do not follow that stereotype at all. However, it *is* true that at any one time, in any couple, it is likely that one person is going to be a bit more outgoing than the other, one person is going to be more committed to their work than the other, one person is going to feel more nurturing than the other, and one person is going to feel more itchy for independence than the other.

Over time, we find that these kinds of things map less and less onto gender. In all kinds of relationships we sometimes find ourselves in the traditionally 'masculine' role and sometimes in the traditionally 'feminine' one. For example, I remember a time when I lived with a man who didn't have much work. I, on the other hand, was going out to a 9-5 job every day. When I got home after work, guess which one of us wanted to talk-talk-talk about everything, and which one wanted to retreat in front of the TV? In relationships with women, I've noticed how often, in an argument, one of us becomes 'the emotional one', getting upset or angry, and the other becomes 'the rational one', trying to calmly talk it out. But who takes on which role varies from situation to situation (unless the dynamic becomes stuck, as we'll explore in Chapter 7).

Acknowledgement that relationship roles are not tied to gender is more useful than claiming that all relationship problems are down to inevitable gender differences. It also makes advice on relationships more inclusive: most books and magazine articles are aimed at heterosexuals because the authors assume that problems are *about* gender differences. Until we challenge the view that a relationship = one man + one woman, and sex = one penis + one vagina, we will never have equality across different kinds of relationships.

We still live in a culture which has strong rules that men and women are different and opposite in various ways. In the rest of this section, we'll explore how these rules are problematic for both women and men who try to follow the rules. In the following section we'll see that, of course, they are also bad for anyone who doesn't follow the rules; for example for people who step outside of the assumption that there are two opposite genders.

First, let's consider the situation for women. The existentialist Simone de Beauvoir wrote about the rules for women back in the 1940s[8] and many of her ideas hold true today. She said that women, far more than men, were defined by relationships with other people. They were taught from a young age that the ultimate things were to be found desirable and wonderful in the eyes of others and to find a husband. De Beauvoir points out that no man would ever say that his main project in life was to get married, but plenty of women do.

We certainly see these messages today, in the idea that the ultimate of female power is to turn all the heads in the room (see Chapter 2). Similarly, women's magazines are still packed with advice about how to get and keep a man. Almost every headline relates to some aspect of this: dating tips, guides to great sex, and advice on dealing with relationship problems. Novels, movies, and sitcoms aimed at women focus almost entirely on romance as The Big Adventure in women's lives (jobs and other aspects of life generally being fairly incidental). The cartoonist Alison Bechdel invented a test which points this out nicely. One of her characters says that for her to watch a movie it has to have at least two women in it, who talk to each other about something other than a man.[9] Think about how many films you know which meet these criteria.

There is great temptation for women to define themselves in relation to other people: it means that they can escape from the hard responsibilities of having to make their own choices in life. We see this kind of escape of adulthood in the way that ideal femininity is often portrayed as childlike: being cute, pretty, vulnerable, and delightful. Think Carrie Bradshaw in her tutu or Sandra Bullock falling over in pretty much every movie in which she appears. Angela McRobbie points out that, as young women become increasingly successful in the worlds of education and work, there is tendency for them to present themselves as even more childlike, to protect against the idea that they might actually be powerful and responsible people:

> she adopts the air of being girlishly distracted, slightly flustered, weighed down with bags, shoes, bracelets and other decorative candelabra items, all of which need to be constantly attended to. She is also almost inappropriately eager to please.[10]

Inappropriately eager to please? What else is possible, when you have been taught from an early age that the ultimate pleasure you can have is to see that you have given pleasure to another person? Check out the adverts aimed at little girls today: they are still all about practising to be beautiful and enticing (make-up, clothes, and fashion dolls), and about caring for others. The most popular toys for younger girls remain the most realistic dolls which wet themselves, get messy faces, and generally require a good deal of care, work, and attention, all in the name of 'play'.

In Chapter 2, we touched on some of the problems that follow from tying a women's identity to the way others see them, when we covered the high rates of body dissatisfaction in women. Diagnoses of anxiety and depression (which are more common in women than in men) are also related to this. For example, middle-aged mothers are at particularly high risk of depression due to the loss of their role as a nurturer and carer when children leave home.[11] It doesn't seem that shifts in gender equality over the last few decades have radically altered the situation. Young women are still often very scared of losing their relationships, often to the point of being out of touch with what they want sexually because they are so focused on pleasing their partner so as not to lose them (see Chapter 4). They are also often uncertain about what they want from their lives due to being hyper-aware of what everyone else wants of them. They express exhaustion at living a life where they have to be good for everyone around them: friends, parents, colleagues, partners. The impossible demand of pleasing all of the people all of the time wears some out, and leaves others despairing when inevitable contradictions arise. Even small choices can become loaded, as their own feelings get lost in the desire to figure out what would be best for everyone else.

In relationships, de Beauvoir pointed out that there is a real danger that women will come to need a consistently desiring and approving gaze from their partner, because that is what they have been taught to require. If that gaze changes over time, as it almost inevitably will in a long-term relationship, there is a risk that women will become angry with themselves, with their partners, or both. If so much of women's focus is on the relationship, and on how they are seen by their partner, it is possible that they will become defined by this and lose, or fail to develop, other aspects of themselves, as well as putting a lot of pressure on their partner to continue to validate them. There can be much rage as women realize just how much of their life they have given over to others, and just how dependent they have become. It can be enticing to not have to make choices and decisions, and to give yourself over to the opinions and demands of others, but de Beauvoir argues that freedom will eventually bubble up regardless. Choosing not to choose is still a choice.

The rules for men are also very restrictive. There is at least some acceptance in our culture that women might want to be 'masculine', because many of the things that are associated with masculinity are so highly valued (being rational rather than emotional, dominant rather than submissive, independent rather than dependent, etc.) However, there is still little acceptance of men wanting to be 'feminine' in any way, because everything associated with femininity is so under-valued. Indeed, the main ways in which heterosexual men still display their masculinity when they are together is by showing that they are not feminine (often through jokes and put-downs).[12]

The strong cultural message that 'real men' show no feelings, and are rational rather than emotional, means that it can be difficult for men to say when they are distressed. They are thus more likely to numb pain through alcohol and drug use or to express it by becoming aggressive and anti-social (anger being one emotion that they *are* allowed to display). Therefore, whilst women are more likely to be diagnosed with 'emotional disorders', men are more likely to be criminalized (seen as 'bad' as opposed to 'mad').[13] This relates to a general tendency for men to be viewed as responsible and independent in ways that women are not, which is bad for women and men. As we have seen, it means that women may be disempowered, infantilized, and stuck in a victim role, not responsible for anything they do. The flip side is that there are huge pressures on men, who may be considered culpable for actions which are equally rooted in distress, and as needing to protect other people (from their partner and family to – in times of war – the entire country). There have been calls to address the 'crisis of masculinity' whereby stereotypes persist of strong, hard, men who provide for their families despite the decline in traditional male jobs and roles which would allow them to do this. This has been linked to the high rates of suicide amongst men (75 percent of all suicides in the UK, for example).[14]

In relationships, the situation is also rather sad for heterosexual men. Heterosexual women are encouraged to have close female friends *and* to form a relationship with a man. Heterosexual men, on the other hand, are taught to be cautious about intimacy with other men (lest they be perceived to be gay), and to treat women predominantly as sex objects. This can mean that they don't have a close, supportive relationship with anyone. The recent wave of 'bromance' movies[15] portrays this tragedy well. Underneath all the dumb humour and gross-out jokes we frequently see an average guy with a close male friend with whom he gets on well: they enjoy the same games and interests, they love spending time together, they know each other inside out. But both of them, of course, have to pursue hot babes. By the end of the film, they have to part company, or see much less of each other, in order to settle down into a relationship with the woman of their dreams, who they have somehow managed to win. This is a poignant ending, because it is quite clear that this woman will neither understand the main character as his mate did, nor have any interest in the things that were of such mutual fascination in the friendship.

The other tragedy of stereotypical masculinity is that, if followed correctly, it will mean that a man can never have a mutually supportive relationship with a woman. Think about all the game-playing advised by the Rules girls and Game boys. This couldn't be the basis for an open and honest relationship. De Beauvoir pointed out that treating women like sex objects, as heterosexual men are encouraged to do, means that they'll inevitably be denied a close, intimate, relationship with an equal. A similar problem will arise if they insist on being 'the responsible one' in the relationship, or on being depended upon and never depending. Interestingly, Neil Strauss comes to the same conclusion as de Beauvoir towards the end of *The Game*. After turning himself into one of the most successful master PUAs in the world, seducing women beyond his wildest dreams and ending up in a Hollywood mansion, he acknowledges that it hasn't been good for him: quite the opposite. His whole sense of himself had become dependent on female attention. He concludes that 'in the process of dehumanizing the opposite sex, I had also been dehumanizing myself'.[16] Researchers have similarly found that women who follow the Rules are no more likely to have a committed partner and a good relationship, and may actually be less likely, given that self-disclosure – rather than remaining mysterious – is a major predictor of relationship success.[17]

You might notice that I have not engaged with the loaded issue of whether things are better or worse for one gender. That is because the question risks reinforcing the problematic distinction between men and women, rather than breaking it down, and also because gender intersects with so many other aspects of our identities that we cannot make sweeping statements. Does an unemployed teenage boy have it worse than a supermodel? Does a young black gay man have it worse than a retired white school-mistress? That said, women have been treated as inferior to men for centuries, and the impact of this needs to be acknowledged. For example, descriptions that professionals make of healthy adults and healthy men are similar, whereas healthy women are described quite differently (less independent, aggressive, competitive and persuadable; more submissive, emotional, and conceited about appearance).[18] This suggests that men are considered the standard of normal humanity against which women are compared, a fact which is also supported by the fact that research nearly always puts the results for men first (in tables and graphs) and women after.[19]

There are certain privileges which go with being seen as the standard of normal humanity (not least of which is being seen as more of an independent and responsible person). The 'male privilege checklist' includes items such as 'If I am never promoted, it's not because of my sex'; 'if I have children and a career, no one will think I'm selfish for not staying at home'; and 'I can be loud with no fear of being called a shrew. I can be aggressive with no fear of being called a bitch.'[20] When I ask students to come up with a 'female privilege checklist', they do it quite easily – but most of the items are about *not* having to take responsibility for things; for example, 'I don't have to initiate sex'; 'people open doors for me'; and 'if a situation becomes aggressive I will not be expected to fight'.

To summarize, the rules of gender are problematic for the women and men who try to follow them, and for the relationships which are based on them. Now let's consider what some alternatives might be to these rules of gender.

Alternative rules

Return to the lists of stereotypical femininity and masculinity you made earlier. Ask yourself the following questions:

- Do you fit into either column perfectly?
- What about people you know?
- Can you think of any men who fit better into the feminine column, and women who fit better into the masculine column?

The way people are is *not* purely tied to whether they are men or women. We can see that just from thinking about ourselves and the people around us. Clearly, there are men who worry greatly about their appearance, for example, and women who find it hard to express emotions. Thinking about fictional depictions, we could point to the characters of Faith and Jonathan in *Buffy the Vampire Slayer*, Cristina and George in *Grey's Anatomy*, or Snoop and Pres in *The Wire* as believable examples of people who fit far better in the other column to their obvious gender. In fact, as we saw before, those who try to fit the stereotypes of masculinity and femininity most rigidly often have the most problems. Sandra Bem's classic research in the 1970s found that 'androgynous' people (those who showed both culturally masculine and feminine traits) were more flexible and psychologically healthy than those who stuck rigidly to gender roles.[21]

But, you might say, what about physical differences? Clearly humans *can* be divided into male and female because they have different bodies and different sex chromosomes. We can't just get rid of the idea of men and women entirely.

It is worth thinking about this quite carefully. Gender specialist Christina Richards suggests that we consider the questions 'How do you know you are a woman?' or 'How do you know you are a man?' to show how tricky these terms are.[22] Take 'How do you know you are a woman?' We might argue that it is because we have 'feminine' characteristics, but what of a female boxer or soldier who seems to contradict most of these 'womanly' qualities? We might answer that it is because we look like a woman: we have long hair and breasts. But what about those who have had a mastectomy due to breast cancer, or lost their hair during chemotherapy? Are they not women? We might say that it is because we are capable of giving birth to children. Again, there are many women who are infertile or past the age of being able to give birth. We might say it is because we have XX chromosomes. But how many people actually know their chromosomal make-up? As we will see, there are people with other chromosomal make-ups who are obviously women. You can try the same activity yourself for 'How do you know you are a man?' If your answer is immediately to locate manhood in the genitals, think about soldiers who have lost or damaged that part of the body while clearly embodying what we culturally consider to be the ultimate in masculinity.

It is also worth remembering that there is diversity across every possible measure of sex and gender, something of which not many people are aware. No way of measuring these things gives us a simple either/or set of opposites that apply to absolutely everyone.

For example, if we start with the physiological level of chromosomes and hormones, we know, perhaps, that the majority of men have the XY sex chromosome, and the majority of women XX. Usually, this means that at certain key stages of development they will be exposed to certain 'sex hormones' which, in turn, means that their bodies will develop primary and secondary sex characteristics (testicles and penis *or* vagina, labia, and clitoris; breasts and fat deposits on hips and buttocks *or* facial hair and a deeper voice). However, we also now know that there is diversity in sex development, and that it is relatively common to be born in some way ambiguously physically sexed. The statistic is between around 0.5 and 2 percent of people, depending on how this is measured. This is similar to the percentage of vegans (lower estimate) or vegetarians (higher estimate) in the US, to give you a feel for how common it is. Examples include people who are born with sex chromosomes that are neither XY or XX, but something else (just one X, XXY, XYY, etc.), and those who have different chromosomal make-ups in different parts of their bodies. Even within purely XX and XY people there are those who are insensitive to certain sex hormones, so that their body is shaped in different ways at birth or at puberty than would be expected for someone with their chromosomal make-up. Jeffrey Eugenides' novel *Middlesex* is a thought-provoking exploration of the experience of a character who has XY chromosomes but 'female' genitals, and is raised as a girl.[23]

Conventionally, medical procedures have been used to ensure that all bodies conform to the 'opposite sex' ideal, creating penises or vaginas when there is any ambiguity. However, in recent years there has been debate over whether this is the most appropriate response. Geneticist Anne Fausto-Sterling has written, for example:

> While male and female stand on the extreme ends of a biological continuum, there are many bodies . . . that evidently mix together anatomical components conventionally attributed to both males and females . . . Modern surgical techniques help maintain the two-sex system. Today children who are born 'either/or-neither/both' – a fairly common phenomenon – usually disappear from view because doctors 'correct' them right away with surgery.[24]

So there is diversity in chromosomal make-up, diversity in hormonal sensitivity and take-up, and diversity in genitals (such that it is not always clear what is a penis or a clitoris). There is clearly diversity in all physical aspects which we think of as male or female (men with higher voices than many women, women who are taller than many men, men with breasts larger than some women's, women who are more hirsute than some men).

At the level of brain function we also might see general patterns of difference in men and women. For example, a difference commonly mentioned in documentaries and popular books is whether activity is more focused in one area (men), or spread across both hemispheres of the brain (women). However, there is diversity in how much focus or spread there is, and there are men who fit the more 'female' pattern and vice versa. There is no characteristic on which we can accurately say that all women score higher or lower than all men. Even when some overall difference can be found between women and men such that, for example, the top scorers tends to be female, and the lowest scorers tend to be male, there is usually a massive crossover between the genders, so that for the vast majority of the population it makes no difference whether they are female or male. Think about sports, for example. The fastest runners still tend to be male, but professional female athletes run a great deal faster than most men. Also, there is change over time, so that today's best women athletes would beat the best men of a few decades ago in many sports.

Remembering back to the previous chapter, it is also important to bear in mind that physiological differences are not necessarily present from birth (or down to 'nature'). All through our lives our brains connect up in various ways due to the situations in which we find ourselves and the learning that we do, so it is just as likely that such brain patterns are a result of socialization (or 'nurture'), and far more probable that there is rather a complex ongoing interaction between our bodies and the world which it would be impossible to disentangle.[25]

When we get to the more social level of the identities and roles that people take up, we also see diversity. Anthropologists have found that there have been times and places where everyone, men and women, have all acted more like the 'masculine' side of the lists you made before, where everyone has acted more like the 'feminine' side, and where the roles have been in some way the opposite of the way they are here and now (such as women being more aggressive and war-like and men being more nurturing and social). It is also interesting to note that the differences between what men are like in two different cultures are far greater than the differences between what men and women are like within the same culture, despite our current cultural desire for men and women to be opposite and different. Also, many cultures have conceptualized gender in ways that are not dichotomous. In other words, in ways that have more, or less, than two gender categories. For example, in Thailand there are six different gender labels on a scale of gender that also incorporates sexual preference and activity (man, gay king, gay queen, kathoey, tom, dee, and woman), and Navajo cultures have a 'third' gender category, 'nádleehí', which falls outside dichotomous understandings of gender. In the past, many cultures believed that there was just one gender (women being a somewhat inferior version of men). The idea of two opposite genders is a pretty recent thing, so understandings of gender can clearly shift over time.

In our own time and culture there are also diverse gender roles and identities. The idea that there is just one dominant kind of masculinity and one dominant kind of femininity has been challenged by research. For example, one interview study with heterosexual men found that they divided up into three different kinds of masculinity. Some of the men did project the stereotypical hard, strong, 'real man' persona. Others drew more on a kind of 'everyday bloke' masculinity, akin to Homer Simpson: 'I'm just a regular guy, nothing special'. And others presented themselves as more alternative, so comfortable in their masculinity that they were able to show their feelings, for example, or paint their nails.[26] Once we add in the way that gender rules intersect with our class, culture, sexuality, and age, we see a real multiplicity. For example, studies have found physical aggression to be part of a white, working class femininity amongst groups of women in the north of the UK,[27] and certain forms of appearance display (clothes, body piercings, and tattoos) are an important part of many young, urban, masculinities.

It is possible that things are changing culturally towards more acceptance of diversities of ways of being masculine or feminine. Researcher Eric Anderson, for example, has found that young heterosexual male students are increasingly comfortable kissing each other and showing other forms of physical affection to their male friends,[28] shifting away from the previous norm of heterosexual masculinity being all about proving how not-gay and not-feminine a man is. Others have pointed out the 'feminization' of the job market (more jobs involving good communication and people skills), which may mean that such aspects become more valued.

We might, therefore, shift from the idea that there are two opposite genders on every level (physical sex, gender identity, and sexual identity) to that of diversity at all these levels. Also, we might shift from the idea that each level defines the next to considering them as separate. As David Gauntlett envisions it, we might move from the model that we saw at the start of the chapter to one that looks more like the one below.

The theorist Judith Butler, on whom David Gauntlett is drawing here, has argued that gender is 'performative'. By this, she doesn't mean that our gender identities are something false that we are putting-on, like an acting performance, but rather that we learn through our lives the appropriate ways of performing gender for somebody of our body type in our society, and through repeating these over and over and over again we *do* our gender (rather than it being something we *are*). Gender is also communicative. We do it in order to say things to other people about how we want to be treated in the world. For example, the function of the gender we do might be to communicate to others the message 'look after me', 'respect me', 'be afraid of me', or 'desire me'.

We do gender through our clothing, our voices, our body language, the words we use, and so much more. The ways in which it is done become apparent when we try and *do* a different gender. When I teach gender, I encourage students to get up and walk around the classroom, greeting each other as a different gender. The results are fascinating. One student said it was the difference between [deep voice, slapping the other person firmly on the shoulder] 'alright mate' and [high voice, excited waving hands] 'hiya'. Clearly she could perform both those genders, it's just that the latter was the one she performed on a daily basis for years and years so it felt more like *her*. Norah Vincent's autobiographical account *Self-Made Man* is a fascinating insight into how possible it is for someone to perform gender differently for a longer period.[29]

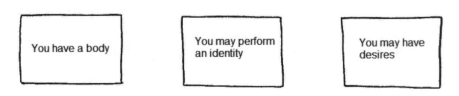

Figure 5.4 Sex, gender and sexuality 2

Beyond rules? Embracing uncertainty

Given the diversity present at each level on which we might understand gender – biological, psychological and social – and the complex ways in which these are intertwined, how might we view gender differently from the 'opposite sexes' idea which we began with? One idea that has been put forward is to see gender on a continuum, rather than as an either/or dichotomy (*either* you are one thing *or* you are the other). This seems to fit if some people are extremely masculine or feminine and some are somewhere in the middle (androgynous).

Let's imagine 7 people, and put them on a continuum of feminine to masculine, based on their appearance (since that's all we have to go on just from looking at them). You might want to think about where you would put yourself on the continuum below.

But we need to question more what we *mean* by masculine and feminine here. There are so many different qualities we are trying to capture when we use these terms. For example, once we got to know these people a bit and found out what they were like, we might put them on different continua depending whether what we meant by 'feminine to masculine' was 'delicate to tough', 'emotional to rational', or 'submissive and yielding to dominant and bossy', for example (see next page).

The problem is that the concepts of masculinity and femininity aim to capture so many different things as to become almost meaningless. One continuum doesn't work. Rather, we need multiple continua to capture all the different aspects that we mean when we talk about masculinity and femininity.

But, actually, even that doesn't work. Remember Chapter 1, where we saw that people were different sides of themselves in different relationships and situations? We could redraw each one of these continua multiple times to capture how tough or delicate, rational or emotional, dominant or submissive, each of those people are in the different situations in which they find themselves. For example, it might turn out that the man on the left of Figure 5.6 is laid back in his family, always going along with other people's decisions, but when he finds himself in the position of having to protect his family he becomes powerful and controlling. Or the woman on the far right might be dominant and bossy in the workplace, but the baby of the family when she gets together with her older siblings.

There are multiple diverse and overlapping ways of being human which may, or may not, be tied to masculinity or femininity.

Feminine   Masculine

Figure 5.5 Gender continuum

Figure 5.6 Alternative gender continua

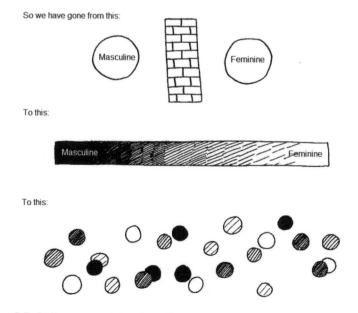

Figure 5.7 Different models of gender

And, in Figure 5.7, those balls really need to move around on the page, changing shade as they do so, to capture the fact that our gender is not something fixed but, like other aspects of our selves (Chapter 1), and like our sexualities (Chapter 4), it is in process and changes over time.

We also need the balls to move around on multiple dimensions, beyond the two dimensions that we have here on this page, to represent the different aspects to which we may be referring when we speak of gender (emotionality, toughness, dominance, nurturing, etc.). We don't have to go far outside the mainstream to see this: think about the ways in which a young girl might demonstrate her femininity (wearing pink, playing with dolls), then think how she might show it as a teenager (wearing skimpy clothes and make-up, going out dancing), as an adult (wearing a suit with a skirt to work, with long hair tied up, looking after her children), and as an older woman (wearing patterned shirts over trousers, spending time embroidering and cooking). And, of course, there are many people who shift gender identities more radically than this over their lifetime, from people who go into a conventionally 'opposite sex' career and change everything including their clothing, attitude and behaviour to fit this; to those who occasionally take on a different gender for pleasure or to entertain others (such as drag kings); to those whose online persona, or avatar, is of a different gender to the one they perform day to day, and who spend a great deal of time being that person; to those who have bodily changes such that they end up in a different gender to the one they were given at birth (their physical body coming to match the gender with which they identify). There are people from all of these groups represented in the continuum cartoons.

It could seem, by this point, that gender is completely flexible and fluid, and that it is great for people to challenge opposite genders and to find different ways of doing gender. There is, however, a strong note of caution to add to this. Although we've seen that there is reason to believe that society is shifting somewhat in recognizing that there are multiple ways of expressing gender which may change over time, there is also a strong backlash to this which insists on holding on to the notion that there are only two normally and naturally opposite genders. We saw this at the start of the chapter when we considered Rules girls and Game boys.

This backlash fits with what we saw in the introductory chapter, about the ways in which we tend to grasp tight onto old rules at times of uncertainty. Nowhere is this more true than with gender. Gender is still the first thing that is generally asked about a baby once the mother has had a scan, often even before anyone asks whether or not it is healthy. And research suggests that people treat babies differently, from the word go, on the basis of assumed gender differences (a crying baby is assumed to be angry if it is dressed in blue, or scared if it is dressed in pink, and the former will be played with much more roughly than the latter).[30] Our language is so gendered that it is virtually impossible to talk about someone without saying what gender they are (him/her, he/she, etc.) We are gendered (and gender ourselves) every time we pick which toilet cubicle to enter (and how outdated are those pictures on the doors?). Also, gender differences seem to be headline news in a way that gender similarities simply are not, despite the fact there are actually far more similarities between the genders overall than there are differences.[31] People seem to *want* to hear that there are differences.

There is also a great deal of discomfort around people who fall outside of the normative rules of gender. Boys are still bullied for being 'sissy' in school,[32] and trans people are seen as an appropriate source of humour in a way that just isn't acceptable for any other group. Ridicule is not the end of it, of course: rates of hate crime against trans people are shockingly high.[33] Also, there is great resistance to those who want to legally define without gender, ticking neither 'male' nor 'female' on the form. Clearly, as a society, we still have major problems with those who blend, bend and break the rules of gender.

In Chapter 10 we will explore further what it is like for people who do step outside the rules in various ways, and why it is important not to assume that this will be an easy, or pain-free, process. However important it is to challenge the rules, it is likely that others will attempt to pressure us into conforming. Also, gender is ingrained within ourselves if we have performed it in certain ways for years and years. Nowhere have I learnt this more than when starting to rock-climb. All around me guys grunt, rage, and shout 'come on' to themselves, as they struggle, fall, or pull themselves over the top. Meanwhile, tears prick the corners of my eyes and hear myself squeak 'I just can't do it', or 'it's too scary'. This is not to say that traditional masculinity is the only – or best – way to go about rock-climbing. Clearly, it isn't. Many men struggle to find the delicacy required to be a top climber, which is reminiscent of the grace of a ballet dancer. But, for me at least, climbing involves having to undo some aspects of conventional femininity in order to develop the 'grrr' required, and recognizing how difficult it can be to rewrite the rules by which I lived for so long.

You might also find it interesting and useful to try an activity which is generally linked with a different gender to the one which you regularly perform, or to do a familiar activity in the way in which another gender might do it. This will help you to experience what it is like to challenge these rules so directly.

It is important, in order for the rigid and damaging thinking about gender to change, that people do start separating out various characteristics and behaviours from gender, questioning the gender dichotomy, challenging why gender is seen as such a vital part of who we are, and otherwise making 'gender trouble', as Judith Butler put it. Recognition of the multiplicity and plurality of gender would certainly be a way forward. Given that the word 'trans' means changing from the gender that we were given at birth, it could be argued that *all* of us are actually trans. How many of us remained in precisely the gender roles that the people present at our birth (parents, nurses and doctors, 20, 30, 40 or more years ago) imagined when they said 'It's a boy' or 'It's a girl'? This doesn't mean that it's not okay to take a look at the circulating, overlapping, masculinities and femininities that surround us and to decide that you're quite happy to be a pink girl or a blue boy,[34] as long as you don't dismiss the rights of other people to be otherwise. It is taking that look that is important, and this is the very thing that we are often too threatened or oblivious to do[35].

Returning to relationships, we have seen that these are not all about gender. Our expectations and assumptions about gender, and how we express it, *are* relevant to our relationships, whatever the gender of those involved. However, conflict generally does not arise from specific differences between the people in a relationship, but rather from the ways we *respond* to any differences between us (with defensiveness and self-justification), which are not tied to gender. We will explore this further in Chapter 7.

Broader, human, themes underlie most relationship conflicts. As we have seen in this chapter when we considered *The Wire*, a common struggle between partners (whatever their genders) is the inevitable tension between freedom and togetherness which comes up whenever two or more people are intimate in any way. This tension has been exacerbated in current culture, with its emphasis on individual independence, on the one hand, and finding love, on the other. Such tensions will come up over the next 4 chapters as we examine exclusivity in relationships, conflict, break-up, and commitment.

Chapter 6

Rewriting the rules of monogamy

What are the rules?

At the end of the last chapter, we saw that a tension present in all relationships is that between freedom and togetherness. Philosophers point out that an unavoidable fact of the human condition is that we are both intrinsically alone *and* unavoidably in the world with other people.[1] We are born alone, coming through the birth canal by ourselves. We will die alone: nobody else can do that with us. We can never truly know what it is to be another person, however close we get to them. At the same time, we cannot escape other people and the impact that they have on our life. As soon as we come to the world, we are in the hands of others without whom we wouldn't be able to survive. During our lives we try to enter the crevices of others' minds and bodies. And, when we begin our final journey, we wish for somebody to be there to hold our hand.

Most of us live right up alongside other people, and most of us care deeply what they think of us to such an extent that it shapes our behaviour on a daily basis. But even if we were to shun all human contact, going to live in a hermitage or purposefully acting against everything that we knew other people wanted us to do, we would still be relating to other people through these very actions – because we would be avoiding them or rebelling against them. As we saw in Chapter 1, our self-identity is utterly bound up in our relationships with others, such that we are even different selves with different people, and the identity we project is based on comparisons we make to others, and how we want (and don't want) them to see us.

This fact of human existence leads to no end of struggle as we pendulum-swing from freedom and independence, to togetherness and dependence, and back again. We build a life with other people, keen for the friendly babble of voices around us and the secure sense of having them there. Then we feel overwhelmed by their presence and irritated by their little ways and long for some space. We head off on our own, loving the solitude, the expanse of the open road – until we start to feel lonely and search for company. We find true love, and happily fling ourselves into the co-creation of a couple unit: a 'we', rather than an 'I'. Then we discover that our partner is not as much like ourselves as we thought they were, or we feel we've lost ourselves in *their* way of seeing the world, and we desperately scramble to escape the situation and to find ourselves again. Alone once more, we relish the stillness of our home and the endless possibilities of a life in which we don't have to take account of somebody else all the time. But, when we see families and couples on the street, we have a niggling sense of something missing and begin to yearn for someone who will understand us and support us again.

As we saw in the Introduction, this struggle has been exacerbated in recent decades as there has been increasing encouragement both for people to pursue their own individual goals in life *and* for them to find security and validation in romantic love (rather than in religion or community, as they might have done in the past). In his book *Liquid Love*, Zygmunt Bauman says that people now are:

> despairing at being abandoned to their own wits and feeling easily disposable, yearning for the security of togetherness and for a helping hand to count on in a moment of trouble, and so desperate to 'relate'; yet wary of the state of 'being related' and particularly of being related 'for good', not to mention forever – since they fear that such a state may bring burdens and cause strains they neither feel able nor are willing to bear, and so may severely limit the freedom they need – yes, your guess is right – to relate . . .[2]

So – we try to form relationships and to get the sense of security that they will last, at the same time as wanting to keep them sufficiently uncommitted that we can get out of them again if necessary. We'll return to this paradox in Chapter 9.

This tension between dependence and independence, freedom and togetherness, aloneness and belonging, plays out in a number of ways in relationships. For example, in the last chapter we considered the common relationship conflict where one partner prioritizes their work over the relationship, and the other person does the opposite. On a more everyday level, conflicts about small household tasks can often really be about people exerting their desire to have the freedom to do things 'their way', rather than having to compromise for the sake of togetherness. Furious arguments erupt over trivial things, like somebody's failure to replace the empty toilet roll, because it represents either the freedom to relax without monitoring in one's own home, or the isolation of not being valued in that moment when the other person thought 'forget it' as they tore off the last sheet of paper. Esther Perel also locates, in this tension between freedom and togetherness, the difficulties that many people experience in keeping long-term relationships erotic. Sexiness requires us to be separate and to surprise each other, while security requires us to be bonded and to know each other inside out. It is a challenge to sustain both heat and warmth in the same relationship.[3]

Related to this, perhaps one of the main ways in which the freedom/togetherness tension plays out in relationships today is in the vexed questions around monogamy. How exclusive does 'being together' mean? And how much freedom are we allowed with other people within that togetherness? Such questions will be the focus of the rest of this chapter.

On the face of it, the rules of monogamy might seem fairly obvious. When we get together with somebody, we are meant to stop seeing anybody else. When we commit to each other in legal or religious civil partnerships or marriages, we make the promise to 'forsake all others', and to be faithful to our partner. If we do stray outside the relationship then we are cheating, being unfaithful, or committing adultery: all of these words reflect the negative light in which such actions are perceived. Doing this means betraying our partner and the end of the relationship if we are discovered.

These rules are apparent in films and TV programmes about relationships. Characters on soap operas are dumped if it is discovered that they have been two-timing. Movies from *Fatal Attraction* and *What Lies Beneath* to *Derailed* and *Contagion* continue to warn against the tragic, and even fatal, consequences of infidelity. Talk shows and tabloids relish revealing the secret affairs of the rich and famous, and we all stand in judgement of their behaviour. Beyond questioning their commitment to their relationship, we question the character and moral fibre of a politician or sports star who has strayed away from home. Women's magazines and urban legends tell stories of wronged women who have shredded their husband's wardrobe, or sold their car for a tiny price, as if this is a justifiable response to uncovering an affair.

Certainly, all mainstream self-help books about relationships assume that they will be monogamous and do not consider any models for romantic relationships other than the (usually married) couple. The average psychology textbook presents pairing off and getting married as an inevitable, natural, normal, and healthy part of development over the lifespan; relationships outside the couple are only considered in the context of cheating and infidelity and the damage this can do. Occasionally, alternatives to monogamy (like swinging, open relationships, or polyamory) are covered in the popular media, but usually in the same kind of 'freak of the week' format applied to 'deviant' sexualities (see Chapter 4). After consideration, journalists and documentary narrators generally conclude that non-monogamy is something that they – and, by extension, all *normal* people – could not handle. It would inevitably end in tears, if not before, then certainly after, bedtime. The possibility of more than one relationship is presented as the enclave of New Age weirdos or of the ridiculously rich and famous, and we are directed back to the normal path of monogamy, and its much simpler rules.

However, any relationship therapist will tell you that the rules of monogamy are not necessarily so clear-cut. Many relationship conflicts and break-ups do indeed occur after somebody knowingly breaks the rules of monogamy. However, many also happen because the people involved have just understood those rules slightly differently. Even if we fully accept the rules of monogamy that I summarized before, we might still be unclear on some matters. After how many dates are we supposed to stop seeing other people? Certainly, sex outside our relationship would be cheating, but is a bit of harmless flirting okay? Does masturbating or looking at online porn count as infidelity? What about the close friend that I have? Is that someone I have to 'forsake' after I commit to my partner? Does it make a difference whether they are the same gender as my partner, or whether they, themselves, are in a relationship?

Considering these questions, we can see that one aspect of the monogamy rules which isn't clear in the phrase 'forsaking all others' is whether we are talking about sexual exclusivity, emotional exclusivity, or both. The current rules demand more sexual exclusivity than emotional exclusivity. Having sex with someone else is definitely infidelity, whereas staying up all night talking with someone else is not necessarily problematic. Indeed it would, generally speaking, be seen as a bad sign if a new partner was unhappy with us maintaining friendships outside the relationship. However, there is certainly suspicion over friendships with people who are the same gender as our partner (or the other gender, if a person is bisexual, due to prejudices that bisexual people can't stick to one gender). It is assumed that such a close friendship always has the risk of becoming sexual. This is also probably the reason why there is often a lot of suspicion, or even a blanket ban, around friendships with ex-parters. It is likely that the rules and restrictions around such friendships are tighter than those around friendships where it assumed that there is no danger of becoming sexual.

Gender also comes into the rules of monogamy, in the expectation that men are rightly and naturally promiscuous and women are rightly and naturally monogamous. This is the sexual double standard which explains why there are hundreds of negative words for a woman who has sex with multiple people, and only a few, mostly positive, words for a man in the same situation.[4] We saw one recent incarnation of this stereotype in the difference between the Rules girls and Game boys of Chapter 5. Such gendered assumptions are problematic in the same way that so many gender generalizations are. Clearly, there are promiscuous women (given a positive representation in the shape of Samantha from *Sex and the City*, after years of demonization), and there are plenty of men, of all sexualities, who are desperate to pair-bond and settle down (indeed this is just what Neil Strauss himself does at the end of *The Game*). Think of Jason Segal's character in *Forgetting Sarah Marshall*, as he tells Russell Brand, 'This isn't Europe. There are rules here . . . you don't sleep with another man's girlfriend'.

Most of the rules of monogamy apply to people of all genders, so we won't consider gender in further detail in this chapter. However, it is worth remaining aware that gender enters into monogamy issues. For example, it might come up in the form of expectations being placed on men to be promiscuous (which can put pressure on them to be so, or can mean that partners will be more suspicious of men in relationships), and in assumptions that women will *not* be promiscuous (which could mean that they are more condemned if they do sleep around, or more forgiven by a partner if they cheat – because it is assumed to be a one-off incident).

The rules of monogamy are fuzzy in places. However, little is done to clarify them. It is unusual for people to have explicit conversations about what the rules for monogamy will be in their relationship. Generally, people assume that partners will share their rules until a situation comes up which reveals that this isn't the case. At that point, the person with the tighter rules can feel insecure about the bonds between them and their partner, while the person with the looser rules can feel that the freedom they had taken for granted is being threatened. The tension between togetherness and freedom is revealed in a way that is raw and exposing for all concerned, as partners evaluate how much they feel free to be themselves, versus how much they are operating as part of the relationship.

To summarize, the rules we have covered here are:

- Relationships should be sexually and emotionally monogamous (with emphasis on sexual monogamy).
- If you break this monogamy in any way then you have done wrong, and the relationship will most likely end if you are found out.
- There are no possibilities for relationships other than monogamy.
- The monogamy rules should not be explicitly discussed or negotiated, therefore they are rather unclear in the details.

Why question the rules?

Built into these rules is the idea that monogamy is the *natural* and *normal* model of human relationships.

David Barash and Judith Eve Lipton's book *The Myth of Monogamy* presents a long examination of why monogamy cannot be said to be the natural way of doing things, either in human or non-human animals.[5] Only a few dozen, out of the approximately four thousand mammal species on the planet, form anything like lifelong pair-bonds with each other. There is a huge diversity of practices, from species of bird where many different females mate with the male that has the most visually-exciting displays, to the bonobo chimpanzees who use sex as a social activity to develop and reinforce bonds with other male and female chimps. Even the seemingly faithful birds in the movie *March of the Penguins* only bond for a season, and find a different partner the following year.

We saw in Chapter 4 that, whether we conclude that monogamy is natural or unnatural, it is generally problematic to assume that any behaviour is good or bad on the basis of whether it is natural or not. We only have to look at behaviours like wearing clothes, taking antibiotics, and being kind to animals or strangers, to see that there are many 'unnatural' behaviours to which people generally adhere and which they see as good. Also, it is probably impossible to tease out all of the complexities of human culture to reveal what people would be like without all the societal and technological influences on them (if we could even call that their natural state).

As well as the idea that monogamy is the natural way for humans to be, many also argue that it is normal: that most people have monogamous relationships. Again, we have seen that there is a problem with equating normality with being morally superior. Extremely high levels of intelligence are not normal, and neither are the acts of self-sacrifice of a person like Mohandas 'Mahatma' Gandhi, Martin Luther King, Jr. or Nelson Mandela, but we wouldn't condemn these people for their abnormalities. The ability to have multiple orgasms or to sing like an angel are pretty rare, but are no less enviable for it.

If we are interested in what is normal, despite these issues, then lifelong monogamy certainly isn't the norm. If we look at the number of different societies in the world (rather than numbers of individual people), then polygamy is definitely the most common relationship structure, usually taking the form of one man having relationships with more than one woman, although there are societies where everyone is allowed multiple partners, and a very few where it is only women who are allowed more than one. Roger Rubin reports that only 43 out of 238 societies worldwide are monogamous.[6] Let me give some examples of the variety of different arrangements. In parts of rural Turkey, a man can have more than one wife and each wife takes on a different role (e.g. one helping him with agricultural work, another doing the domestic labour). Many Toda women, in Southern India, marry a man's brothers as well as the man himself. In Nigeria, Abisi women marry three men on the same day (two being arranged marriages and the other a love marriage). In some New Guinean societies men are expected to have sexual relationships with other men before they form relationships with women later in life. In many European, Canadian, American, Australian, and New Zealand urban centres, 'trial marriages' are most common, whereby people cohabit for a while prior to making any legal commitment. There are also tribes, in these centres, in which having more than one sexual partner is the norm.[7]

It is certainly the norm to *claim* monogamy, but whether it is the norm to *be* monogamous is another thing. People living close to a swingers' club recently organized a petition to have it closed down because they found it offensive. The owner commented that this was ironic because it was a well known 'secret' that several of the local community were having affairs with each other's spouses. That was seen as acceptable, because it was kept hidden. According to recent statistics, as many as 60 percent of men and 50 percent of women have had sex with someone other than their spouse whilst married.[8] Add to that the number of people who realize that they had different monogamy rules (so it feels like one of them has been betrayed by the other's behaviour, even if there isn't a clear case of an affair), and we have a majority of people.

So, we could say that non-monogamy is the norm in our culture, but that it usually takes the form of secret, hidden, infidelities rather than something that is openly known about by all involved. While some couples may know full well that it is going on but pretend not to, the more common story is that of the person who is stunned when they find out that their partner has had an affair. They are then either left bereft when their partner goes off with the 'other' person, or left questioning their trust when their partner assures them that it will never happen again (and what then becomes of the 'other' person?). The discovery of an affair often marks the end of a relationship, or at least causes considerable unhappiness amongst all concerned.

Despite the commonality of affairs, there is still a strong idea that we *can't* be attracted to, or have love feelings for, more than one person at once. However, many people do have strong feelings and attraction for more than one person simultaneously at some point in their life, and it is even something that is becoming more commonly portrayed in the media. Two blockbuster movies which came out in the same year (2006) included plots in which a woman loved two men. In *Superman Returns*, Lois was portrayed as loving both Superman and her new husband. In the second *Pirates of the Caribbean* film, Elizabeth (along with much of the audience) was attracted to the rogue Jack Sparrow as well as the more conventional hero, Will Turner. It seems that movies, and many soap operas, admit the possibility of loving more than one person, but the character is usually presented as having to make a choice. It is interesting that we readily accept someone loving more than one child, sibling, or friend without their love for one of them diluting the love for others, but when it comes to romantic or sexual love most people cannot accept it happening more than once at a time.

We might, therefore, question the rules of monogamy, because we can see that there are actually other ways of managing relationships globally; and because we can question whether monogamy in its current form is working for people, given the high rates of secret affairs and separation (and the pressure and pain these cause). We can also point to the common experience of people having loving or sexual feelings for more than one person at once, and wonder about ways in which this might be resolved, other than by the forced choice of staying with one person and rejecting the other entirely.

Perhaps the most important reasons for questioning the rules of monogamy is the fact that they *are* unclear and they do differ between people (even though we might like to think that they don't). A recent study found that one third of young people in monogamous relationships didn't agree on whether they had discussed what monogamy meant to them with their partner, and over half of them disagreed on whether the rules of monogamy had been kept or not.[9] It would be better if we were able to be open and to negotiate and agree upon our monogamy rules.

Anthropologists Katherine Frank and John deLamater studied a wide range of heterosexual couples.[10] Some were monogamous without any infidelity, some were monogamous but having secret affairs, and some were openly non-monogamous in various ways (in open marriages, swingers or polyamorous – in multiple relationships). The researchers found that it was difficult actually to differentiate between these categories of people in the ways in which they were managing their relationships, or the conversations that they were having. This suggests that any separation between monogamy and non-monogamy might be a problematic one. Rather, we should see that there are a wider variety of ways of managing this aspect of relationships. Therapist Tammy Nelson also reports that many of her clients continually revisit the rules around monogamy in order to maintain their relationships over time.[11] The term 'new monogamy' refers to monogamy that incorporates some openness.

It is clear that *all* relationships have rules around monogamy, whether these are explicit and talked about, or implicit and taken-for-granted, and that these vary widely between relationships. Consider the following examples.

Jacqui and Taz have a relationship in which neither of them are allowed to spend time alone with members of the 'opposite sex' because they, and their community, view any such contact as inherently sexual and therefore risky.

Caroline and Beth have committed to their relationship with a civil partnership ceremony. Caroline knows that she has to be careful not to be too friendly with other women because Beth would find it threatening and become insecure.

When Simon got together with Jemima, he had to stop spending time with his ex-girlfriend because Jemima felt that such contact was completely out of order now that he was with her.

Geoff and Kim are in their mid thirties and recently got married. Neither would ever have sex outside their relationship, but Geoff has an old schoolfriend, Sue, with whom he is close, and with whom he sometimes goes travelling. Kim has a gay best friend, Charles, with whom she goes out partying most weekends.

Natalya and Ian have been married since they were 23, and they have two children together. Ian doesn't know that Natalya occasionally spends lunch-times with a work colleague at a hotel, where they have sex. Natalya doesn't know that Ian goes to lap-dancing clubs when he's away on business.

Geraldine and Pat have a 'don't ask, don't tell' policy in their relationship. When their kids came along, Geraldine went off sex and she is okay with Pat having occasional flings – as long as she doesn't have to hear about it.

Bobby and Jo are in their twenties and live together. They are happy in their relationship. Both of them occasionally have a bit of a flirt and a kiss with a stranger if they're out at a nightclub with friends, but they know that it doesn't mean anything.

Serena and Pete have been married for years and still have an active sex life. However, there are some desires that neither of them can satisfy in each other, so Serena doesn't mind when Pete goes off to have casual sex with men he's met on the internet, and Pete is fine that Serena writes sexy stories about her favourite TV characters, which she posts on a website viewed by her online friends.

Eric and Cliff are a professional couple who live together in London. At weekends they go out cruising nightclubs together. Sometimes, one of them will bring another man back for sex and, occasionally, they'll both like the same guy and have a threesome with him.

Pearl and Tony are swingers in their fifties. A few times a year they go to a club or party where Pearl will go off with another man and Tony with another woman. They've been doing this for years and find that it livens things up a bit.

Amer and Len are a couple in their thirties who consider themselves in a primary relationship with each other. Both also have secondary relationships with other people whom they see for dates every week or so. They generally get on well with each other's other lovers, whom they refer to as metamours.

Nancy has two husbands, although she is only married to one of them legally. They all live together and are bringing up their kids. They are part of a close network of polyamorous people and they all have sexual friendships with others in the group.

Harriet, Ann, Priya, and Loz are a poly-fidelitous quad. That means that they all have sexual relationships with each other, but none of them are looking for other relationships or sex outside of their unit.

The point, here, is that it might be more useful to see monogamy as a continuum rather than an either/or thing. It isn't just a matter of deciding to be monogamous or not, but rather of where our relationship stands on the continuum of monogamy, and whether all of the people involved can agree on that. Figure 6.1 presents one possible alternative way of thinking about monogamy. We could imagine two continua of what we might call emotional and sexual monogamies.

Think about where you would like to be on each continuum (imagine it as a scale of 0-10 if that helps, with 0 being a completely closed relationship and 10 being a completely open one). You could provide a number, or draw an X at the point on the line where you think you would generally like to be (although, of course, this might alter over time). Then think about where any past and current partners, lovers, or friends, would be on these scales, how that has come about, and whether everyone involved is content with that.

Of course, this is only one alternative way of seeing monogamy (compared to the either/or monogamous/non-monogamous model). Also, it might not make sense to everyone to tease apart love and sex in these ways. Some people might see emotional closeness and sexual contact as always linked together. Others might imagine further continua beyond these two to make sense of their relationships, such as proximity (from living with one person to many); how vulnerable they can be around someone (from having only one person they 'let in' to many); or time (from having one person they see much more than everyone else, to having many

---

Continuum of emotional closeness/love

Monoamory   ━━━━━━━━━━━━━━━━━━━━━━━━   Polyamory

One close intimate relationship &   *Multiple close*
no close relationships outside this   *Relationships*

Continuum of sex/physical contact

Monosex   ━━━━━━━━━━━━━━━━━━━━━━━━   Polysex

No sexual or physical contact   *Multiple sexual*
outside the relationship   *encounters*

Figure 6.1 Monogamy continua

between whom they divide time). There could also be different continua for different forms of sex. For example, some of the kinky people we met in Chapter 4 vary in terms of whether they have one main dominant or submissive partner, or whether they play with different people in this way. This might be separate to the rules they have around non-kinky sex.

Rules about emotional and sexual monogamy are something that all of us have to negotiate in our relationships. This is true whether we are careful about who we socialize with outside our partnership in case that becomes threatening, or we 'forsake all others' sexually whilst retaining close friendships, or we open our relationships up in some way. One problem is that, while people who have explicitly non-monogamous relationships of some kind might spend time and energy negotiating these rules, most people just assume that everyone will have the same rules that they do. Often, it can be a huge relationship crisis when we realize that the thing we thought was okay is actually extremely troubling to our partner. And, of course, not all openly non-monogamous people do this communication perfectly either (as we will see later). Certainly, most trip over unshared rules, or realize that they haven't negotiated everything they need to, when a problem comes up. Wherever we fall on the continua of monogamy, there is frequently the taken-for-granted assumption that our partner/s will be in same place as we are.

Alternative rules

The rules that different groups of people put in place when they do step outside of the conventional rules of monogamy may be helpful to all of us when negotiating our own rules of monogamy, particularly if they have been tried and tested by communities over a stretch of time.

Estimates of the proportion of people in openly non-monogamous relationships vary from 15-28 percent of heterosexual people[12] to around 50 percent of bisexual people and gay men.[13] The types of openly non-monogamous relationships which have been most written about in recent years are gay open relationships, swinging, and polyamory.[14] Broadly speaking, swinging and open relationships involve couples who openly have sexual (but generally not love) relationships with other people. Polyamory (or poly) involves people having multiple love relationships which may also be sexual. There are various different possible arrangements for this. For example, some have one primary relationship and other, more secondary, ones. Some have two equal relationships (a V structure). Some form a triad, quad, or family, of people all of whom are involved with one other, perhaps also living together. Others see themselves more as an individual with various (sexual and non-sexual) relationships in their life.

Beyond swinging, gay open relationships, and polyamory, there is a huge internet phenomenon of couples seeking singles and singles seeking couples for sex, which tends to be done more secretively (although it is open in the sense that those involved all know about it). Linked to this is the activity of dogging, where people meet in secluded lay-bys and car parks to watch others having sex, or to be watched. There are various forms of cybersex which don't involve people meeting in person. Open non-monogamy is also the norm for the Game boys mentioned in Chapter 5 (although how accepting they are of their partners also being non-monogamous is not so clear). The hook-up culture which is emerging in some colleges and universities tends to involve casually sexual, or fuck buddy, arrangements which are not monogamous.[15] Finally, there are many people who renegotiate their relationships in unique ways due to their circumstances: for example, when giving talks on this topic, I've heard of couples who've incorporated a new person into their relationship rather than breaking up after an affair, and about people who've kept two partners in different houses, with all their family members knowing of this and referring to their two 'aunties' or 'grandfathers'. Many people negotiate such relationships but don't make it widely apparent to other people.

Clearly, a huge stigma remains around openly stepping outside the rules of monogamy. As we've seen, non-monogamy is frequently ridiculed or dismissed as being too immature or complicated to contemplate. People in openly non-monogamous relationships complain that when monogamous relationships break-up nobody ever blames monogamy, but when their relationships break up it is often taken as evidence that polyamory or open relationships can't really work anyway. There is no legal recognition of more than one relationship, and many people fear how they would be treated at work, by neighbours, or in schools, if their arrangements were out in the open, particularly if they have kids. This is despite research suggesting that children who grow up in such families do just as well as those in monogamous families (and may actually be better off in some respects, such as having multiple role models, incomes, and people for support).[16]

Turning to the rules which people use to manage open non-monogamy, perhaps the most common is to draw a clear distinction between love and sex. Many swingers, and people in open relationships, allow sex outside their main relationship but put strategies in place in an attempt to prevent strong emotional bonds from forming with those people. Common examples of rules include not sleeping over with anyone else, not having sex with anyone else in the house you share with your main partner, not seeing other people more than one time, or considering anyone outside the main relationship as simply a plaything. Some couples keep certain forms of sex (such as genital sex or anal sex) sacred within their relationship and don't do this with anybody else.[17] This separation relates back to the continua of love and sex which we explored earlier.

There are two main ways in which swingers and gay men in open relationships tend to keep the extra sex they are having as non-threatening as possible to their main relationship. Some do it by minimising the amount that they know about what each other are doing, and others do it by maximising this information (even to the extent, in some cases, of actually having their partner present any time they have sex with someone else). An example of the first strategy would be the 'don't ask, don't tell' policy, whereby both people know that their partner is sexual with other people but agree never to talk explicitly about it. At the other end of the spectrum, an example would be partners always sharing the details of what they

---

Continuum of privacy/disclosure

Complete disclosure   Complete privacy

Share everything   *Don't share much about your*
about your lives   *lives outside the relationship*

Figure 6.2 Privacy continuum

have done with other people, perhaps to the point that it becomes an exciting part of their shared sex life. You might want to think about how much you like to know about the rest of a partner's life (whether or not your relationship is open in these ways). On a spectrum from preferring complete privacy to total disclosure, where would you place yourself?

Some polyamorous people draw similar boundaries around the activities which are, or are not, permissible in various relationships.[18] Because polyamory is about emotional, not just sexual, connections, there may also be rules around things like time, space, and closeness. For example, in some primary/secondary arrangements it might be that only primary partners live together, or that secondary partners are only allowed a certain number of dates each week or month.

While some openly non-monogamous people use explicit rules or contracts to keep their relationship secure, others deliberately resist any rules or lists of activities which are, or are not, okay.[19] Some people feel more free if they have clear boundaries around what is and isn't acceptable, whereas others feel more free if they are trusted by their partner to make whatever decisions seem right to them for themselves and for the relationship. In the latter case, there is a strong emphasis on self-awareness and open communication to ensure and display trust, commitment, and the stability of the relationship. You might think, again, where you fall on this spectrum in your own relationships. Do you prefer a clear set of rules and boundaries, or would you rather emphasize freedom and see your relationship as a work in progress to be continually negotiated?

Whatever their contract, or lack of one, most openly non-monogamous people say that it is important to demonstrate some form of specialness in each relationship. This can be done by keeping certain activities, locations, or times, sacred within a specific couple (or triad, quad, or family). Some say that this is

---

Continuum of boundaries

Clear contracts   Ongoing negotiation

Agreed set of rules about   *Trust in each person*
what is and isn't okay in the relationship   *to make good decisions*

Figure 6.3 Boundary continuum

particularly important when one partner is in 'new relationship energy' (a honeymoon period when they have just started seeing a new partner). You might find it useful to consider the ways in which you do, or don't, mark the specialness of a relationship. How do you like to demonstrate how much you value it, and have it demonstrated to you? Are there times when this is particularly important?

What can we all take from these strategies which openly non-monogamous people have had to learn by stepping outside of the conventional rules? The polyamorous motto is 'communicate, communicate, communicate', so perhaps the major thing is to communicate both with yourself, about how free and together you want to be in relationships, and with others, so that they are aware of where you are, and can let you know whether they are in similar, or different, places. It is important to recognize that there are losses and gains to both ends of that spectrum. Being more free means having less say over what the people in your life do; being more together means you'll have to compromise more around your own desires. Most of the spectrums we have covered in this chapter relate to this wider one of freedom/togetherness. At one end, we have more clarity, security, boundaries, and sharing; at the other, we have more freedom, openness, individual privacy, and autonomy. People may be at different places on the different continua, and where they place themselves will also vary over time.

Often, in relationships, there is an idea that there is a right and a wrong place to be on such continua. For example, some people have a shared assumption that they should do everything together, and the person who wants more space and privacy feels guilty about it. Others have a shared assumption that everyone should be very free, so the person who feels jealous and insecure thinks they are wrong for feeling this way. It can be helpful to question such notions of right and wrong (as we did in Chapter 3) and instead to respect everyone's right to be where they are at on the continua we've covered. Then, we might think carefully about agreements which could meet the different needs which are in play,[20] and how these might be gentle and flexible, rather than rigid and constraining. In Chapter 9, we will cover further the kinds of commitments we might make to one another when in relationships, and we consider in the next chapter how conflicts around them might be negotiated.

Beyond rules? Embracing uncertainty

By covering these forms of open non-monogamy I am not proposing that they are in any way better than monogamy, nor that any form of open non-monogamy is

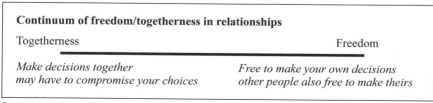

Figure 6.4 Freedom continuum

superior to any other. As we have seen, distinctions between monogamous and non-monogamous relationships are false splits which depend on who is drawing the line (and perhaps it is better not to draw a line at all). Also, as I mentioned in the Introduction, there is a strong and problematic tendency for those who step outside of the rules to grasp the new rules that they come up with just as tightly. An example of grasping new rules in openly non-monogamous relationships comes in the form of the search for the 'poly grail'. This is where people rigidly try to ensure that their relationship conforms to some mythical ideal of what they think it should be like (for example, a couple searching for an idealized bisexual woman who will be attracted to both of them, or people insisting that anyone they get involved with has to move in with them to form a triad or a quad).

When you ask non-monogamous people what the biggest challenge they face is, the answer is generally the surprising 'time management', rather than the expected 'jealousy'. Another way of grasping open non-monogamy too tightly is to assume, as Jamie Heckert puts it,[21] that, because you can go anywhere, you must go everywhere. Having too many relationships can mean not having enough time or energy for any of them. Some polyamorous people have invented the word 'polysaturated' for this particular state.

None of this is to dismiss open non-monogamy. Rather, the point is to acknowledge that any relationship style grasped too tightly can become limiting and brittle, and that there is a huge temptation, when stepping outside the taken-for-granted rules of monogamy, to cast around for any other set of rules that might be available and to grasp hold of them even more tightly. There is not one way of doing non-monogamy, just as there is not one way of doing monogamy; rather there are plural monogamies and non-monogamies which blend into each other and overlap. Perhaps the emphasis should be on finding a style of relating which fits the people involved, rather than on searching for a relationship style to shoehorn people into.

Something that is worth questioning in both monogamous and non-monogamous relationships is the common privileging of a certain kind of romantic, sexual, love over all others. In Chapter 3 we saw some of the problems with our current ideals of romantic love. In open and multiple relationships there is a risk that these problems will be squared and cubed, rather than being decreased. People may take even less time alone, and may be more likely to assume that they can get everything from their partners (after all, don't they have four of them now? Surely that is enough?) They may assume that this great new kind of love they have discovered really *will* conquer all problems, in a way that monogamous love did not.

Open relationships and swinging can maintain the privileging of romantic love over all other forms, because partners in the couple tend to be viewed as more important than other sexual relationships. How does it feel to be the 'extra' man or woman who is told that they are not allowed to sleep over, or that it is 'three way or no way', or that they must be content with one date every other week? Similarly, polyamory can, in some forms, privilege romantic relationships. Someone with multiple partners may have even less time for their friends, family, and colleagues than someone with one partner, and these relationships may be relatively inflexible to change over time (for example, conflicts or break-ups may occur if a long-term secondary partner wants to become primary or vice versa, or if one person in a triad or quad doesn't want to live with the others any more).

Jamie Heckert and Eleanor Wilkinson both argue for dismantling the hierarchy whereby romantic and sexual love is prioritized over other forms of love. This would involve a shift in focus from the polyamorous idea of multiple *lovers* to the notion of multiple *loves*. Wilkinson lists some of these as 'familial love, love for friends, neighbours, community, or love of the planet'[22] and Heckert adds self-love to this list, lest we forget that we need some solitude and care for ourselves (see Chapters 1 and 10). You might relate this back to the activity we did in Chapter 3 about the different needs we have met in different kinds of relationships, and in Chapter 1 about the different selves that emerge in different relationships. Christina Richards also puts forward models for how people might experience themselves as different genders in different relationships[23] (see Chapter 5). Given that we are all plural people in relationships with other plural people, then perhaps it is more realistic to say that we are *all* in multiple relationships, even those of us who regard ourselves as monogamous with one partner. We might even consider the ways in which we do or do not nourish and value all those different relationships (between the different sides of ourself and of our partner) (see Chapter 9).

Let's examine one specific aspect of this romantic love hierarchy, before moving back to explore some other aspects of the 'multiple loves rather than multiple lovers' idea. This is the distinction that we tend to make between lovers and friends. This is related to monogamy because we often lack ways of understanding close, but non-sexual, friendships, and this, in turn, may pressure such friendships into becoming affairs.

Vivien Burr and Trevor Butt say that the love/friendship categorization is an example of our common way of seeing the world in either/or dichotomies (as we have seen previously in the book with men/women, good/bad, and normal/abnormal).[24] Like those other dichotomies, there is a hierarchy in place: romantic love is valued over friendship. We don't have legal or religious ceremonies to celebrate and confirm our commitment to our friends. There are precious few self-help books devoted to managing friendships.[25] We have no special day, like Valentine's Day, for celebrating friendship. We are bombarded with images of the perfect couple, but there are a limited number showing the perfect friendship, and most of these are aimed at children and teenagers (think of cola adverts for example), giving the message that friendship is something pre-love, perhaps just practice for the 'real thing', when we won't need to invest so much in friendships any more. TV programmes like *Friends*, which seem to celebrate the importance of friendship, still end by pairing the characters off with partners, and this is the tragedy we saw in Bromance movies in Chapter 5.[26] Generally, something in us is not satisfied by endings in which friendships are begun or cemented. No fairy tales finish with the hero finding a close friend or two to hang out with. There is a sadness in *Casablanca* when Ingrid Bergman gets on the plane and Humphrey

Bogart is left to begin his 'beautiful friendship'. Only children's films seem to be comfortable celebrating close friendships. The Disney Pixar movies developed further and further away from requiring a romantic love interest (it was there for Buzz and Woody in *Toy Story*, less so in *Monsters, Inc.*; *Finding Nemo* explicitly rejected any love relationship between the main characters, and *Up* focused on an unusual friendship between an old man and a boy).

Burr and Butt give the example of a man and a woman, both married, who meet at a writing class, hit it off well and become close. Immediately, rumours start to circulate about whether they are having an affair. Their spouses are uncomfortable and suspicious, and the man and woman themselves begin to feel awkward and unsure around each other because their emotional attachment is such that the word 'friend' feels an inadequate description, even though neither of them particularly wants to have a sexual relationship. Because the categories of friend and lover are considered to be mutually exclusive, anything that doesn't fall neatly into one or the other will be squeezed into the one that offers the best fit. The existence of these either/or categories exerts a pull on people's behaviours, so that these two people might 'find themselves' having an affair, feeling like they had little control over what happened, or their friendship might drift away from the intensity that it had since that is so threatening to the way we understand relationships. There is a similar theme in recent 'fuck buddy' movies such as *Friends with Benefits* and *No Strings Attached*. While the possibility of a sexual friendship is opened up, the characters inevitably end up in a conventional Hollywood-style romantic relationship.

The hierarchy between love and friendship is illustrated in the idea that, if we're not sexually interested in someone, we might decide to be 'just friends' with them, implying that this would be so much less than a romantic relationship. If we are interested, we become 'more than friends'. It is useful to think about what these hierarchies means for how we treat the people around us and what we expect from these people. One thought experiment is to wonder what it would would be like if we were to treat our lovers more like friends and/or our friends more like lovers.

What if we treated our lovers more like friends? We saw in Chapter 3 that the privileging of love puts pressure on love relationships. Think about starting a new relationship: this person hasn't spent as much time with you as some of your oldest friends and you haven't yet told them about all the major events of your life but, somehow, because you've had sex, you expect them to telepathically know how you're feeling and to respond perfectly to every situation in which you find your-selves. Also, we can handle our friend having opposing attitudes to us on some of the things we hold most dear, but a lover can disagree with us on something as simple as whether it's okay to miss the movie trailers and it is a major issue. It is easy to take lovers for granted. We may not be as grateful when a lover puts them-selves out for us as we would if a friend did the same. We might not be so appre-ciative when they give up their evening to comfort us when we're low. We might take our irritations and frustrations out on them by being snappy, unfriendly, or quiet without explanation in a way we'd never do with a friend. Perhaps we should take few moments, each time we're being irritable with a lover, to ask ourselves 'How would I treat a friend in this situation?' In Chapter 8 we will also consider whether shifts in relationships would not need to be quite so 'all or nothing' (stay together or break up) if we could imagine categories in between lover and friend.

What if we were to treat our friends more like our lovers? Might it be good to put a bit more romance into our friendships? With lovers, we often celebrate by making a big thing of anniversaries or Valentine's Day, or by spoiling them on their birthdays. We show our appreciation for them with little gifts and cards. We leave them a note when we depart in the morning after an enjoyable night together. We make time for them. Many of these things could be incorporated into friendships. We could send a friend a homemade CD when we hear they've been low. We could schedule in a regular lunch date. We could send a bunch of flowers to an old friend to let them know we're thinking about them even though we haven't seen each other in a while. We could arrange, each year, a day with a friend to specifically focus on our friendship, perhaps going away for a weekend together doing something we both enjoy, maybe acknowledging the day we met or cemented our friendship in some way. Perhaps friendships could also benefit from some of the 'state of the relationship' discussions we may have with lovers. It might be easier to let friendships drift or to avoid talking about a problem because we're not generally expected to reflect on, or work at, our friend relationships. In Chapter 9 we'll think about the kinds of commitment we might make to all types of people in our lives. Might we look after friends when they're sick, for example, have physical intimacy such as hugging or snuggling, or be there for them in a crisis.

Returning to Heckert and Wilkinson's idea of recognising multiple loves in our lives, this certainly includes challenging the distinction between love relationships and other kinds of relationship, such as friendship. It might also suggest that we unpack the notion of friendship a little further. What kinds of friends are there? What hierarchies do we put them in? Perhaps we privilege those with whom we have a biological and/or historical relationship (such as family) over those we have chosen to be with; or it could be that we are more likely to take for granted those we have a biological or historical relationship with. What of colleagues? Many of us have colleagues we spend more time with than some of our friends, family, or lovers, such as partners in business or in the police force, people who serve together in the military, or people who write together. This starts us questioning the basis on which we evaluate intimacy (something we will return to in Chapter 9): is it time together, proximity, emotional intimacy, physical intimacy, or something else?

Heckert and Wilkinson's ideas are about more, even, than our relationships with human beings. Many people have closer relationships with companion animals than they do with some of the human beings in their lives. We might also consider our relationship with the environment around us. How many of us have places we love? The first place we lived? Our favourite holiday destination? I think about my own relationships with cities. When I moved out of London, for example, I found that London and I were much better together when we were in a long-distance relationship than when we rubbed up against each other every day. Consider times of day: I used to have a relationship with the time between midnight and two in the morning: a loose, rumpled time of fuzzy edges, drunken camaraderie with strangers, and greasy gutters. We broke up and I hardly ever see that time any more, but I do have a new relationship with the time between six and seven a.m.: it is a sharp, silvery grey, raw and empty time, but I'm growing to love it.

Obviously, the question of how we relate to other people, creatures, and the world around us, have much broader implications than the quality of our own experience, in terms of sustainability and how we care for our environment. There is even a word 'ecosexuality' for relationships which are designed specifically with sustainability and eco-friendliness in mind.

As with our identities, genders, and sexualities, we can see that our relationships are therefore plural rather than singular. And, as with those other aspects of ourselves, they are also in process rather than static. As Heckert puts it, relationships are fluid rather than fixed: they are ever-changing and in a constant state of becoming. This understanding is important when we come to points at which we realize the relationship has changed, as we will see in Chapters 8 and 9.

Let's return, finally, to the place at which we began this chapter: the tension between freedom and togetherness. An implication of seeing relationships as multiple and in process is to recognize that we simply can't possess, control, or fix the people with whom we're in relationships (as some forms of relating attempt to do). Rather, we can enjoy the people that our partners are when they are with us, recognising that they are inevitably other people in their other relationships, of whatever kind, and that that is okay. We can also recognize that each relationship will inevitably shift and change over the time that we are in it, meaning that any rules or contracts we have are likely to require renegotiation in the future, and that the positioning of any boundaries is also likely to change. This changing nature of relationships will return, as a key theme, in the next three chapters, as we consider times of conflict and break-up, and what we can realistically commit to our relationships.

Chapter 7

Rewriting the rules of conflict

What are the rules?

The main unwritten rule of conflict is that it shouldn't happen at all. According to the rules of love that we explored in Chapter 3, The One should be everything to us and should telepathically know all our needs, so conflict should be unnecessary. Once we've found the right person and publicly declared that we are together, we are required to keep proving, to ourselves and to others, how good the relationship is. That means pretending there are no problems. It is shaming to be overheard rowing by our neighbours, to acknowledge to colleagues that we look tired because we had an argument with our partner last night, or to tell our family that we are going through a rough patch, because it brings the whole relationship into question.

This can also mean that we do not communicate much with partners about the difficult stuff of managing a relationship day after day, year after year. If conflict is something to be avoided, then we also want to avoid any potentially dangerous conversations which might precipitate an argument.

Towards the end of the last chapter, we saw that an alternative rule for relationships is 'communicate, communicate, communicate'. It may seem that we *do* communicate a lot about relationships already. We spend a lot of time gossiping about all the people we know and how they manage their relationships, deciding who makes a good or bad match, and analysing their arguments and break-ups. We pour over celebrity stories in magazines and newspapers which evaluate every aspect of each person's relationship, doling out blame and praise. However, all of this is communicating *about* relationships. It is much less easy to communicate *in* relationships. We want to bring up a small issue with our partner about who does what around the house and the words stick in our throat every time we try to initiate a conversation. We're left with angry feelings after an argument which appeared to be resolved, so we spend hours imagining what we might say and becoming enraged about it, rather than daring to confront the issue with the person concerned. We realize that we want to spend less time with someone than we have in the past, and we let it drift and risk them becoming hurt and confused, rather than simply saying something.

So, conflict is to be avoided and not spoken about. But obviously we *do* conflict in relationships, so what are the rules for conflict when it ends up happening despite our best efforts? In order to explore this, let's think about a concrete example of conflict. I'll give you my example in a moment but, first, you might find it useful to come up with your own example to consider through the rest of this chapter. If so, take a moment to write about a recent conflict you had with somebody close to you (it doesn't have to be a romantic relationship). Be completely selfish about it: write it entirely from your perspective, in the present tense, so you can get back into what it was like at the time. How does the conflict start? How do you respond? How does the other person react? How do you feel? What's it like in your body? What do you think of them? Where does it end up? Don't worry about the other person's perspective, just let it all out.

Such stories can help us to pinpoint key elements of the implicit rules of conflict. Here's an example of a conflict from my perspective, which you can consider, along with your own story, to examine what rules are in play here.

It's the weekend, so we decide to go for a walk in the country. I'm not sure about it because I have work I need to do left over from the week, but I feel listless so agree to the break in the hope that I'll return feeling more motivated. As we walk across the meadow in the sunshine, however, the tension in me clenches tighter rather then being released. You notice that I don't seem relaxed and comment on it. I feel immediately defensive. Are you saying I'm too uptight? I remember a niggle from a conversation we had last week. I'd tried to tell you about a new project I was considering and you didn't seem very enthusiastic. Maybe it's partly your fault that I'm stressed out. I bring it up and you bristle a little. *You* are fine. *You* are having a perfectly nice day. It is *me* who has the problem.

There it is again. You're not valuing me. I'm telling you I felt bad about something and you're not listening at all. I point this out, with a helpful reminder of a few other times when you've done this previously. You say that you don't see the point in talking about it when I'm being like this.

A hot tear trickles down my hot cheek and falls onto the hot, dry ground. I feel knotted up from stomach to throat and something is bubbling up inside and leaking out of my eyes. I do *not* want to cry. It seems to reinforce the distance between us: you, cool and calm and loose, me sweaty and twisted and tense. My shoulders hurt from hunching up as I walk, while your arms swing free. In my horror at your seeing, but being baffled by, my pain, I protect myself with more attacks. They boil up inside me and spit out at you like sparks. How *can* you not see how much pain I'm in? How *could* you respond in such a way when you knew it would hurt me? You bark back that it was me who started this, that I always take it out on you when I'm stressed, that I'm being irrational.

We're in the middle of a cornfield. Green hills roll above us beneath a clear blue sky. But the beauty of our surroundings only makes it worse. You go quiet and, in the silence, my head roars. I know you can't care about me at all, otherwise you'd reach out to me and say kindly things. You must be disgusted by my tears. I keep trying to brush them away, to clearly and calmly explain how rotten I feel, but you just look dismissive. I want to walk away but I need to *prove* to you that you're being unfair.

Time contracts to a pinpoint and there is just us, in pain, in this field. It feels like this is all there has ever been and all that ever can be.[1]

Because of the tendency to avoid conflict, when it does happen it can feel like a terrible thing, as if everything is at stake and the whole relationship is in question. You can see in my example how a niggling tension escalates all the way to a serious crisis in a relatively short period of time.

Another element of conflict is the desire to locate blame. When I feel bad, I'm desperate to find a reason for that feeling so that it can be sorted out and will hopefully disappear. My partner is closest to hand, so it is very easy for me to start wondering if they are the source of the bad feeling, as I do in this example. Inevitably, there will be some disagreement or issue between us that I can pick up on. Similarly, when they feel my anger turning towards them, my partner also seeks to find the cause of the pain they now feel, and my current behaviour is the obvious suspect. The conversation quickly becomes less and less about the issue that we started talking about and more and more about who is right and who is wrong. As we've seen throughout this book, we tend to see the world in dichotomous, either/or ways: good or bad, man or woman, emotional or rational. When we're in the heat of conflict, this seems to polarize even more, such that we *know* that one of us must be right and one of us must be wrong. The possibility that we are being the 'bad guy' in any way seems so preposterous, and so terrifying, that we'll do almost anything to prove that it is otherwise – and that means proving that our partner is really the one who is wrong and bad.

Another thing that happens is that we are often very reluctant to step away from the conflict, perhaps because it feels so important to prove that we had a legitimate point, and because we are dismayed at the fact that our partner is clearly unhappy with us. We tend to grasp hold of the conflict tightly and keep shaking it in the hope of reaching a resolution. If our partner is as embroiled in it as we are, then we will both keep hold of it like this.

Finally, an element of many conflicts in intimate relationships is the sense that we know exactly what the other person is thinking about us. Relationship psychologists call this 'metaperception': the perception we have of how someone perceives us. In times of conflict we tend to be utterly convinced that we know what the other person is thinking about us, and we often respond to *that*, rather than to the content of what they are saying.

This chapter focuses on conflicts in partner relationships, but much of what we cover here applies to conflict more broadly, between people in different kinds of relationships and even between groups of people. One of the reasons this area is so important is that, if we can learn how to be better with conflict in our closest relationships, perhaps we can get better at dealing with conflict on a much wider scale. The examples of conflict in this chapter are between two people, but many of the same things apply when more people are involved (as when there is conflict between more than two partners in the multiple relationships described in the last chapter, or in any family or setting where more than two people live or work together).[2]

It is also important to say that, in this chapter, we're not covering conflicts which are generally regarded as abusive, for example when one person physically attacks the other, or makes them do things by force. Some of the ideas we cover may well be helpful even in such extreme situations, but they require additional understanding, guidance and support which are beyond the scope of this book.[3]

A summary of the rules of conflict so far, is as follows:

- We should avoid conflict at all costs, and avoid bringing up any potentially difficult issues which might lead to conflict, because conflict would be a sign that something was wrong with the relationship.
- If conflict does arise, one person is right and the other person is wrong.
- We must keep at it until it is resolved.
- It is vital that we win the conflict and justify ourselves, otherwise it might turn out that we are the bad guy – and that would be intolerable.

Why question the rules?

The first reason to question these rules is that conflict *isn't* something that can be avoided in relationships. In fact, trying to avoid conflict prevents us from communicating about important things, which may well put them under greater pressure. Ironically, attempting to prove that our relationship is perfect is likely to lead to problems festering, rather like an unattended wound. If we act quickly to address such an injury it may be painful but, if we fail to act, there may be much more damage requiring that we have to sever the whole limb.

However compatible people are, there are bound to be things about which they disagree, whether that is something as seemingly trivial as how often they need to vacuum the house or as seemingly vital as deeply-held religious or political beliefs. Also, as we share more of our lives, our time, and our living space, we are increasingly likely to rub up against these differences.

Carol Tavris and Elliot Aronson argue that our most intimate relationships are the most dangerous places to be because they are where we are forced to confront ourselves and to learn how we are capable of behaving. This is not always a pretty sight.[4] Perhaps if we embarked on love with the awareness that it is likely to be one of the most challenging, frightening, and personally demanding things we ever do, rather than with the expectation of an easy happily-ever-after, we would be better prepared for the patience, courage, and skill that is actually required to be intimate with another person.

The philosopher Jean-Paul Sartre proposed that, quite opposite from conflict being avoidable, actually human beings are *unavoidably* in conflict with each other.[5] That is what he meant by his famous quote 'Hell is other people'.[6] We are inevitably in the world with other people (as we saw at the beginning of Chapter 6) and, for Sartre, that means that we are inevitably in conflict, because the presence of other people limits our freedom. Going back to the metaphor we used in Chapter 1, the gaze of other people can easily fix us – like a pot in the kiln – meaning that we are no longer free to shape ourselves in whatever way we like. We desperately try to free ourselves from the hold that other people have over us, just as others try to free themselves of the hold we have over them. The only options out of this situation, as Sartre saw it, are to either make the other person an object for us, or to give in and to let ourselves become an object for them. We can fix the other person, or we can fix ourselves.

Lest this all seems abstract and philosophical, consider how it plays out in our romantic relationships. You might imagine that the last thing people would want to do when they are in love is to fix someone: to turn them into an object. But, going back to Chapter 3, this is often exactly what we do. Think about what we are yearning for in love: we want someone to be The One who will be everything for us, who will save us from being alone and make everything better through their love. Right there we are making them an object for us, rather than accepting them as the full, complex, flawed human being that they inevitably are. And, if they fail to deliver, then we might well start niggling at the bits of them that we don't like so much, or which don't fit the image of the perfect partner we had at the start. It is so easily done. We start gradually pushing them to be just a little more caring, just a bit less untidy. Without us noticing it, this dynamic grows until we're shocked to realize that we've become a nag, always on our partner's case, trying to make them into the person we want them to be and to fix them that way.

So that is turning someone else into an object, but what of turning ourselves into an object (the other way in which Sartre said that people handle conflict)? Surely, nobody would want to do that to themselves? Actually, fixing or objectifying yourself is extremely common, and it comes back to the sense that we are lacking, which we explored in Chapter 1. A lot of the power of falling in love comes from the fact that we find ourselves fixed in the gaze of another person in a quite wonderful way. This person dancing opposite me in a nightclub, sitting across from me over a candlelit dinner, or lying next to me in a hotel bed, gazes at me in adoration. The vision of myself which I see reflected in their eyes is of the person that I would dearly love to be. It's like they see all of the good stuff and none of the bad. As long as they look at me in that way, perhaps I can pretend that there *isn't* any bad in me. Maybe they are right and I really *am* that loveable through and through. No wonder that, at such times, love feels like a drug which we can't get enough of.

This fixing can happen in all kinds of ways in relationships. We might find ourselves in love with someone whom we regard as older and wiser. When they look
at us, we see reflected this fabulously sexy young thing, and we love being that
person. We move into their house and happily take on the identity of being 'X's
partner'. We hang on their arm at parties and hang on their words in conversations.
We let them make all of the decisions and enjoy being the carefree one who gets
looked after. Alternatively, we might find ourselves in love with someone who is a
little damaged and vulnerable. When *they* look at us, we enjoy the vision they have
of the strong rescuer, the one who is going to nurture them and cherish them and
make them whole again. Enticed by this view of ourselves as the warrior knight in
shining armour, we fix ourselves as that for them, letting our own needs go unspoken as we focus on being the person we see reflected in their eyes.

We can, therefore, be drawn into fixing other people for our own benefit, as well
as into fixing ourselves for the benefit of somebody else. In most relationships an
element of both these things happens. The fact is – as Sartre pointed out – freedom
is pretty damned scary. Most of us do not like being faced with the realization that
our life is our own to create with our choices, and that the mistakes we make along
the way are also our responsibility. We don't want to bear the weight that there is
no given meaning or purpose to our existence, but that we have to make it up as we
go along. How much easier to search for somebody else to make our life meaningful for us by being The One. How much simpler to fix ourselves as something for
other people, and to pass the buck over to them to make all of our decisions.

However, neither of these strategies work well. Freedom has a tendency to bubble back up whether we want it to or not. When we try to fix someone for us they
soon get tired of our niggling and nagging and resist our attempts to change them
from a beast into our idealized handsome prince or perfect princess. Either we stay
in a relationship where we always poke and push, and they always resist this and
become hurt by it, or the relationship breaks down. When we try to fix ourselves
for somebody else it similarly doesn't tend to work. If we give up our own life to
become someone else's perfect partner, we often find that there is an underlying
sense of loss, or irritation, and we begin to resent the choices being made on our
behalf. If we give ourselves up to being someone else's rescuer, we often resent
it if they don't allow themselves to be saved. Equally, it can be difficult if they
suddenly do become much happier and don't need us any more. What we yearn
for in all of these situations is for the positive vision that the other person has of us
to remain, no matter what. This isn't sustainable, because all of us are imperfect
(as we saw in Chapter 1). Eventually, the other person will see our flaws and that
will feel dreadful. Or they will continue to gaze at us in adoration, and we'll lose
respect for them because we know we are not actually that great.

A further problem is that when we fix other people in relationships (e.g. as
our mentor or the victim whom we are going to look after) we also become fixed
(e.g. as just 'X's partner' or as the rescuer). Remember Neil Strauss, in Chapter
5, saying that by dehumanizing the opposite sex, he ended up dehumanizing himself? This is what he was talking about. As Terry Pratchett's great sage, Granny

Weatherwax puts it, 'Sin, young man, is when you treat people as things, including yourself, that's what sin is'.[7]

Sartre pointed out a further problem with us giving up freedom for another person. That is that the person with whom our partner initially fell in love *was* free. If we then give up that freedom in order to be something we think our partner wants us to be, then we won't be the person that they fell for any more. They won't feel the same way about us. We may well pick up on this and try even harder to become what we think they want us to be, which, of course, they will like even less. This is a tragic pattern, whichever side you are on. However desperately the one person tries to make themselves into what the other person wants, they take themselves further away from actually being it.

This is human conflict. We want to give up our freedom to other people so that we might be seen (and therefore see ourselves) as completely good and not lacking. But when we give up our freedom we find ourselves wanting it back, especially if we fear that the other person *is* beginning to see us as bad and lacking and fear that they will now fix us in *that* way. In Sartre's play *No Exit*, one character, Garcin, implores another, Estelle, to be the one person in the world who does not see him as a coward, for that will mean that he truly isn't one. Perhaps we all nurture a hope that The One person will come along and prove to us that we are not what we most dread being. But intimacy makes it impossible to hide what we least want our partners to see.

Returning to specific moments of conflict in relationships, it is helpful to recognize these desires to fix and be fixed, which are often in play. In my example I hated the idea of being fixed by my partner as irrational or uptight, and a lot of my energy went into resisting that: trying to prove that being stressed was understandable and that I had plenty of justification for my behaviour. As the conflict went on, both of us strongly resisted being fixed as the bad guy. We both desperately wanted the other person to go back to seeing us as the lovely and loveable partner we were used to them seeing, not as this monster. We struggled to free ourselves from the negative gaze of the other person, while also struggling to get back that more positive gaze so that we could see ourselves reflected well in their eyes again and convince ourselves that we were not really so flawed.

Tavris and Aronson argue that relationship problems generally come down to self-justification. People get stuck in patterns of justifying themselves to their partners whenever a conflict occurs. In justifying themselves, they attempt to shunt all the blame onto the other person, criticizing and condemning them rather than understanding and/or forgiving their behaviour. Why do we have such a strong need to self-justify? Because of that underlying fear that we are really lacking, that our partner may see that, and that, if they see it, we will become fixed in that way forever.

When we enter a conflict with that fear that our partner will pick up on something negative about us, we are far more likely to assume that that *is* what they are saying. If I am worried that I might be an irrational person, and if I think that would be a terrible thing to be, then my partner doesn't need to say much for me to jump to the conclusion that this is what they think of me (even if it is the last thing in the world that they actually think). As we saw in Chapter 1, we have a lot of these fears that we might be flawed or terrible people, often left over from bullying at school, from the way our family members saw us when we were growing up, and/or from previous relationships.

Stephen Batchelor writes about the commonality of misperception. He says:

> 'I misconstrue things: like entering the pottery shed in the yard to discover a snake in one corner. My heart accelerates and I am frozen with fear. Only when my eyes get used to the light do I realize it is a coil of hose'.[8]

In conflicts, we are like the snake phobic entering the pottery shed. As we saw in the Introduction, people are always searching for patterns or meanings in things. In our visual perception we make sense of the shapes and colours that fall on our retinas on the basis of previous experience: that collection of lines is a chair; that blob of white on blue is a cloud. In our social perception we also make sense of other people's behaviour using the theories we have developed over the years, based on our past experiences. In both cases we are quick to fix our perception. For the snake phobic that long coil must be a dangerous viper, there is no other explanation. For the person who has been hurt in relationships before, their lover's silence must be coldness that means that they don't care about them any more.

In conflicts, we always bring our past experiences to the present situation. These are what make up metaperceptions: our assumptions about what other people think of us. The idea that we telepathically know what our partner is thinking is a particularly dangerous one. It is much more likely that our partners are a screen onto which we project all our fears and insecurities about what we are convinced – and ashamed – is the truth about ourselves. In the face of such threat, we desperately cast around for a solution. Run away? Fight this person we love who has suddenly become a monster? Destroy this horrible twisted pain at all costs. There's a snake in the pottery shed!

Another major aspect of conflict is escalation. As we've seen, arguments don't tend to stop with one self-justification, or casting of blame. Psychologists of all kinds of conflicts (from pub brawls to warfare) have noticed a similar pattern, which goes something like figure 7.1.[9]

This cycle goes round and round in an upward spiral. One person says something. The other person hears and interprets it in the light of their experiences and values. They respond to what they heard rather than to what other person actually said. It then seems to the first person that the other person reacted out of proportion so *they* become defensive, and so on. Consider this process in your own conflicts.

Certainly, we see this pattern in my conflict: my partner goes quiet and I interpret this (the roar in my head) as condemnation of me, when there may be many reasons why they have stopped talking (a deliberate attempt to give me some time, or their own sense of powerlessness in the situation, for example). Each thing that I say in the conflict seems to yield an overly defensive response from my partner, just as

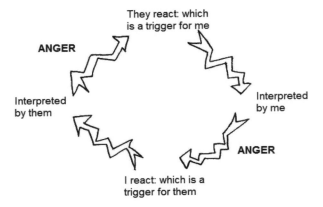

Figure 7.1 Escalation of conflict

the things I say seem out of proportion to them. Often, they *are* out of proportion as responses to the specifics of this situation, but each person is bringing to the conversation all the previous times in their lives when something similar happened, so it feels a lot bigger, and more loaded, to them. The weight of the current situation brings down the weight of every time something similar happened in the past. No wonder we feel so crushed by it, as if everything about ourselves and the relationship is at stake.[10]

We saw at the start that one common rule of conflict is that there is always someone right and someone wrong. It is tempting to search for the 'good guy' and the 'bad guy', hoping that figuring out whose fault it is will end the fight. But relationships are co-constructed: we build them together between us, and that includes the conflicts and arguments as well as the more peaceful times. As Kenneth Gergen says, nothing we do can mean anything unless there is another person there to make sense of it.[11] My extended hand doesn't mean anything without you to pull me into a hug or to glare at it. It is hard to get into an upward spiral of aggression if only one person is reacting and interpreting things through their own blinkers. A good argument takes at least two people to misperceive things, to feel put down, and to lash out because of it.

What we need to do in such situations is to break the upward spiral and to get it spiralling back down again: to de-escalate the situation. Often it only takes one of us to back down, and to start taking responsibility, for the other person to follow suit. But, as I'm sure you know, this is extraordinarily difficult to do in the heat of conflict. For all the reasons we've explored, we want to stick with the argument until it is resolved and we are vindicated.

Alternative rules

Now that we understand better what is going on in a conflict, we can start to imagine a different approach to our standard tactic of avoiding it at all costs or going in barrels blazing if it does happen, desperately trying to defend ourselves and to prove the other person wrong.

We have seen that we are always implicated in conflicts. Our own fear of what the other person might see is the root of all those over-reactions and self-justifications. Therefore, as we suggested in Chapter 1, the first step is not about how we relate to the other person at all, but how we relate to ourselves.

On a basic level, you probably know that conflicts go far worse if you are in a bad way already. When we are tired and overstretched we are much more likely to respond poorly to situations, to jump to conclusions, and to fail to see the full picture as I did in my example. Also, we are more likely to take short cuts to try to escape the situation, rather than really hearing what the other person is saying. This is what my partner does when they tell me to chill out rather than listening to what I'm bothered about. If we are serious about being kinder to our partners in conflict, and in general, we can start by ensuring that we look after ourselves.

Looking after ourselves can be divided into two types: kind self-care and reflective self-care. Kind self-care maps on to the gentle way of being which we explored in Chapter 1, while reflective self-care maps onto the firm. I'll give more examples of this in Chapter 10 but, for now, kind self-care includes things like taking a hot bath or giving ourselves half an hour in a café, while reflective self-care might be writing in a journal or meditating. Both help with conflict. When we treat ourselves as people to whom it is worth being kind, it is easier to be kind to others when things are difficult, and to remember that we deserve kind treatment ourselves. When we build space for reflection into our lives, we cultivate self-awareness, so we are more able to see what *we* bring to conflict situations, and to respond less defensively. For example, in my conflict, some time out the week before might have helped me to realize that something was niggling me about how my partner responded to my new project. I could have reflected on whether they were just distracted, or had really responded dismissively. In the latter case I could have picked a good moment to bring it up (not when I was totally stressed out) and done it in a less confrontational way.

Reflective self-care helps to improve our awareness of the past experiences which we bring to the current situation, and the expectations and assumptions these have left us with. Over our lives we gather a certain amount of baggage: backpacks, hold-alls and suitcases full of all the bad memories, tough lessons learnt, and negative patterns we've seen in the things that have happened to us. Each piece of baggage is kept closed by a fastener, but these are easily opened by pressing a button and springing the catch. It is easy for people to inadvertently press those buttons when they interact with us, particularly if they're not aware of what our baggage is, or where we are carrying it. Also, if we find ourselves in a situation similar to one we've been in in the past, that can push a button. When this happens the bag pops open and there is our messy stuff, all over the floor.

One useful form of self-reflection is to start to list our baggage. We'll need to revisit this list because we will pick up baggage, and put it down, as we journey through life. Perhaps you have a heavy schoolbag hanging from your shoulder, digging in painfully, full of all the tough stuff that happened growing up. Maybe there's a big rucksack on your back from your first long-term relationship, containing all the difficult things you learnt about yourself during the painful break-up. Are you trundling a huge wheelie suitcase behind you which keeps tripping you up, full of the patterns you see through your past relationships, fearing that you'll always end up hurting people, or being hurt yourself?

A helpful key to our baggage is our emotional reactions. We might notice a flood of anger or fear, a chain of blaming thoughts, the fantasy of punching someone, or the fact that we raise our voice or run away from the situation. We usually try to forget such painful responses, dismissing them as over-reacting or beating ourselves up for feeling them. Instead, we might turn and address them directly, assuming that they are sensible responses to *something*. Thinking back to Chapter 2, we might tune into our bodily sensations to access our baggage (like the hunched shoulders and knotted stomach of my conflict). Bodies often remember things in a powerful way: we notice we feel empty abandonment when someone is walking on ahead of us, or that we flinch away when someone reaches out to us in an argument. What's that about?

If we are more aware of our baggage, we may be able to tell our partners about it when things are calm, so they are more able to recognize it too, in times of conflict. Of course, often the way we find out about baggage is when something does hit our button and we find ourselves exploding or crumpling before we can do anything about it. So we need also to give ourselves a break, rather than harshly expecting ourselves to be perfect at conflict and berating ourselves when we are not. Remember the gentle and firm mode of self-relating that we covered in Chapter 1.

When I think about how baggage gets in the way in the conflicts, I'm always reminded of a particular A. A. Milne story.[12] Winnie-the-Pooh and Piglet have set a trap for a heffalump. Pooh unwittingly falls into it during the night and gets a honey jar stuck on his head. When Piglet comes along to the trap in the morning and sees Pooh bumping about and crying mournfully for help, he is sure that he's seen a heffalump and runs off shrieking. In conflicts with our partners we often see in them a monstrous heffalump because that is what we're expecting, and fearing, that we will see. Really, it is just our poor partner who has got stuck in a trap and needs our help to get out.

We can, therefore, see that making sure that we look after ourselves, and building some time into our lives for our own self-reflection, is valuable in enabling conflicts that do arise to be dealt with with more kindness and awareness.

Self-care also comes in during the conflict itself. Something which is recommended in virtually every book on relationship therapy or conflict resolution is 'time out'. This is perhaps the hardest thing to put into practice when a conflict occurs. The last thing we want to do is to walk away from each other and to sit by ourselves. We want to Sort It Out. If we do find ourselves alone – maybe because our partner had to go to work – we are likely to sit there boiling, going over and over the argument in our head, trying to figure out exactly what to say when we return. We are unlikely to take the time for kindness and reflection.

When things are already heated, continued discussion will often escalate the situation, whereas time out can enable us to cool down and return in a less volatile state. It is worth remembering this when we first feel the rising sense of indignation and self-righteousness. This usually means we're in danger of saying something we'll regret, and it would be worth getting half an hour or so by ourselves. Particularly, it is worth avoiding the temptation to fire off a quick angry email, text message, or comment on the person's social networking page, but rather to write down what we want to say, coming back to it when we've cooled down.

It can be helpful to talk about time out with partners when things are calm: what are the telltale signs we might observe which mean that one or both of us needs a break from a discussion? How can we say, in those moments, that we need some time out? We won't always manage it because conflict is so sticky, but it can help to think about it in advance. It is also worth considering *where* we will go to get that time out. If everyone has their own room in a house, that is great but, if not, there needs to be an arrangement. One person living in a small flat curtained off a bit of the living room that was her space where she wouldn't be interrupted. Other people use a long shower, or the garden. Once there, we can remind ourselves to try not to stew on the conflict or hone our argument, but rather to consider what we bring to the conflict and also to build some compassion for our partner.

Once we've considered why *we* might be responding so heatedly to the argument, we can reflect on how it might be from our partner's point of view, bringing in what we know about them, as well as the imagination to see that things may look different from another point of view. In conflict we tend to get stuck in one story: our own story of what has happened. The challenge is to put down our story, and to open up to other possible stories that might be there, before coming back to hold all the possible stories simultaneously (ours and the other person's). I'll say more about the power of stories in the next chapter. For now, it is about remembering that you are likely to clutch *your* story of the conflict tightly. Through gentle self-understanding maybe you can loosen that grip. And, once you have done that, perhaps you can firmly tell yourself to let that story go for a moment. It is not helping anybody, however true and incontrovertible it might seem. Then you can open up to the possibility of other ways of seeing the situation.

At this point, it might be useful to return to the conflict you considered earlier in the chapter. Try writing about this conflict again but, this time, pretend that you are the other person involved. Write it in the first person (I, me, etc.) from *their* perspective, again in the present tense. Imagine how they might feel, what they might think of you, and why they *know* they are so completely right.

I have done this for my own conflict so that you can see what this might look like. It wasn't too hard because I have been on both sides of this kind of conflict (with different people, and with the same person). That may well be the case for you as well. Sometimes you are the one who is stressed out and cruising for an argument; sometimes you are the one surprised by the other person's sudden prickliness. Sometimes you are the person who gets really upset; sometimes you are the one trying to force the other person to see it rationally. This is what I call relationship karma: what goes around, comes around. We can tune in to that and remember what it is like to be on the other side of the dynamic. Pema Chödrön has written about how we can use our own difficult feelings as routes to compassion for other people.[13] Sometimes relationships get more stuck in one direction (as we saw when we considered gender dynamics in Chapter 5), especially when we are fixing ourselves and other people. We'll return to how we might deal with such stuck dynamics in the last section of this chapter.

Here is my conflict, told from the other side:

It's the weekend and I'm looking forward to some down time together after not seeing each other much during the week. We decide to go for a walk: not my cup of tea, really, but you love getting out in the countryside, and you seem a bit wound up so I go along with it.

As we walk through the field, I can tell you're still tense. I begin to tense up too, some constriction in my throat, and it pisses me off. Why should I feel bad just because you are? I swing my arms in an attempt to relax. I even say something about how walking can be good for stress, to encourage you to enjoy the break.

Suddenly we're talking about a conversation from last week that I barely remember. Apparently I wasn't enthusiastic enough about one of your plans. I'm under attack, and just when I was doing my best to help. It feels grossly unfair. I have a sick sinking feeling in my stomach because this is a familiar conversation. I'm going to be accused of hurting you any minute. I try to stop it in its tracks by pointing out that it is a lovely day and we should just chill out and enjoy it. That is totally the wrong thing to say. I know before the words are out of my mouth.

We're walking through a stubbly cornfield, the ground is dry and cracked and scratchy with straw. I feel scratchy and raw too. You carry on and on at me. It's like nothing I say could possibly be right. I'm squeezed into a corner and I want to escape. I didn't even want to be here. I want to be at home where it's cool and quiet.

We lapse into silence and I feel like you're punishing me by closing down the conversation. You obviously don't think I'm good for you, and probably I'm not. I hate being this person – I *hate* it – the person who has just hurt the person they love. It is way too much responsibility, this ability to reduce another person to tears. It's crushing me like a great weight. I can't bear it. If I can just talk us back through from the start of this ridiculous argument then you'll be able to see that this is about your stuff, not mine, and we can get past it. But the more I explain, the more the tears stream down your face.

Eventually, I shut down because it feels two damned hard. Your whole body is turned away from me now. You obviously can't stand to be close to me. Two people who're supposed to love each other stuck in this stinking field, staring at each other like strangers.

Beyond rules? Embracing uncertainty

Once we have taken time out from a conflict, it is useful to consider how we might return to the other person in a way that doesn't attempt to fix them, or ourselves, given that we know how tempting it is to do this. Simone de Beauvoir suggested that this was possible when we commit to affirming the freedom of ourselves and the other person.[14]

This presents a radical alternative to the situation we considered at the start of this book. We saw how we desperately want to belong in a relationship *and* to reach our own individual goals. This seemed like an irreconcilable tension. But perhaps de Beauvoir's re-imagining of relationships allows for both togetherness *and* freedom. It acknowledges that we need relationships of different kinds in order to meet our own goals, and that we must embrace the freedom of others in order to have positive relationships with them. In such mutual relationships, instead of treating other people as objects for ourselves, viewing them in terms of what they might offer to us and manipulating them to reach our own goals, we treat them as full and complex people who may see things differently to us and who have their own dreams. We are open to who they are, rather than wanting them to see things the way we see them; and we are with them right now rather than expecting them to be as they, or other people, were in the past.[15]

This kind of relationship isn't easy. We will always fall back into something more like the fixing-and-being-fixed model which we explored earlier (so we shouldn't beat ourselves up about that). But it offers us something to aspire to: a different way of being in relationships and conflicts. When we treat the other person in a mutual way, and respect their freedom, they are more likely to do the same for us in return.

We can see what such a way of relating looks like in practice if we return to the ideas from Chapter 1. It is about being gentle and firm with others in the same way that we are gentle and firm with ourselves. So the foundation is in gentleness: patiently listening to the other person; desiring to help rather than hurt them; recognizing how hard it is when we feel desperate and under threat; and being ready to forgive others for the kinds of behaviours that we know that we, ourselves, are capable of in such circumstances. Along with gentleness, there is also the firmness whereby we expect to be treated in the same ways ourselves; and that we won't accept unfair criticisms, take all the responsibility for a conflict, or remain in a situation where we are regularly hurt.

As we saw in Chapter 1, part of gentle and firm relating involves seeing both ourselves, and our partners, as plural and in process (rather than as singular and static). When we take time out for self-care, we are reminded of our own plurality and process. We don't have to be so scared of being fixed by the other person, because we know that there are many sides to us and that we change. So what if they see some uncomfortable sides of us? We know that this is not all that we are. Maybe we have been a bit of a bad guy in this confrontation, but we can acknowledge that and apologize, because we know that we are not always that way.

Importantly, this same multiplicity and change over time is true of the other person. That means recognizing that there are many sides to this person that we love, so we should not treat them as if they are always the way that they are being at this moment. Also, we can remember that they change, so when we go back to them they will not necessarily be the same as they were when we were arguing.

In the rest of the chapter, I'll draw on these ideas to propose some practical suggestions for coming together and communicating about a conflict after we have taken time out.

Humanizing each other

We might start by taking time to humanize our partners before talking about the difficult issue: deliberately engaging with parts of them other than the part with which we were in conflict. Many psychological studies have found that it is much more difficult to be cruel to someone when we're seeing them as a fellow human who can feel pain and pleasure like us, rather than when we're dehumanizing them (like a torturer putting a bag over his victim's head, or a nation calling another nation animal names in a time of war).[16] Gergen reports a helpful strategy with public conflicts, such as those around abortion in the US: in small groups, people first mingle, sharing aspects of their lives *other than* their views about the issue. Later, when they talk about the issue, they all get a few minutes to talk uninterrupted about how they got involved, what the heart of the matter is for them, and any uncertainties they have. By getting people to talk to each other initially and then to open up about their personal histories and *why* the issue is so important, they can see each other as full human beings rather than just as the enemy.

You might think that it should be easy to humanize our partners. After all, we love them and know them intimately. But, as we have seen, we are capable of switching to seeing our partner as our enemy and even as a complete monster. So we might decide to make time to connect with each other prior to a potentially tough conversation. If we've just had a nice meal together where we've made an effort to hear all about each other's day, it might be harder to be cruel. After that, we might make time to really listen to them, having already imagined how it might be from their perspective. We could aim to hear why it is so important to them, and what meanings the issue has for them which we have not thought of. For sticky conflicts, it is worth scheduling a specific amount of time for one person to be listened to, and then for the other.

Listening

In arguments, we often say 'How *could* you?' We are usually disinterested in hearing an answer to this question. But imagine it removed of all the heat and aggression. This is the person we love and care about and generally think is a wonderful human being. *How* could they say what they said, or do what they did? If we can ask ourselves that question in a genuinely curious way we will see that there are probably many reasonable and understandable answers to it. They haven't become a monster overnight; therefore, it is most likely that they were in a difficult situation. Let's find out how that was for them. Many conflicts escalate because people just really want to be *heard* and aren't being.[17]

The point of listening is to truly try to understand and show that you get what they are saying. You don't need to see things in the same way, or come round to agreeing with them. Rather, you are open to the fact that they might see things differently to the way you do, and able to be moved by their suffering. Being heard is likely to put the other person in a frame of mind to hear you too. It is important to avoid interrupting or leaping in with your interpretations, and to demonstrate that they have your full attention. Try to build up the most complete picture that you can about what it was like for them. Remember that things mean different things to different people. For some, a raised voice is part of the cut and thrust of enjoyable debate; for others, it feels threatening. Bursting into tears can be seen as a legitimate expression of pain or a manipulative attempt to shut down conversation. Make sure that any questions you ask really *are* questions, rather than accusations or challenges. Finally, summarize what you've heard, using their words, and checking whether it is accurate or whether they want to add any more. Make it clear that however they feel is an acceptable and understandable response, rather than giving them the impression that you're doing this special listening thing because you think they're being emotional, crazy, or irrational.

Talking

When it is your turn to speak, take responsibility for your own feelings and way of seeing things. It is tempting to put our emotions onto other people and to blame them for 'making us feel' angry, hurt, or upset. Marshall Rosenberg argues that we put people into emotional slavery when we assume that they are responsible for our feelings.[18] So, instead of saying 'you made me feel rotten when you told me off like a child', we might say 'I felt bad when you said that I didn't pull my weight around the house' (making sure the words accurately reflect our feelings). It is easier for our partner to empathize with this and not to feel blamed, so the conversation may avoid degenerating into blame and self-justification.

Rosenberg also argues that we disempower other people when we assume that we are responsible for their emotions. It is easy to become invested in how those close to us are feeling. We might find it unbearable that they are upset and want to do anything to cheer them up, or feel that we couldn't handle them being angry about something we'd done. It is useful – if very difficult – to remind ourselves that how other people feel is *not* our fault. Neither is it our duty to make them feel differently; in fact, that is quite disrespectful to the pain they are feeling. It is much easier to value and understand our partner's emotions if we're not taking responsibility for them. My partner in my conflict was tense partly because they had taken on the job of making me relax.

It is also worth avoiding extremes. It is easy to accuse somebody of *never* doing any chores, or *always* nagging, because that is what they are doing in this moment, or to say that nobody you've ever known has been as touchy, bossy, or lazy as them, leaving them feeling abnormal and defensive. It is also worth avoiding deliberately pushing the other person's buttons. It can be enticing to poke at something that we know is a sore spot for the other person, especially when we are upset and they seem coldly calm and rational. It can bring them down to our level. But pointing out the other person's flaws will only increase their defensiveness.

It is important to take responsibility for the parts of a conflict that you *do* feel responsible for, but not so much that you take all the blame. There is likely to be responsibility on both sides. Taking too much responsibility is like the visitor who breaks an ornament which has great sentimental value to us. They become so upset about having done this that we end up comforting *them*, rather than being comforted for having lost our treasured object. Instead of allowing guilt to overwhelm us when we feel that we've done wrong, we can accept that it is okay to make a mistake, that it is not the end of the world or a sign that we are a terrible person. Then we can accept responsibility and sincerely apologize. For example, if you've realized that a situation reminded you of something in the past, you could say, 'I'm sorry I got angry when you commented on my essay. I realize now that it reminded me of how my dad criticized my schoolwork. I felt vulnerable showing you something that was important to me and I should have told you that'. Clarifying the things for which you do feel responsible can start that downward spiral of de-escalation. Similarly, being open about our own areas of uncertainty can break through the 'right and wrong' dichotomy.

Once you have both had your say, you may well find that there is nothing left to do, as all you both needed was to be understood. However, obviously there are some circumstances in which decisions do need to be reached and people have differing goals. What if one person wants to move out of the city and the other wants to stay living there? What if you have different ideas regarding having children? Dossie Easton and Janet Hardy suggest writing a list – together – of all the possible solutions, even those that might seem ridiculous, then each person, in turn, crosses out suggestions that they couldn't live with. Then you decide together to try one solution for a given length of time, after which you will re-evaluate and either stick with it a while longer or try something else.[19]

Another sticky situation is when we have become fixed in one dynamic such that we conflict regularly, always playing out the same roles. For example, one person always bursts into tears and the other tries to prove that it wasn't their fault;

one person always tries to get away with things, and the other points this out, feeling like their parent; or one person will do anything for a quiet life and the other wants some drama. What can we do with such stuck dynamics? First, we can bring them into awareness. Seeing the dynamic for what it is can loosen things up. We can also deliberately try to access other sides of ourselves: the normally parental person being playful and childlike, the emotional one being rational and calm, or the normally peace-loving one being dramatic. You can increase times in your relationship when you get to be these different sides of yourselves, for example through certain leisure pursuits, working on a project together round the house, or being with a group of friends who bring that out in you. If none of this works, some relationship therapists[20] suggest prescribing the problem: take a week trying to act exactly like the dynamic in which you have got stuck. This helps to reveal it more clearly, and it may become so ridiculous and tiresome that you start to find a way out of it.

In all relationships there will be some conflicts in which you realize that you are actually on the same page and it was a misunderstanding; some where you feel differently but can find a compromise; and some where you may always feel differently because it is based in different values, perhaps related to the continua we explored in the last chapter. Those latter tensions will crop up occasionally throughout the relationship, but you can at least be aware of them and spot them more easily when they come up.

To summarize, here are some guidelines for communication which are alternatives to the rules with which we started the chapter:

Taking time out

- Think about what you bring to the situation: the baggage that might have been triggered for you.
- Imagine other possible ways in which your partner might be seeing the situation.
- Remember that you and your partner are complex and change over time: you are not fixed as you were in the conflict.

Coming together

- Reconnect and humanize each other.
- Listen and show that you have heard your partner's story.
- Tell your own story, owning your feelings, taking responsibility for your part in it, and expressing uncertainty.

In the next two chapters, we will keep hold of these ideas for mutual relationships, and gentle and firm treatment of ourselves and others, while we explore two of the most challenging times in a relationship: when we break up, and when we stay together.

Chapter 8

Rewriting the rules of break-up

What are the rules?

Much of what we explored about conflict in the previous chapter applies also to relationship break-up, but at these times such dynamics are often even stickier and difficult to extricate ourselves from. Break-ups, like conflicts, are generally seen as something to be avoided at all costs, perhaps because they are perceived as a sign, not only that the relationship has failed, but that we ourselves are a failure: at relationships, and perhaps even as a person. The tendency to polarize people into right and wrong, good and bad, is almost overwhelming during break-ups as we, and everyone around us, are drawn into the casting of blame. Given the potential of being revealed as a failure, and this magnetic polarization into good guys and bad guys, there is also a strong urge to self-justify: to explain our actions as reasonable in the face of the wholly unreasonable behaviour of the other person. Thus, it is also common for conflicts to escalate during break-ups to intensities of anger and despair from which it is extraordinarily hard to come back with any kind of mutual respect intact.

We see this play out in the break-ups which occur in romantic comedies, bromances and sitcoms. The rules of break-up here are as follows. The break-up should take the form of an explosive argument during which you admit to all of the things you secretly despise about that other person, perhaps ending with the claim that you never loved them anyway. The dumper should be wracked with guilt and the dumpee devastated and the object of much sympathy (unless it was their adulterous behaviour that instigated the break-up in which case this is reversed, see Chapter 6). Afterwards, neither partner should speak to each other for months, years, or – ideally – ever: they should delete each other from their lives entirely. If they do have the misfortune to bump into their ex (which seems a particularly common occurrence in New York city, despite its vast population), they should look stunningly attractive and be in a new, perfect, relationship in order to win. Ideally their ex will be having a bad hair day and will be alone. At this point they should pretend that they want to stay in touch but never actually do so (as we saw in Chapter 6, friendships with exes are treated with suspicion).

Think also about the language surrounding break-ups: the relationship is *broken*. We have *split* and *separated* from someone. It is *ended* and they are now our *ex*. Everything suggests finality: something that is over and relegated to the past.

Many of these rules relate back to those we covered in Chapter 3 about love more generally. If we believe that there is The One waiting out there to complete us, then break-ups are dangerous times which call this belief into question. We thought that *this* person was The One, and now the relationship with them is ending. There are only two possible stories to explain this:

- Story one: they *were* actually The One for us and now we are losing them.
- Story two: they were not The One after all.

If the first story is the case then we are in a desperate situation having lost the very thing that makes life worth living. We are destined to a life alone, knowing that our happily-ever-after has been and gone. Any relationship we form now could only be a pale shadow of the perfection that we had. And because this person that we were with was The One for us, it must be our fault that the relationship has ended. This proves that we really are a hopelessly flawed human being. The person we loved so much no longer wants to be with us, perhaps even despises us; therefore, our guilt is overwhelming. We have messed up so badly it's hard to know how to carry on.

Given the depressing nature of story one, we can see why most people post break-up opt for story two instead: the person they've broken up with was *not* The One after all. However, because we thought they *were* The One all the way through the relationship, taking this option involves working hard to revise the story of the relationship. We need to explain how there were always telltale signs that it wasn't right, how this person must have been some kind of imposter.

Such stories are powerful during break-ups. We tell the new story of the relationship to convince ourselves, and others around us, that this was not really The One, and that the break-up was not our fault. For example, the song *14 Years*, by Guns 'n' Roses, looks back on a broken relationship, saying that the 14 years the couple spent together were years of silence and pain which are now gone for good. It seems unlikely the the entire relationship was this bad, otherwise why would the singer have stayed in it? Elsewhere, he acknowledges that it was only in the last four years that he realized how bad things were, but clearly he is now looking back over the entire relationship and rewriting it as purely painful and wasted time.

Think about the stories you've told around your own break-ups if you've had relationships which have ended. What was your tale of what happened during the split? Did it include attributions of blame and, if so, at whom were they directed? Did your story of the time you spent together change after the end of the relationship, compared to what it was before?

There are two different kinds of stories in romantic relationships: the stories we tell together and the stories we tell separately. For example, we often tell the story of the beginning of a relationship together. We keep reminding each other of how we met, when we fell for each other, the first time we kissed and so on. We build a coherent story of our beginning and we tell this together to friends and family, to each other on anniversaries, when we make up after an argument, or when we feel particularly loving towards each other. When we break-up, on the other hand, we tend to tell our stories separately. Each person goes away and tries to make sense of what happened. They tell their friends about it, and often come up with very different ways of explaining what went wrong. This is why break-up stories are generally much less similar to stories of how people got together.

These stories are not constructed in a vacuum. The culture around us is full of bigger stories of getting together and breaking up which we draw upon when we go through these times ourselves. We don't necessarily tell our own stories deliberately in certain ways: it is more like there's a script that's already out there. It is much easier for us to read the lines that are written for us in the script than it is to toss it away and improvise. Do you find yourself singing lines from songs to yourself when you start a new relationship? Are you remembering that scene from *Pretty Woman* the first time you have a bath at his place? Or that scene from *(500) Days of Summer* when you walk along the street and it seems like everyone might burst into song? Similarly, the pain of the break-up comes with familiar lines 'It's too late baby', 'Everything we say and do hurts us all the more', and we draw on other lyrics to get though it: 'I will survive', 'Gonna get along without you now'. We match our pain to that moment when Aidan screamed at Carrie 'You *broke* my heart!', when Peter curled up on his hotel floor in *Forgetting Sarah Marshall*, or when Harry recounted how the moving men knew about his separation before he did in *When Harry Met Sally*: 'Mr Zero knew'.

We talk, talk, talk, to all our friends, who have their own stories, similarly shaped by the world around them, and this helps us to shape our story too. Perhaps this person we're breaking up with is to us what their ex was to them: the person we needed to be with in order to learn this particular lesson before we could move on and find somebody perfect. Perhaps, like them, we can retell the story of our relationship to reveal our ex-partner as somebody who was hopelessly damaged, or quite abusive. Our friends may well be invested in helping us tell our story in this way because it validates their experience.

During a break-up, our story becomes the focus of our attention. We rehearse it in our minds last thing at night, first thing in the morning, going over every detail of our time together and the key moments of our split, shoring up our version of events until it is rock solid and incontrovertible. It becomes vital to be the one who has the last word. Seeing it the other person's way just isn't a possibility any more.

Stories are not just told in words between friends or repeated in our minds; they find their ways out into the world as well. Think about those urban legends of people throwing their ex's clothes out of the window, or sending emails to their whole inbox telling everyone all the terrible things they did. Those stories bubble up in our own imaginings of revenge and retribution. Perhaps we even follow them through, in letting a piece of information slip that we know our ex wouldn't want to be known, or allowing a mutual friend to take our side. How many images have we seen of the wronged party throwing their drink at their soon-to-be ex, slapping them across the face, or turning from them and walking away? There can be a sense of rightness as that scene we have seen played out so many times on the screen finds a way to play out through our own bodies and mouths.

In extreme cases, we know of physical attacks, and even murders, that occur during break-ups. We may think we would never carry things that far. But it is worth reflecting on times – during a relationship crisis – when we have imagined such things. Perhaps we have wished that the other person would do something obviously outrageous (like being caught cheating), so that we could justifiably become enraged and cut them out of our lives. Maybe we have fleetingly fantasized that our partner was in a fatal accident so that we would be free to continue with our life with all the sympathy that goes with such a loss, and none of the guilt of being the one to end the relationship. Post break-up, we may have felt it unbearable that our ex still exists in the world, somewhere out there saying the same loving things to someone else that they said to us. We may have wished them off the face of the planet, or hoped that some terrible tragedy would befall them, perhaps to make them feel the way we feel right now. We rarely admit such thoughts to anyone but they are there, as a capacity – even if never acted upon – in all of us.

When clients in counselling let therapists into those sides of themselves, it becomes clear just how common it is to have at least brief moments when we wish the most horrific things on the people we love, or have loved. In relationship therapy, when people are breaking up, we hear these things given voice. The warring couple on the TV show *In Treatment* both admit to fantasizing harm towards the other.

Break-ups have the potential to reveal the very darkest sides of ourselves: the potential thieves, vandals and abusers that lurk somewhere inside everyone. And this is understandable because we are in an intolerable situation. The person who used to validate our existence and reflect back an adoring vision of us has ceased to do so. The reflection of ourselves that we now see in their eyes is tainted and rotten in just the ways we have always feared. From seeing the best in us they now see the very worst. It is extremely hard to keep hold of the mask that we present to the world in the face of this: knowing that somebody so close has seen underneath and that they are now out in the world with such knowledge of us. All the more explicable, then, that we want to ensure that all of the bad stuff stays loaded upon our ex-partners. They are the ones who are wrong, not us, and anything negative we do feel towards them must be entirely justified.

Our ex-partners are likely to feel just the same way as us: that their very selves and existence are under threat. So they work hard to paint *us* as the bad guy, in conversations with us and with mutual friends. This reinforces all that we are thinking about what a terrible person they are, to be so cruel.

To summarize, the rules of break-ups are as follows:

- Break-ups signal the failure of the relationship, and potentially of ourselves.
- There is always a good guy and a bad guy in a break-up, and it is vital to figure out which is which, and not to be the bad guy.
- If we have broken up with someone, they must not have been The One after all, so we should be relieved.
- We should never speak to our ex-partner again following a break-up. It is over.

Why question the rules?

Why might we question the rules of break-up? The first reason is a pragmatic one. Given how intertwined our lives become when we are partners, it is often very difficult to disentwine everything once we have separated. Perhaps the most obvious example of this is the common situation in which people have children together and then separate or divorce. In most such cases, parents have to continue some form of relationship with one another in order to maintain a relationship with the kids, so the rule of never speaking with, or seeing, their ex-partner again becomes problematic. It is well accepted that it is better for everyone if parents can be civil to each other, address problems that arise together, and not engage the children in stories of good guys and bad guys. It is extremely difficult for everyone if they hate each other and are intent on demonizing each other to those around them. It is tough for people in this situation, because these old break-up rules still dominate in our culture, but they need to find a way to do something different.

It is not just in situations when people have children that a non-amicable split can be damaging. When we are together we may well build up a group of mutual friends and become very close to each other's family or old friends. There is a risk, given our rules of break-up, that all of these people will feel forced to pick a side, and this often causes rifts amongst friends and communities beyond the break-up itself. I've known networks and communities which have drifted apart following too many break-ups in quick succession. Each break-up brought up tough memories and feelings in everybody else, who then sided with the person whose situation felt most similar to a situation they had been in themselves. Also, there can be multiple losses following a break-up, for those who lose their friendship group or the people who've begun to feel like their own family, as well as their partner.

Additionally, we often have roles in each other's lives beyond being partners. We may be work colleagues as well. One of us may have a caring role for the other person (for example, if they have a long-term illness). We might share property ownership or have joint savings. We may share a beloved animal. All of these things mean that a complete separation of any involvement in each other's lives is likely to break more than just the relationship. So, we are either left with extra losses and grief to deal with, or with the need for some continuing relationship with our ex. Increasingly, there are practical issues which make it virtually impossible to stop seeing each other, or even to move out of shared accommodation in times when money is tight and jobs are unstable.

Another type of damage that break-up can do, if we follow the rules, is damage to ourselves. As people live longer, it is highly likely that we will go through more than one relationship during our lives, and also more than one relationship ending. According to the rules, after each of these we should quickly acknowledge that that person was not The One for us and keep searching. But this fails to recognize that such break-ups involve losing someone just as surely as a bereavement does. Our partner may have been somebody with whom we were extremely intimate, who saw sides of us that we didn't show to anybody else, and with whom we shared huge amounts of time every day, perhaps sleeping next to each other, breakfasting opposite each other, and caring for each other when we were ill. If we delete them from our lives overnight then it is a similar wrench to how it would be if they had died, in that they can feel just as lost from our lives and, certainly, the version of them that they were when we were together is no longer available to us.

Of course, bereavement has an additional degree of finality which break-ups never have, and it is seldom useful to compare different kinds of pain in order to say that they are equal, or one is more than the other. However, it is worth remembering the potential forms of grief associated specifically with break-up, such as knowing that the one you loved is no longer yours but *is* still out there, and that there is someone in the world who may hate you and wish you ill, both of which can be enormously hard to cope with. If we keep expecting ourselves to get over it and to move on, we could be denying ourselves the time we need to process what has happened and to look after ourselves. So it might be helpful to imagine how we would treat ourselves if it *was* a bereavement, and to remember that break-ups can be a heavy burden which we are likely to carry for some time, particularly if we keep rushing straight into new relationships in order to dull the pain of the previous one ending. Similarly, we might think about how we treat colleagues and friends when they have gone through a break-up, and appreciate the level of pain they may well be feeling.

Another aspect of self-damage occurs when we layer one story over other potential stories. We saw earlier that we are likely to pick story number two (that the other person was not The One and it is All Their Fault) over story number one (that the other person was The One and it is All My Fault). However, even if we stick rigidly to story number two, it is likely that story number one will remain somewhere underneath it, like a troubling spectre, haunting us with its presence. As we saw in Chapter 1, everyone has that nagging doubt that perhaps they are fundamentally not okay: that something is wrong with them which makes them a bad and flawed person compared to everybody else. The ghost story tells us that this is true: we couldn't make it work with this person, and that must mean that they saw what was so terrible about us. We really *are* unloveable, just as we always feared we were.

The thing about denying story one and only listening to story two is that story one may well get bigger and louder underneath as it demands to be heard as well. Stories have a lot of power when we tell them over and over again, but we can also give them power by trying to pretend that they don't exist. Better to face story one, and to remind ourselves that it is understandable to have self-doubt after such a tough time; that relationships are all co-constructed, so it is unrealistic to place all the blame upon ourselves; and that we know that we are imperfect – so is everyone – but that doesn't mean we can't have good relationships in the future.

We sometimes go the other way after a break-up. Story one becomes louder and louder so that we can no longer hear story two. We find ourselves drowning in guilt and grief, feeling that we really are terrible people, and despairing that we will ever love or be loved again. At such times, perhaps we need to access some of story two, again remembering that relationships are co-constructed. We might allow ourselves to feel some anger and resentment towards the other person, instead of feeling that this is unacceptable. Story one often becomes overwhelming when we are the person who instigated the break-up without some seemingly legitimate reason for doing so (for example, when we realize that our feelings for the other person have changed, rather than ending the relationship in response to some clearly abusive or infidelitous behaviour on the other's part). Story one can also take over if we were the responsible one, or the rescuer or nurturer, in the relationship, and we have had to admit that we wanted to be free again, or that looking after the other person had become too onerous.

Ironically, when we instigate a break-up ourselves, rather than the other person instigating it or it being a mutual decision, people around us often assume that it will be *less* painful for us. Sympathy tends to lie with the dumpee rather than the dumper. Again, it isn't useful to get into comparisons of amounts of pain. Each break-up is experienced uniquely by each person and will be related to all the past experiences that they bring to the situation. Also, being the one who is dumped does have extra challenges to do with the uncontrollability of the situation and the sense of powerlessness for something for which you may have been quite unprepared. However, the 'two stories' idea alerts us to the fact that the instigator of the break-up may be more likely to tell story one than story two, because they find it harder to paint themselves as the victim. They are, therefore, also worthy of sympathy, because guilt and self-doubt are heavy burdens to carry. The assumption that dumpees hurt more than dumpers is worth questioning.

We might also question this whole idea that there are two, and only two, possible stories. We will come back to the idea of multiple stories later in the chapter. For now, let's just stick with the idea that, even with these two stories, it might not be a case that *either* story one *or* story two is true, but rather that *both* story one *and* story two are valid. In other words, instead of our ex being all bad and us being all good, or vice versa, there may be good and bad in both of us.

As a culture, we may be getting to the point where we are more able to cope with this possibility. If you look at the superhero movies and comics of the mid to late twentieth century, they were pretty simple: there were the heroes, and there were the villains. Lately, things have become more complex. Films like the *X Men* series, or the recent re-imaginings of *Batman* or *Spiderman*, constantly remind us of the closeness of hero and villain. They often start in similar places. The hero may have moments when they strongly consider, or even carry out, villainous activities, and the villain may display moments of heroism. Such movies encourage us to question what good and bad even mean. We have to accept the dark side in the hero, and we may find ourselves cheering the villain, or at least understanding them.

This suggests that we *can* cope with the idea that good and bad can coexist in the same person instead of needing to polarize everybody into 'us' and 'them', the good guys and the bad guys. However, it is not an easy thing to do. We would still like the security and certainty of a world where such distinctions were easy. Perhaps we yearn back to those old tales of heroes and villains, cops and robbers, even as we enjoy the postmodern complexity of *The Dark Knight* or *The Wire*. In something as personal and challenging as a break-up we easily slip back into either/ors. Love turns to hate and the utterly wonderful person we were with becomes the complete bitch, or the total bastard.

Perhaps this is related to the rule we examined in Chapter 3: that The One is everything to us, our perfect match, our ideal. If we didn't place such high expectations on people when we were with them, perhaps we wouldn't need such a complete flip to them being all bad when we are no longer together: either totally accepting or totally rejecting them, with no other options available. Whatever the case, we can certainly question this good/bad, love/hate, right/wrong, thinking that underlies the rules of both conflict and break-up.

The tendency towards polarization in break-ups also relates to the tension between freedom and togetherness which we've considered several times in this book. In Chapter 6, we considered Zygmunt Bauman's suggestion that we always try to keep relationships secure and bound together at the same time that we attempt to keep bonds loose and disposable in case we want to get out. We want relationships to save us and to prove to us that we are okay, but then the gaze of the other person becomes too fixing, their expectations of us too constraining, and we we want to be free to be ourselves again.

Wanting to be free *and* to be bound up with another person often manifests itself in all-or-nothing ways: we go from being utterly committed to a relationship to wanting to escape it entirely, with no middle ground, sliding from 'we are together and they are great' to 'I want to escape and they are terrible'. They are a good guy, and then they are a bad guy.

Whatever the stories we tell through break-ups, there is also a danger that we will become fixed, not just in the story of one break-up, but in the story of many. Many people come to see patterns in their relationship endings just as did Rob Gordon, the character in *High Fidelity*, (as we saw in the Introduction). People become convinced that there must be something wrong with them because people always leave them, or that love will never last for them because they never manage to maintain it over time. They think they are destined to always get hurt, or to always end up hurting the people they love. They are sure that they must have terrible taste and cannot trust their own judgement, or they decide that intimacy with another person is just too painful, given all the conflict, and try to opt out of it entirely.

When we have been through a break-up or two, following the rules, we are likely to approach the next relationship with baggage heavy on our shoulders. It may seem to push us inexorably towards a similar dynamic to that which we had in previous relationships, in the hope we might get it right this time. Or it might push us in the opposite direction, towards a dynamic which seems totally different to the one we feel we can't risk again. But this will have different and difficult challenges, maybe putting us on the opposite side of a past dynamic so that we finally realize what our ex-partner was going through with us. It is worth exploring and questioning our overall story of 'me in relationships' as well as the specific story of the most recent relationship that has ended. It is helpful to realize that we are likely to project our history onto our next relationship, and useful to proceed with some awareness of that.

Alternative rules

What might alternative rules of break-up look like? Certainly, there are cultures and communities in which the rules are quite different; for example, where it is more common to remain friendly with ex-partners than it is to cut them out. This often happens in smaller communities where many acrimonious break-ups would be too damaging to the community as a whole, for example in some bisexual, lesbian and gay networks in big cities. It is not that bad break-ups never happen within these groups, but it becomes easier to do break-ups amicably when there are stories available to us beyond those which follow the rules we set out at the start. In such communities, for example, we may be able to point to people who have remained close to previous partners, or who have negotiated different ways of being in one another's lives which fit somewhere between exes and partners.

On the other hand, when there is only one way of seeing things available to us then, however much we want to do things otherwise, we can feel forced into a corner. For example, when things become difficult in a relationship, we might try to think and talk about how we could shift it into a form which would work better. However, if all that surrounds us are the mainstream rules, we will feel pressure to read such conversations as break-ups. Other people in our lives will assume that, for example, moving out of shared accommodation, spending less time together, or deciding not to be sexual any more, equates to having broken up, even if other aspects of the relationship (such as emotional closeness or shared goals) have remained the same. Despite our best intentions, others may then feel that they have to take sides, deciding which of us to support and which of us to blame, and that puts further pressure on us to feel that we are breaking up.

Maybe one thing that we can offer when friends are going through a tough time in their relationship, or breaking up, is to consciously avoid picking sides or supporting any kind of all-good or all-bad depiction of those involved. We might think that we're being kind when we shore up our mate's story of what a bastard or bitch their partner or ex is. However, is it really helpful to encourage someone to think that they have no responsibility in matters and that the other person has it all? Might we be colluding in hiding away that ghost story that it really *is* their fault, which only gives it more power? Might we fan the flames of the conflict, such that it will be even more difficult for those involved to find their way to a compassionate relationship?

It is certainly tough, during a break-up, when a friend points out that you are behaving in a way that isn't acceptable or kind. But perhaps we can have more respect for a friend who had the courage to do this (as long as *they* are kind about it) than we have for those who just agree about how terrible our ex was, even though they used to like them perfectly well when we were together.

As we explored before, maybe the most important thing that we can do around break-ups is to resist the urge to write, rehearse, and tell one particular story of events so that it becomes concrete, rigid and fixed. As we saw in Chapter 7, there is value in learning how to let go of our story and to remain open to other possible versions of events, both for ourselves and for the others involved. Once we understand all the reasons why we might be drawn to simplistic good guy/bad guy break-up stories, it might be easier to do this.

Perhaps we are fortunate when our lives allow us to hear, later, our ex's story of our break-up. This alerts us to just how different our stories of exactly the same events can be. This was brought home to me one time when I found out that both myself *and* my partner genuinely thought that the other person had been the one to end the relationship. We had both been present in the same conversation and had heard the same words spoken, but they had gone away with the impression that I had broken up with them, and I had gone away with the impression that they had broken up with me. This goes back to the idea from Chapter 7 that we are so primed to hear what we expect and fear in times of conflict that we often completely misconstrue what the other person has said. After the break-up we both waited for the other person to come and find us, and read the other person's silence as a sign that they didn't want to stay in contact, rather than realizing that *they* were waiting for *us* to get in touch.

How can two people do that? How can they come away from exactly the same conversation with such different understandings of what had happened? The answer lies in stories. When things become difficult between us we tell our stories to make sense of the hurt we are feeling and to explain how things could have led up to this point. These stories do not just describe the facts of what happened: they are more important than that. They *do* something for us. They have vital *actions* as well as being simple collections of words to convey events. This isn't deliberate. It's not like we sit down and think 'how can I tell what happened to portray my own role in as good a light as possible', but that is what we do nonetheless. Examples of things our stories *do* include explaining how something so good could have become so painful, and allocating blame to the other person so that we don't have to take responsibility for behaving unreasonably ourselves. The stories portray us in a positive light to ourselves and to the other people to whom we tell our story. And, as we go over it in our own minds and in conversations with our friends, they became more concrete and clear and easier to accept as the truth of the matter.

We pick out memories of our time together that support our story and use those to illustrate it, rejecting any that don't fit the version we wanted to tell. We draw on stories of other people we knew, or from films we've seen and books we've read, to help strengthen our stories, telling them in a way that people can recognize.

I might tell the story that my partner was to blame for the break-up because they never let me be on my own: it was their insecurity and need for constant contact that stifled and suffocated the relationship. They might tell the story that I was to blame for the break-up because I was so volatile, always bursting into a rage about little things in a way they couldn't predict, so that they were constantly on edge waiting for an explosion. I bring in memories of when my partner begged me to stay at home rather than going out and potentially meeting new people. They bring in memories of the time that I blew up because the computer wasn't working properly. I say that my irritability was due to them never giving me enough space. They say that their occasional insecurity was due to my being so fiery and unpredictable.

Psychologists Potter and Edwards analyse times in public life in which people, such as politicians and journalists, tell very different stories of the same event.[1] This reveals that memory is something that we *do* as an action, rather than something objective that we simply have somewhere in our head like a tape-recording. It is tempting to attempt to get to an absolute truth of what has occurred, especially when things are painful. And, when two stories differ hugely from each other, it can seem that one *must* be an accurate representation and the other a tissue of lies. However, this is rarely the case. Instead of trying to tease truth from fiction, it can be more useful to be aware how different people can come up with different versions of events and each believe them to be completely true.

In my example, both people used different memories to back up their versions of the break-up, telling the history of the relationship in different ways. I drew on the times when I'd said that I wanted time with other friends and my partner had become insecure, perhaps erasing times when they'd encouraged my activities. They drew on times when I'd lashed out at them unreasonably, perhaps erasing times when I was calm and mellow. We used different words to describe the same circumstances with a different flavour ('rage' versus 'irritation', 'slight insecurity' versus 'stifling need for constant contact').

Psychological research demonstrates what a malleable thing memory is. We can implant memories in people that never even happened (for example by asking them to imagine childhood events, such as getting lost in a shopping mall, and then asking them about it a few years later: they will believe that it really occurred). We can alter someone's memory by the use of leading questions (showing a film of an accident and asking 'how fast were the cars going when they hit each other?' versus 'how fast were the cars going when they smashed into each other?').[2] There's a whole area of 'eyewitness research' which shows how hazy memories can be in legal cases.

In a break-up, we have good reason to let our memories of the relationship and ending swing in certain directions and not others. Memory is such a flexible thing that, by telling and retelling these stories of the past, we probably really *do* now remember the same events in different ways.

Finally, we know that people make different attributions when their relationships are in a good place versus when they're in a bad place. Researchers have found that we tend to attribute the causes of events either to personal factors (it's because someone is that kind of person) or situational factors (it's because of the situation they were in). In the first blush of new romance we tend to put all the good things our partner does down to personal factors and all the bad things down to situational factors (they bought me chocolates because they're such a kind person; they were late for our date because work was so hectic). When we're in conflict, the attributions are reversed. We put all the good things down to situational factors and all the bad things down to personal factors (they bought me chocolates because they happened to be in the shop; they were late for our date because they're so disorganized and careless).[3] Tavris and Aronson write that, during break-ups, people revise their whole relationships in this way, such that their stories blame all the bad things about their partner on personality flaws, and explain any good things away as just down to the situation.

It can be scary to realize that there is no true story to be found through our break-ups; rather, there are many different stories which could be told through the same set of circumstances and all of which are equally valid. We are often powerfully driven to locate the truth that we feel must be there in order to relieve the pressure, but that rarely works because it just means that we have to dismiss one of the stories as lies (our own, or the other person's) because they are *so* different. Rather, the way forward is to recognize that there are many different stories available to make sense of the situation, and the one we choose will probably be based on our own needs and fears, not on how objectively valid it might be.

The existential therapist Irvin Yalom quotes Nietzsche as saying that 'there is no truth, there is only interpretation'.[4] Yalom reminds us that, even within one person who has gone through a break-up, there are many different stories which they will tell at different times, depending on how they feel, or what else is going on. For example, here is an adapted list of the stories that one client of his told in therapy about why she broke up with her new partner:

- I'm cursed and destined to lose everyone I love.
- I'm scared of getting too close, because the other person might see me and discover that I'm not really an okay person.
- If I fell in love with this person I'd have to acknowledge that my last relationship was really over.
- If I fell in love with this person it would prove that I didn't really love my previous partner.
- I've had too many losses in my life: I can't survive another one. Better to end it now.
- I hate being helpless. If I fall in love again they'll have the power to hurt me if they become angry with me. I'm not going to let that happen again.
- If I stayed with this guy, I'd have to commit to him and I want to keep my options open.

So what is the way forward? It is helpful to recognize that there are always many different possible stories around each event or situation. Once we are aware of this, we can assess whether the story we are telling is the most useful one. Perhaps we can choose a different story that enables us to build in the other person's perspective. Or, perhaps the awareness that the other person is likely to be telling a different story to ours can help us reach a place where we can hear their story. Each person recognizing the other's story and understanding why they need to tell it in this way can help us to reach some kind of reconciliation or compromise. Maybe, eventually, we can tell a new, joint, story which incorporates elements of both versions in it and makes sense of things in a way which allows the relationship to continue in some form.

Telling a new and different story like this is not easy. It is hard to let go of the story you're currently telling for many reasons, including the following:

- It has become a habit, because you've told it for such a long time. It is hard to get out of habitual ways of thinking. Like someone giving up smoking, you find yourself automatically reaching for the cigarette someone offers you, or thinking in those old, familiar, ways again.
- You get something important out of the story; often the idea that you are the good guy and have behaved well. Questioning it is threatening, like an earthquake that will leave you shaking. It is easier and safer to stick with your story than to face your role in what happened.
- Our stories are often those that are most easily accessible: those we read in magazines, see in films, and hear from our friends. It's difficult to reject the standard stories and tell things in a different way to the people around us. Culturally taken-for-granted stories (like the story that break-up is all one person's fault) are difficult to question.
- If we are hurting, as we often are during break-up, we tend to see things in simple, polarized terms. More complex stories that reject the conventional ways of seeing things and allow diverse perspectives are hard to hear.

Beyond rules? Embracing uncertainty

With this idea of being open to multiple stories, we find ourselves once again embracing uncertainty. As we've seen throughout this book, that is not something which comes easily. It is particularly hard to do when we are hurting so much. We want to find something sure and certain to cling to: an anchor in the storm. Particularly, we want reassurance that we are okay, given our underlying fear that we may not be. Ironically, grasping that anchor is what will pull us under, whereas allowing ourselves to float free on an ocean of multiple possibilities can see us to calmer waters. We need to hold on to many stories, even when they might be in contradiction, rather than searching for one simple truth.

Let's consider a few practical ways of exploring alternative stories. First, we might remind ourselves of different attributions which are possible for our partner's behaviour. We can think up situational alternatives to personal attributions when we are going through a tough time. For example, if they don't call you after an argument your personal attribution might be that they don't care, whereas a situational alternative would be that they, like you, are going through a very stressful time. You could make your own lists of behaviours you've found tough, and practice coming up with alternative, situational, attributions.

Psychologists have found that everyone is capable of horrendous behaviour when they are in a bad situation. In times of conflict and break-up, when we feel attacked and at risk of losing everything, we are particularly prone to lashing out, running away, saying the first thing that comes into our head, putting the other person down to make ourselves feel better, and all kinds of harsh, cruel, unthoughtful, and manipulative behaviours. If we can face our own potential to behave in such ways and understand the situational context in which they occur, perhaps we can forgive our partners for similar behaviours, recognizing that they are in distress too, and that such reactions are understandable.

Another useful activity for recognizing multiple stories is to explore the different emotions we're feeling. Four common emotions after a break-up are anger, grief, guilt, and relief. You could give yourself time to write as many things you can think of about the relationship and break-up under the headings 'I am angry at you for . . .', 'I feel a sense of loss about . . .', 'I am sorry for . . .', and 'I am relieved that . . .'. This helps us to realize that, even for ourselves, there is not just one story. We might struggle with this exercise if we've been taught that certain emotions are off-limits to us: those 'boys don't cry' and 'girls don't get angry' messages that we receive growing up (see Chapter 5). Avoiding certain parts of the emotional range can be just as damaging as focusing only on some. So the story that we are not at all angry about what happened, because we don't get angry, can be just as destructive as the story that it is all their fault and we are *only* angry. Similarly problematic are stories that we're too tough to be sad about it, or that we never feel guilt because it's a pointless emotion.

What of the rule that break-ups are endings which relegate the relationship completely to the past? It is useful to recognize, first, that even breaking up does not end the relationship and, second, that when we stay together with someone the relationship will still end in various ways. This questions the idea that break-up = ending, and staying together = continuing. The situation is much more complex than that.

What is meant by this? Well, we saw earlier that many people who break up have to maintain a relationship because their lives are intertwined. They may redefine their relationship as co-parents, housemates, extended families, friends-with-benefits. We can wonder, in such cases, what the word 'break-up' even means. What has broken here? What has ended? Perhaps the concept of *change* is more appropriate than *ending*. There are many ways in which we can be in each other's lives: we can live together, we can share roles (like parenting or being business partners), we can spend lots of time in each other's company, we can have shared goals, we can be sexually intimate, we can be each other's support in times of crisis, we can be financially interdependent. If we move away from the break-up model, it becomes possible to change one of these aspects without necessarily changing all of the others. Which ones aren't working any more? Which ones still are? Is the word 'ex' really appropriate for someone who remains in our life in important ways?

Even if we do break-up and decide never to see each other again, anyone who has been in this situation knows that you remain in a powerful relationship with the other person. They set up occupancy in our heads. We have internal conversations with them. We think we see them on the street until we realize it is just someone with a similar dress or gait. We remember them whenever a certain song, scent, or place, reminds us of them. This relationship may last the rest of our lives. Many people in their seventies still have such relationships with their first partner, or their ex-wife whom they haven't seen in years. So the concept that relationships end and we move on is a problematic one.

On the flip side of this, when we do stay together with someone, rather than breaking up, we still have endings with them. As our bodies change, there are times when we have to let go of an activity we always did together (like certain sexual practices or hobbies). We might realize that a certain topic of conversation always leads to conflict and decide not to go there any more. Somebody's difficulty sleeping might mean we start sleeping separately when we used to sleep together. One of us may change job and the role that the other person used to take supporting our career stops being necessary. If we have children who grow up, or parents who come and live with us, the dynamics of our relationship change again.

All our lives are in process, so we constantly lose old versions of ourselves to be replaced by new ones. For some, this is the very reason we break-up. We find ourselves saying 'you've changed', as if this is a blameworthy thing and not simply a fact of life. Alternatively, we could recognize that any relationship will involve change and loss. We could acknowledge that one day we will lose this person entirely (whether this is through separation or death). And we could recognize that up to that point we will lose the person we started out with a little bit at a time, as they – and we – inevitably become somebody different. Mark Epstein tells the story of Thai monk Achaan Chaa who held up his drinking glass and said 'the glass is already broken'.[5] He imagined the day when it would be knocked over and shatter, which made every moment he had with it precious. In the same ways, our relationships are already broken. Acknowledging this can help us to remember how precious they are, however they shift and change over time. We will come back to this idea of embracing change in the next chapter, when we consider alternative forms of commitment.

There is a risk in shifting from the idea of relationship ending to relationship changing, however, and that is that we might grasp hold of this idea too tightly in the hope of avoiding the pain of endings and break-ups. A couple of times I have insisted with partners that we are not breaking up, we are just 'changing the nature of our relationship', expecting that this change will then happen immediately to everyone's satisfaction. This is disrespectful to the pain and loss that both they – and I – were experiencing. We can grasp onto the idea of changing in a naïve way which longs to keep hold of all of the good parts of our relationship and none of the bad bits. What is required is a more nuanced understanding of what good and bad mean anyway (see Chapter 3), how each person experiences the situation (see Chapter 7), and the complexity of the tangled place in which we find ourselves during relationship crises and times of change. We'll return to this in the next chapter.

Rather than expecting an easy shift from partnership to friendship, for example, or to a different form of partnership, we need to acknowledge that the process is unlikely to be simple or pain-free. As with needing time out from a conflict, we may need time out from the old dynamics of a relationship before new dynamics can emerge: time to grieve, to process what has happened, and to let the heat go out of situation so that we don't come to each interaction so loaded with heightened emotion that we can't hear the other person, however hard we try.

When we are apart, though, it can be easy to dehumanize our ex and to fix them as just the person they were during the break-up. Contact – when we are ready for it – may help to remind us that this is still a complex, changing, human being, who was in a tough situation and who is not the same now as they were back then. Remembering that we, ourselves, are plural and in process can stop us from fearing that we are fixed as the person our partner saw us as being during the hard times: the person we were during the good times is us, too. We can more readily set our partners free to continue with their lives when we are not desperate for them to come back and validate us. Acknowledging that the other person is plural and in process can remind us that the parts of them we loved so much are still them, just as much as the parts of them that we find difficult.

Reminding ourselves that our ex-partners are human beings in process is also useful if we find ourselves, in the heat of a break-up, wishing suffering upon them. Undoubtedly they *will* suffer pain, beyond any we could wish on them, as they go through life facing the inevitable struggles, hardships, and losses, that come with human existence. They will also have moments of wonder and triumph. If we wish that they could feel how we are feeling right now, relationship karma means that they probably will. Remembering this can take some of the heat out of our anger and stop us from getting caught up in stories of revenge.

Another alternative way to view our exes is to think of them as the people with whom we have reached the height of intimacy. What could be more intimate than showing the most vulnerable sides of ourselves to another person during a break-up? Perhaps we can view these people as the most valuable and precious relationships in our lives, instead of hating them or relegating them entirely to the past.

This points us towards an alternative to looking back through our relationships and coming up with patterns about how we 'always are' in relationships. If we have had more than one partner in our lives, we can do the activity from Chapter 1 (about how we are different people in different relationships) for them. Again, we may find that we were different selves in different relationships. It doesn't make sense to regard ourselves as a static person who always does everything in the same way. When we regard ourselves as static selves this can become a self-fulfilling prophecy as it becomes more comfortable to behave as we have done in the past, even if it is painful for us. Even the story 'I'm a bad person whom everyone leaves' can be more comfortable than changing to a new story which is unknown.

We've seen that we tend to equate success with staying together and failure with break-up. This means that we often feel more scared each time a relationship ends, and enter the next one with expectations that it will end in pain. Because of this, we may become harder and more self-protective over the years. My friend Linette told me of a woman she'd met who challenged her on this way of thinking. The woman said she'd learnt important things, about her self and about other people, from every relationship she'd had. Instead of feeling more wary of each new relationship after the breakdown of the last, she eagerly launched into them, knowing that they would probably be transitory, but valuing them nonetheless for the ways in which they would enrich her life. Linette said that hearing this woman talk was like looking at one of those optical illusions where there are two pictures in the same image (like the vase or kissing faces in the Introduction). Both of these stories of our relationship histories are possible through the same series of events.

To end this chapter, there is one burning question which we haven't addressed so far. That is how we know when to break up and when to stay together. How do we tell whether this is a bad relationship which needs to end, or whether it is a bad time in the relationship which we need to ride out? What is the right decision?

These questions may be in need of some rewriting too. We can challenge the idea that there are right and wrong decisions (as we did in Chapter 3) as well as replacing the either/or approach with a model of change (as we've done in this chapter). But how do we know when there is a need for *some* re-evaluation of the relationship? A few possibilities we might consider include:

- One or more people is feeling increasingly constrained in the relationship.
- There is such tension between our major values that we can't move forward without one of us completely compromising what we hold dear.
- We can't agree about how we communicate together and can't hold onto our stories being equally valid. Instead, we both keep trying to change, or dismiss, the other person.
- The kinds of stuck dynamics which we explored at the end of the previous chapter seem intractable and resistant to shifting.

Nobody else can tell you when a relationships has reached some irretrievable point because nobody else really knows. While we might wish for an answer, we should mistrust anyone who claims to offer it. However hard it is, we need to embrace the inevitable uncertainty of these situations.

Martine Batchelor's metaphor from Chapter 1 can be useful for relationships here. Remember that she imagines that we have a precious object in our hand. If we grasp it tightly (clinging onto the relationship), we can't see it or use our hand. If we hurl it away from us (rushing into break-up), we don't have it any more and we damage it. If we open our fingers slowly and let the object sit in the palm of our hand, we can see it for what it is. Then we can decide to put it down or to pick it up again.

Chapter 9

Rewriting the rules of commitment

What are the rules?

So we reach the final topic of the book: commitment. Now that we have explored rewriting our rules of ourselves, our bodies, love, sex, gender, monogamy, conflict, and break-up, what do our relationships look like if we *do* decide to commit to them? What kinds of promises, if any, might we make to other people, and expect from them?

Let's start by thinking about the vows we'd feel comfortable making to a partner, and those we'd like them to make to us. If you're in a relationship, then consider what you'd promise to each other if you had some form of commitment ceremony (or what you *did* promise, if you've already had one). If you don't currently have such a relationship, but would like to in future, then think about promises you'd like to make and have made to you. You might also think about the form you'd like such a ceremony to take. Is it important to make promises publicly or privately? If the former, who would be there, and why? Where would you hold it? What is commitment about for you?

If you haven't thought much about such questions before, it may be interesting to answer them now, and then to come back to them at the end of the chapter once we have explored the kinds of commitments people make to each other.

In the Introduction, we saw that committing to relationships continues to be highly popular, despite all the evidence of uncertainty in relationships. Weddings seem to be recession-proof;[1] more young gay, bisexual, and lesbian, people seek marriage rights and have marriages and civil partnerships where those are possible;[2] and many of those in non-monogamous relationships (see Chapter 5) commit to each other and seek greater legal and public recognition for their relationships.[3] If anything, committed romantic relationships have become more important to us, not less, as religious beliefs have declined and personal freedom has increased.

This first part of the chapter will consider the vows and promises which people commonly make to each other in marriages, civil partnerships, and commitment ceremonies in Western Europe, Canada, Australia, New Zealand, and the US.[4] These are generally rooted in the marriage ceremony of the Christian church, even when they are secular ceremonies. Therefore what I'm saying does not apply to all religious and cultural contexts, although similar themes run through many of the major world religions. These are also the vows we hear in soap operas, popular music, and Hollywood movies that are consumed around the globe. It is worth considering the vows and promises that people you know are generally expected to make, which may, of course, differ from these.

Perhaps the key aspect of commitment, as it is generally presented to us, is the promise of 'forever'. Women frequently leave out the 'obey' part which used to be in the vows; being the same gender is no longer quite the obstacle it was to committing; and non-religious people have developed secular ceremonies. However, both marriage and civil partnership vows clearly state that people will *always* love and protect their partner, that they will do so all the days of their lives, and that they will be together until *death*. The listing of 'for better, for worse, for richer, for poorer, in sickness and in health', underlines this message. We are promising 'forever', whatever happens.

Because the promise of together forever is so deeply ingrained in our culture, from the fairy-tale happily-ever-after to the commitment ceremony to the pop song ('I will always love you', 'I'll love you till the day I die', 'endless love', etc.), it is no wonder that our very definition of a successful relationship is whether it lasts. Whenever I speak at conferences about openly non-monogamous relationships I am asked how successful they are. I start my answer by checking with the questioner what it is that they mean by 'successful'. They are often quite surprised to be asked, because they thought that everyone would automatically understand, but they respond by saying that they meant whether or not such relationships last over time.[5]

As well as promising to *stay* with someone forever, we also promise, in such vows, to *love* them forever. Clearly this relates back to what we considered in Chapter 3 about the meaning of love. Such vows support the idea of The One. The person we commit to is *the* person we have found to love, and the idea that we *can* offer to love them forever, whatever life throws at us, is presented relatively unproblematically. It is interesting to contrast this with to the way in which falling in love is presented. Falling in love is beyond our control, something that just happens to us, like a thunderbolt or a natural disaster, whereas, in commitment, love is something we have so much control over that we can confidently predict that it will continue, unchanging, for the rest of our lives.

Most vows also include an element about being true to each other, or faithful, or sometimes 'forsaking all others'. So it is clear that some form of monogamy is integral to conventional commitment. We won't cover this in depth because it has a whole chapter of its own (Chapter 6). However, it is useful to relate this chapter back to Chapters 3 and 6 to see how the rules of love, monogamy, and commitment are interwoven, and how similar questions may be asked of all of them. There is also a line in most vows about 'having and holding', which suggests that committing involves giving yourself to another person such that you belong to them and they to you (you *have* each other). Of course, this is reinforced in many of the songs of love, in which lyrics like 'you belong to me', 'you're mine', 'I'm yours', and 'I give myself to you' are commonplace.

What of the more implicit promises that we make when we commit to one another? During the exchange of rings in many ceremonies, people promise to worship each other with their bodies, and to endow each other with all their worldly goods. This suggests that a committed relationship will be a sexual relationship, and that our money and property will be pooled, such that we will live together and have joint finances. In Chapter 6, we saw how love and sex are intertwined, such that sex is seen as the defining feature of a relationship and there is pressure on relationships to remain sexual. In this chapter, we'll spend more time on the other implicit expectation: that being in a relationship means sharing our money and cohabiting. Also, there are assumptions for most people that committing to someone means committing to spending a certain amount of time (daily, weekly, yearly) with them. For example, we may assume that we will always share an evening meal, sleep together, vacation together, and spend public holidays with each other.

Finally, committing to each other, for many people, means implicitly signing up to an agreement about the future. In relationship therapy we often bring the assumptions about what this means out into the open, because problems often occur when people don't have quite the same expectations. People frequently have a mental list of 'check boxes' for their life together, based on what they regard as 'normal', or what everybody else does. This list often involves most or all of the following: meeting The One, moving in together, having some formal commitment, buying property together, having children, and retiring once those children have left home. Of course, there are differences in the check boxes for different individuals, groups, and cultures, in terms of both the content of the list and the age at which these things are expected to happen.

You might like to spend a moment considering whether you have such a checklist for your life and, if so, what the key items on it are for you. Which, if any, have you ticked off already? At what ages do you hope to tick the other items off? Has the list changed at all over your life so far? Are all the items there shared by the other people in your life? Where do the items come from? Again, you might find it useful to revisit this list once you have read the whole of this chapter.

To summarize, the rules of commitment that people commonly follow – either explicitly or implicitly – in relationships are as follows:

- We will stay together forever, through whatever happens, and won't break up.
- We will love each other throughout the relationship (see Chapter 3).
- We will be monogamous (see Chapter 6).
- We will belong to each other.
- We will be sexual throughout the relationship (see Chapter 4).
- We will share our lives (usually pooling our money, living together, and sharing time).

- Together, we will tick the check boxes expected of people in a relationship in our culture (e.g. moving in together, having a commitment ceremony, buying our own place, having children).

In the rest of this chapter, we'll first consider how we might re-interpret these rules if we do want to stick with them but don't wish to interpret them too rigidly. Then we'll explore the alternative forms of commitment that are possible if we reject the standard vows. Finally, we'll explore other possible ways of conceptualising relationships such that the commitments we make, and the people we make them to, are viewed differently. Of course, all of these options are valid, and many of us will combine aspects of all three (sticking with some of the rules, reinterpreting others, forming some of our own, and coming up with our own understandings of relationships more broadly).

Why question the rules?

One major reason to question these rules is that they are implicated in the two different kinds of suffering that we experience in relationships: that is, breaking up from relationships, and staying in relationships which are painful. This may seem paradoxical, but the pressure to make such big forever promises is both the thing that encourages us to run away from relationships when the going gets tough, and to cling onto them even when they aren't good for us any more. Sometimes we are so overwhelmed by the prospect of commitment in an uncertain world that we can't face it at all, or we make a commitment and then break it at the first sign of trouble. Other times we feel so trapped in the expectation that we *will* make such commitments that we don't feel able to alter them, even when they aren't working for anyone involved and haven't for a long time. We might, therefore, question the rigid form of these commitment rules, both for encouraging relationship breakdown *and* for inducing people to stay in destructive relationships.

The rules listed before are those which mean that we often feel like a failure when we end a relationship (see Chapter 8). We might feel that we have failed (as partners and/or as individuals) if we leave when we find that we can't love someone in the same way consistently for 50 or more years. This may be, for example, because our sexual feelings change over time; because living together is difficult; because we develop loving or sexual feelings for other people; because we have different check boxes on our lists (or different times by which we expect to meet them); or because we find ourselves wanting different levels of freedom or privacy.

In addition to these pressures around leaving relationships, the same rules can put us under pressure *in* relationships. Many people worry about whether they and their partner love each other *enough*, especially when the quality of love, and the ways in which it is expressed, have changed since the start. Similarly, there is no quantifying the extent of heartache that occurs because sexual desires have changed over time, because one or more partners have developed sexual or romantic feelings for others, or because people realize that they have different expectations and values.

For many people, the focus on forever weighs heavy on a relationship. When problems do occur, they are a terrible burden – because we feel that we must remain in the current situation for ever and ever. This means that difficulties are exacerbated, rather than potentially bubbling up and then going away again. There is also a danger that we will feel bad about ourselves at times when it is difficult to love our partners. As we saw in Chapter 7, there are times in the best of relationships when it is hard to love someone who is seeing us at our most vulnerable and who is conflicting with us. Pressure to be together forever can also mean that people jump out of relationships quickly because this thought of forever is intolerable when, actually, it may have been a problem that could've been dealt with.

We can question whether longevity and endurance are the best measures of a successful relationship. In Chapter 4, we saw that our current focus on whether or not the sex we are having is normal has overshadowed the (perhaps more important) question of whether it is enjoyable for those involved. Similarly, the question of how long our relationship has lasted can overshadow the (perhaps more important) question of whether it is an enjoyable, nourishing, and positive aspect of our lives. For example, would we value a relationship which lasted 10 years but was miserable for the last 5 over one which lasted 5 years where there was an amicable split? Would we value a relationship where people fought in front of their kids every other day over one where they decided to become co-parents rather than partners, and remained on relatively good terms? Should we prioritize longevity over quality?

Finally, in relation to the rule of loving each other forever, it is important to realize that people express and reaffirm their love for each other in different ways. In long-term relationships it is useful to check out how each person understands that they are loved. For example, one person may feel loved when it is clear that others still desire them sexually; one person may like to be told 'I love you' regularly and to be treated romantically; and one person may think that actions speak louder than words and feels loved when others have made the effort to do the domestic chores. In a relationship, those people might all feel they were strongly demonstrating their love to the others (by being sexual, romantic, or practical), but the others wouldn't be feeling loved at all.

The rule of belonging to each other can mean that people are not aware of the inevitable tension, in all relationships, between togetherness and freedom, which we have explored throughout this book. However much people feel that they belong together, there will be times when they tug towards a bit more freedom. For example, one person might think that it is up to them what decisions they make about their work, whereas their partner might think that all decisions that impact on both of them should be made together. In another relationship, one person might feel that they should always drop everything if their parents or siblings need them, whereas their partner might feel that this puts them at a lower priority and that isn't appropriate. If we acknowledge that there will be tensions between togetherness and individual freedom, then we may find these aspects easier to acknowledge and work with than if we insist that we totally belong to each other. We may also want to think about how we conceptualize belonging. Does this person 'belonging' to us mean that they always have to be a particular way, or can they change and display different sides of themselves and still be ours (see Chapter 7)?

We might also question the implicit assumptions about sharing that are involved in commitment. For example, the assumption that we will live together doesn't always function for those whose work takes them overseas (like those in the military or those who travel a lot on business). It is easier for such people to negotiate ways of being together which work for them if others don't assume that their relationships are somehow lesser because of it. Similarly, the concept of pooling money can be complex. What if the people involved have different beliefs about what it is worth spending money on? What if one earns a lot more than the others? What if – as is increasingly the case – one or more people has family to whom they give support? Should new partners be expected to support them too? It may well be necessary to think carefully about money and resources and to fit different practices to different situations. This can be hard if everyone around you thinks that partners should simply share all their worldly goods.

Similar issues arise around sharing time. For example, it is so unlikely that our sleeping patterns will be identical that we might well want to question the common ideas that we should always go to bed at the same time, sleep alongside each other throughout the night, and get up at the same time. This is especially true in times of stress or illness. In reality many people don't follow these rules, having separate beds or separate rooms. It may well be better to appreciate that there is a diversity of ways of sleeping (from completely together to completely separate), which may also change over time. This links with the issue of having separate space. It is commonly assumed that it is a bad sign for partners to spend time apart. However, as we saw in Chapters 1 and 7, some separate time is essential to keep us feeling okay in ourselves and to deal with conflict when it comes up. As well as thinking about how we spend time together (on a daily, weekly, or yearly basis), we can think about how we spend time alone, and with other people in our lives, without feeling guilty about this.

Finally, we might question the utility of checklists of expectations. The major reason for questioning this is that it can be so hard for people when the boxes don't get ticked for whatever reason. It can be difficult, for example, if they are unable to afford their own house, or if they find that they can't have children in the way in which they had assumed they would. Similarly, if the check boxes are tied to a particular age or life event (in my 20s, before I'm 40, while my parents are still alive, after I retire, etc.) then it can be very difficult if they happen earlier or later than expected. Of course, we are unlikely to go through life with no sense of what we'd like to accomplish up ahead. But when the check boxes feel as if they are given to us with no alternatives, it is worth thinking about where they actually came from and what we gain and lose from them. Who wrote the list? Are all of the things on it things we really want? If we do want them, do they have to happen in the way we imagine, or might there be other ways of making them work? Given that we don't *really* know at what point the end of our life will come, is it really sensible to have fixed dates by which such things need to have occurred?

Of course, when we question the rules of commitment what we are talking about is our *interpretation* of these vows or commitments. The rules are only problematic if they are adhered to too rigidly. Most of those offering counsel to people tying the knot would not tell them that they will always love each other in the exact same way that they did when they met, or that there is something wrong with their relationship if they don't continue having sex the way they did on their honeymoon. We might be happy to commit to the whole list of rules if it was acknowleged that the way these commitments are expressed will change over time.

As we saw in Chapter 6, we often enter relationships with the assumption that our own rules are shared by our partner. Then situations arise which bring this into question. Relationship therapy often involves bringing the implicit rules we have out into the open and acknowledging that it is okay for people to draw their lines in slightly different places. If we do decide to commit according to the rules listed before, perhaps the most useful thing we can do early on is to go down the list and discuss what each rule means to each person.

- *Staying together.* What does being together mean? Are there aspects of our relationship which might acceptably end, or change, over time, or do we need things to stay pretty constant?
- *Always loving each other.* What does loving each other mean? How do we each like to express love and have it expressed towards us? Can this shift over time or do we want consistency?
- *Being faithful.* What does monogamy mean? Where do we each draw our lines on the continua of emotional and sexual monogamy (see Chapter 6)?
- *Having each other.* What does belonging to each other mean? How much freedom do we want, and in what arenas of life? Which choices should we always make together? Are there areas of our lives that we want to keep private from others?
- *Sharing our bodies.* What does being sexual mean? How do we each like to express desire and have it expressed towards us? Can this shift over time, or do we want consistency?
- *Sharing worldly goods.* What does sharing our lives mean? Which aspects is it important for us to share, or to keep separate? Think about money, space, time, and roles, particularly.
- *Planning a future together.* What are our check boxes for the future and the ages at which we hope certain events will happen? Might these change, or are we fairly wedded to them?

If we and our partners are on the same page, great. If we have different ideas on some of them, which is likely, then perhaps we can accept and respect that, and work towards reaching a compromise. In some cases, it is likely that we will have to agree to differ, and appreciate that this is an acceptable tension in our relationship of which we are aware and which will probably come up several times during our lives together.

Alternative rules

We might, therefore, decide to stick with the conventional rules of commitment but communicate more about how we understand each of them, recognising that they won't necessarily mean exactly the same thing to others as they do to us.

What if we go further than this and decide that, for us, these standard rules of commitment are *not* the main things that we want to promise to one another? Might there be alternative rules of commitment which would apply better to our situation?

A good place to start with such rewriting of rules is the idea, which we have touched on several times in this book, that relationships shift and change over time. This is the reason why many people who question the rules of commitment do so. Their point is that, if we know that we won't be quite the same people tomorrow, next week, next year, or next decade, as we are today, how can we promise that both our feelings (loving somebody) and our behaviours (being with them in particular ways) will remain the same?

Let's start by exploring this on a basic level. Up until now, we've discussed commitment as if it was a one-off thing that happens at one specific point in a relationship. Obviously this is not the case, even if we do have a commitment ceremony. We still make commitments, whether implicitly or explicitly, throughout our relationships.

Reflect on this for a moment. What commitments would you expect to make to another person, and have them make to you (whether or not they are spoken aloud), at the following points in a relationship?

- Having kissed or flirted.
- Having been on a date.
- Having had sex.
- Saying that you are seeing each other.
- Going on holiday together.
- Saying that you love each other.
- Calling each other 'partner' or 'spouse'.
- Living together.
- Having a child together.
- The other person getting long-term sick.
- You deciding to care for a relative.
- The other person deciding to work abroad.
- Having broken-up.

I've put these in the rough chronological order of an imagined relationship, but obviously many relationships have a different order to this (e.g. housemates who get together may live together as their first commitment, and many people may have a casual sex encounter and then build a more emotional attachment). Also, of course, not everyone will do all the things listed here as part of their relationship.

Hopefully, from this you can see what rules, for you, come attached to each stage of a relationship. Again, it is useful to compare this list to those of other people in your life. This alerts us to the fact that the same commitments may not be applicable all the way through the relationship, or for all people.

Some people take this idea a stage further, arguing that it isn't possible to predict how they're going to feel in the future. Commitment is something that they do on a daily basis. Instead of making one-off promises in a commitment ceremony, they start every day by recommitting, reminding themselves what they can offer. They might have forms of relationship ceremonies with partners, but these would be about celebrating the relationship that has happened rather than making promises about the relationship to come.

Being present

Jamie Heckert explores this concept of time and relationships.[6] He says that we spend a lot of our time in relationships in the past or in the future, rather than in the present. When we are future-focused we seek reassurance that our partners will be there for us forever, that the relationship won't change, and that their love and positive view of us will remain stable. We don't enjoy the present moment because we are thinking about how it will be in the future, trying to ensure that it will stay safe enough and/or exciting enough for us. Perhaps we spend our time planning to buy the perfect house, or to change job so that we can spend more time together. Perhaps we try to persuade our partner to spice up our sex life, or to become more ambitious. If we ever do reach any of those aspirations, another aspiration comes to take its place. We live our relationship in a series of 'if onlys': if only we lived together, if only we could improve our sex life, if only we had more money. To paraphrase Thich Nhat Hanh, we only ever have the hope of fulfillment some day if we never find fulfillment in the here and now.[7]

When we are past-focused, the things that we do in the present are only done because they mean that we will be able to say that we are 'the person who has done that' when we are in the future. We treat the present as if it is already the past. Think about the way we treat an evening out or a weekend away with our partners. Often, we are so intent on having a nice time that we become stressed out, or we are shaken if anything doesn't go to plan and feel that it has been ruined. We focus on creating the kind of memory we want to look back on. Sometimes we become obsessed with recording these memories in photographs or in our diary or blog. When we do this, the present has become all about making a good past, rather than about appreciating it while we are in it. This is not to say that photographs, diaries, or blogs are bad things, necessarily, but they might be questionable if we use them as ways of avoiding being in the present moment.

Focusing on ticking off the items on our checklist is another way of being past-focused. We become all about being the person who has checked those boxes, ideally at the appropriate times. That means that we rarely appreciate the here and now. In fact, it might feel as if time has sped past shockingly fast, because we don't fully experience anything but just rush on to the next check box. The same can be true when we focus on making notches on the bedpost of the kinds of sex or sexual partners we've had, like some of the Game boys we met in Chapter 5.

An alternative commitment which we might make, if we are skeptical of promises about the future, is the commitment to try to stay with our partners in the present. Being present involves recognising that it is very human to fall into habits of going over the past, or planning for the future. We don't beat ourselves up for doing so. Instead we gently draw our attention back to the present when we find ourselves drifting away from it.[8] For example, when having a wonderful day with a partner we might want them to promise that we'll have many such days together in future. However, we could come back from that desire for security to the present which is still *being* wonderful right now, and which nothing can take away from us. We might similarly ask ourselves whether watching a sunset together would really be enhanced by taking a photograph or imagining how we'll describe it on our social networking site.

Commitment to the present can also be valuable at difficult times in our relationship. When we're struggling, we often get hung up on the future or on the past. We desperately thrash around because we're terrified that we will stay stuck in this appallingly difficult place forever (which ironically often traps us even more, like the person who struggles to get out of quicksand). Or we put pressure on improving things because it will be so horrible to remember in the future that we had a bad holiday, or a ruined day, or a spoilt summer. If we can gently bring ourselves back to the present moment, without all that future and past focus, then we can deal with it more calmly and wisely. We can remember that everything changes and shifts, so we are *not* trapped here. Just like past struggles and conflicts, this will likely have blown away by this evening, tomorrow, or next week. Also, we can properly tune in to what is actually happening, instead of trying to force it to be something else. Then we will be better able to hear what we, and our partners, are experiencing (see Chapter 7).

Flexibility

If we want to base our commitments to each other on the recognition that people and relationships change over time, then another commitment we might make is to be flexible. The rules of commitment generally focus on reassuring us that things will not change substantially, that we will stay together in a relatively stable way. Instead, we might recognize that change is a fact of life, and that everything is impermanent. Then we might come to value flexibility and capacity to change, as well as consistency and stability. Like the monk Achaan Chaa, whom we met in the last chapter, we might recognize that the glass is already broken when it comes to relationships. They will end one day. In this case, we might appreciate the relationship more. Paradoxically, trying to keep relationships safe and secure with rigid rules and contracts can make them more brittle and unstable. They can easily break if something unexpected happens, and people may feel trapped inside them. Although it may feel less stable, flexibility can mean that a relationship is *more* safe and secure because it is able to adapt and change over time and situations in the way that something fixed and rigid cannot.

What does flexibility look like in practice? It might involve being ready to change aspects of our relationship which others regard as fundamental, recognising which parts of it work well for all concerned, and which don't work so well. For example, some people find they are great for each other until they try living together, at which point they get on each other's nerves and start taking each other for granted. Is this a reason to end the whole relationship? Or could they try being together under some alternative form of living arrangement: living separately, or in a group of people, for example? If we do decide to cohabit, we might question the assumption that this necessarily means that we will always share a bed, eat together, pool finances, go shopping together, send cards from the both of us, or combine our DVD collections. We can be prepared to alter some of these rules if they don't work so well for us. Flexibility is about being prepared to adjust the rules as we go along. For example, if we find that one person is always nagging the other about his or her spending, the rule 'we share our money and talk through all potential purchases' might change to 'we don't comment on other people's spending habits, unless it's affecting their ability to pay their share of the bills'.

Similar flexibility might apply to the checklists we have for our relationships. In addition to talking openly about such mental lists early on, we might be open to the fact that they are likely to change over time. We may well find new interests, passions and goals which may alter, for example, whether we can promise to cohabit, to have children together at a particular time, or to have each other as our only, or primary, confidant. Of course, it is not easy to be completely flexible and open about such things. It is very human to want the kind of stability and safety which comes with commitment promises. However, our relationship may be more likely to survive, in some form, if we accept the way that other people, and ourselves, change over time, adapting to that rather than making the statement 'you've changed' as a fatal accusation (see Chapter 8).

Going back to the 'who knows what is good or bad?' story in Chapter 3, we might also remember times when we finally stopped resisting a change a partner made and found that it turned out to be good for us. For example, it may be that when we stopped jealously trying to prevent them from spending time with somebody else, we realized that we were equally free to enjoy time with other people in our lives. Or that when we stopped trying to hold them to their original plan about where we would live, we realized that we too might like to try a different kind of living situation. Flexibility towards the checklist also means that we might be better able to cope during the times when it turns out that we are unable to tick a particular box. Any relationship will inevitably bring both what we want *and* what we don't want. We may find that some of the things we didn't think we wanted were actually valuable and useful, whereas our rigid pursuance of what we *thought* we wanted was actually constraining, and we didn't always like it when we got it.

Another thing to keep in mind is that the sides of our partners that we dislike or find difficult are often intrinsically tied to the sides of them that we most value. Their nagging may be the flip side of the deep caring they have for us. Their tendency to be a drama queen may be tied to the extroversion which drew us to them in the first place. The outspoken passion which they bring to an argument is the same passion which they bring to our most loving moments. As we saw in Chapter 1, we need to be very careful when we are tempted to tweak either ourselves or another person in ways that suggest that they are flawed human beings who need fixing. It is likely to fuel the self-doubt that they already have, and it may well backfire – if they do decide to make changes – as we find that the things that were so precious about them have changed as well.

Compassion

Following from this, another thing we may want to commit to each other is compassion. In Chapter 7, we saw how this was a vital element in times of conflict. Compassion is the capacity to see things from the other person's perspective; to appreciate the situation they are in and how this might be impacting on them. It also involves recognising the plurality and changing nature of other people, rather than fixing them as they are in this moment.

Stephen Batchelor has an activity for building compassion which I will adapt here for partners.[9] You sit and close your eyes, imagining your partner in front of you and becoming aware of the mood that the idea of their presence evokes in you. You then consider what it is about them that makes you feel that way. Are you freezing them in a certain moment? You can remember how your impression of them is constantly edited and updated and has changed since yesterday or last week. You can notice how your perception of them is wrapped up in your own feelings: it has become hard to disentangle them from the 'emotionally charged image formed by [y]our own desires and fears'.

In order to look at your partner from a fresh perspective, you can then do a visualisation. Imagine them being born, coming into the world vulnerable and fragile. Follow them as they grow from toddler, to child, to adolescent, to adult, all the way up to the day when you first met them. Imagine all their hopes and fears, triumphs and tragedies, before you even knew of their existence. Think of them now as a unique person who values their feelings and ideas in the same way that you do your own, however strange they might seem to other people. Then continue into the future, watching them grow older through the inevitable illnesses and changes of ageing, and finally to their death.

Freedom

This brings us to the final commitment that we might consider making to our partners: that of freedom. In building compassion, we recognize that our partner is an autonomous person in their own right, not just someone for us. This brings us back to those ideas of de Beauvoir and others which we explored in Chapter 7. We recognize that, in order to be free ourselves, we need to embrace the freedom of our partner, and we gently remind ourselves to treat them as a mutual, full, and complex human being, rather than as a thing for our own purposes.

An example of applying freedom occurs at those difficult times in relationships when we find ourselves quantifying what we get from our partner and what they get from us. Generally, when we are in this frame of mind, the balance sheet comes up unequal and we are convinced that we give more than we get. When we embrace the freedom of the other person, and aim at mutuality rather than some kind of quantifiable equality, we can move away from relationship accounting to a more compassionate understanding of how things may look from their perspective. We can question what it means to 'give' and to 'get', anyway. We can remind ourselves that we are not responsible for their emotions and they are not responsible for ours (see Chapter 7). We can embrace the fullness of this person, rather than just looking at them through the lens of what they are for us.

In addition to this, authors such as Esther Perel have argued that some degree of freedom is essential for long-term sexual relationships. As we saw in Chapter 4, it is useful to question the excessive importance which is placed on sex as foundational to a relationship and as a barometer of its success, as well as acknowledging that sexual desire will ebb and flow, and widening out our understanding of what is meant by sex. However, many people see the erotic aspect of their relationship as very important, and recognising the separateness and freedom of our partner is key to sustaining, and developing, this over time. Freedom enables the playfulness and imagination which is required for eroticism to coexist with domesticity.[10]

To summarize, if we rewrite the rules we might consider the following alternative commitments:

- Being present.
- Flexibility.
- Compassion.
- Freedom.

Of course, true commitment to the freedom of others would involve committing to these things without expecting or assuming that we would get the same commitments back in return. We can clearly state what we want in a relationship, but also make it clear that this does not mean that we *expect* it, and that it is fine for the other person to say if it is not something that they can offer to us. If that is the case, then it may be that the relationship needs to change, or to end in its current form, and that is okay.

Beyond rules? Embracing uncertainty

If we continue this theme of freedom further, we come to a question that we have considered previously in this book: whether we treat our partners differently to the other people in our lives.

The standard rules of commitment suggest that partners are different because they belong to us, and are therefore 'ours' in a way that other people in our life are not. But, if we commit to the freedom of our partners, this is no longer the case. We recognize that treating someone as The One might not be such a wonderful thing to do to them. Rather, it may fix them in ways which constrains their freedom and makes them into something for us. Therefore we could attempt to let go of the yearning for The One and instead embrace all of the relationships in our lives (see Chapter 3). We could question distinctions that are made, for example, between friends and lovers (see Chapter 6). This might help us to break down the toxic hierarchy between singledom and coupledom (see Chapter 3), replacing it with the conceptualisation that we are all in constellations of relationships with other people, and that we are alone at the heart of this (see Chapter 6).

In Chapter 6, we saw that people often put rules and contracts in place to protect and secure certain relationships and to keep them special and separate. If we are present to our partners, and flexible in recognising that they will change over time, will we need such rules, contracts, and borders around our relationships? Instead, might we accept that both we, and our partners, will get different things from the different relationships? If we are compassionate, and embrace our partner's freedom, might we aim to accept and respect the different sides of them that emerge in different relationships (see Chapter 1) instead of trying to keep something special and sacred about them to ourselves?

We have seen how common it is to seek something in relationships which is for us, rather than for our partners. For instance, we may fear that we are flawed, due to negative messages we have received, and we may look to partners to prove to us that this is not the case, and to fill any perceived lack (see Chapters 1 and 3). As well as treating our partners as objects for us, this puts them under pressure, as we demand that they be everything to us and that they rescue us from the pain of the past (see Chapters 7 and 8). An alternative commitment is finding ways to treat *ourselves* gently and firmly, embracing our own plurality and process, such that we don't demand the impossible from our partners (see Chapter 1).

Once our partners cease to be the people from whom we demand this huge task of validation, what is it that sets them apart from others in our lives? Perhaps a totally rewritten form of commitment does not distinguish with whom commitments are made. We may commit similar things to everyone.

For the remainder of this chapter, we will consider what our commitments would look like if they were made to all of the people in our lives, rather than just those we regard as partners.

Some people try to completely flatten any hierarchies between the people in their lives, for example by refusing to say that some are more important to them than others. However laudable this aim, if rigidly applied it can be painful for those involved. Inevitably, we *do* treat different people in different ways, and it can be hard if they *feel* these differences at the same time that we insist that there are no differences, really. For example, there will be people with whom we spend more time, people with whom we are more sexual or physically intimate, people we see on a more everyday basis, people whose life projects are more bound up with our own, and people with whom we just connect better and find it easier to be around.

Therefore, as a starting point, we might reflect upon what the important aspects of relationships are for ourselves, and for those around us. For example, we saw in Chapter 4 that, for many people, a 'relationship' is what we have when we are sexual with someone. But others have questioned this way of distinguishing relationships by having non-sexual intimacy (in the case of asexual people, for example), or people with whom they are sexual but whom they do not count as partners (see Chapter 6). We might distinguish our relationships on the basis of to whom we currently feel closest, but that could deny that a friend we have known since we were 9 years old knows us in different ways because we have so much shared history. We might find that the people with whom we spend most time are colleagues, rather than partners.

How important are the following aspects in distinguishing the importance of the relationships in your life? Are there any other aspects that you would add to the list?

- Being sexual or not.
- Being physically tactile or not.
- Spending lots of time together, currently, or not.
- Living together or not.
- Having a shared history or not.
- How emotionally open you can be with each other.
- Whether you share projects and goals.
- Whether you feel you can really 'be yourself' around them.

Do the other people in your life agree with these things in relation to their own values about relationships?

You might find it useful to sketch out your own preferred way of relating to clarify how you conceptualize it. For example, in Figure 9.1 I have drawn a common way of viewing relationships in terms of the importance of different people in your life. The sexual relationship is prioritized over others, and your partner is viewed as the other half of a whole with yourself.

I offer an alternative conceptualisation which some people may prefer to this importance hierarchy. In this model, closeness is depicted by a series of concentric circles. You are in the centre, with space around you, recognising your aloneness and need for solitude. Then there is the inner circle of the closest people in your life: perhaps the people you could call up at two in the morning if you were having

Figure 9.1 Common model of relationships

a crisis, or the people you would live with if the opportunity arose. A little further out are the other people whose lives are entwined with yours and with whom you spend time regularly, and with whom you talk about the stuff of your lives. Then there is your wider circle of friends, then acquaintances, and so on. Family members aren't assumed to be in there by virtue of being related, rather, they are included if they actually are close people in your life. Boundaries between circles are permeable and people's positions shift over time.

In this model, all relationships are conceptualized as forms of friendship. This could be another useful possibility to explore because it may mean that we value our friendships more and recognize that the same skills apply to them as to other relationships (see Chapter 6). Instead of treating friendships as something that children have before they embark on 'proper relationships', we could value

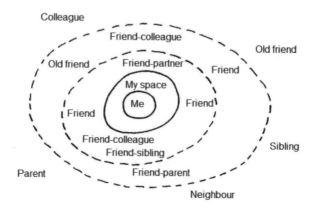

Figure 9.2 One possible alternative model of relationships

friendships in and of themselves, and prioritize the development of friendship skills in childhood as something that could prepare people for all kinds of relationships in later life (sexual, collegiate, family, etc.) Hopefully, this would also address the problem of bullying which erodes so many young people's self-confidence, leaving them the self-doubting self-monitors we met in Chapter 1.

Of course, if we go back to the ideas of Heckert and Wilkinson at the end of Chapter 6, we may not stop at considering the *people* in our lives. If we conceptualize our lives in terms of multiple loves, rather than multiple lovers, we may include companion animals, places we love, the world around us, particular times of day and, importantly, ourselves.

Might we then make the kinds of commitment which we imagined earlier to all of the loves in our lives, including ourselves? Remember that those were:

- Being present.
- Flexibility.
- Compassion.
- Freedom.

Being Present

We might aim to come to each encounter, with any of the people in our lives, open to who they are at this moment, rather than expecting them to be exactly who they were last time we saw them, recognising that there are multiple sides to both them and us (see Chapter 1).

For example, the therapeutic approach of transactional analysis suggests that we all have at least three different sides to ourselves: parent, adult, and child.[11] When we are parents, we look after people, or lecture them. When we are adults, we are reasonable, and treat others as equals. When we are children, we respond spontaneously, often emotionally, to situations. You might think about the people to whom you are close: when have you seen them, and yourselves, as the parent, adult, and child versions of themselves? These ways of being mean that there are at least nine different possible ways of relating to another person (all the combinations of parent, adult, and child).

Of course, there are many different ways of being beyond these three modes. Therapist Andrew Samuels lists the following nineteen ways in which we can be in relationships with others, and there are bound to be more as well: warrior, terrorist, exhibitionist, leader, activist, parent, follower, child, martyr, victim, trickster, healer, analyst, negotiator, bridge-builder, diplomat, philosopher, mystic, ostrich.[12] Samuels suggests cultivating the ways of being on this list which don't come so easily to us.

Being present to someone means being with whichever side they are at the moment and, potentially, allowing ourselves to respond in ways which are open to that. For example, we might find ourselves being nurturing if someone is being childlike, or attentively listening if someone is in leader mode. Being present to ourselves and others means accepting these plural selves. Sometimes, we are not in a good place to be with the way the other person is right now, and that is okay. Being present to ourselves means letting ourselves be who *we* are, and perhaps taking some time out and coming back when we're in a different place (see Chapter 7).

Such openness and presentness can be difficult to maintain all of the time, particularly with people we see every day. It is likely that we will fall into taking them for granted and treating them as if they are always the same. Perhaps it is worth building in time with the specific aim of being present to them. Can we have a protected date night with a partner or friend? A lunch with a close colleague at which we agree not to talk about work? Can we ensure that we spend time with our family members individually, instead of always all together, when we tend to fall back into old ways of relating? It is worth thinking about what we most share with each person and building in time for that. Also, we can demonstrate our commitment to being present by not being contactable to other people during such protected time.

Of course, if we are committing to this with the people in our lives then we need to commit it to ourselves as well. Can we create space to really be with ourselves doing the things we most enjoy? Going back to Chapter 1, such space will involve being kind to ourselves and giving us time to reflect on our lives. What are your preferences for this, and can you communicate this to others? You might find it easy enough to take time out walking the dog in the morning, or taking a bath when you get home in the evening. Or you might prefer to have a whole evening to yourself with nobody else around, perhaps needing the people you live with to schedule social events on a specific night to allow you that.

Some solitude helps us to be more present to other people. On a basic level, it means that we are more comfortable in ourselves and in silence, so we won't be so desperate to fill time in other people's company with chatter and activity. We can let ourselves be with them and let whatever happens, happen. Also, we can spend time alone making sure that we are not being with other people in certain ways just because this is expected of us. For example, we might feel that we have to have sex with someone because we had sex with them before, or that we have to see them every weekend because we are calling each other partners, or that we should work together because we've collaborated on projects in the past. Doing these things because we feel we should do them, rather than because we want to, is not really present to ourselves or to the other people involved.

Flexibility

The related commitment of flexibility involves accepting the fact that we, and others in our lives, will change over time: that we are a work in process. In the last chapter, we met a woman who said that she began each relationship knowing that it would be transitory, but valuing it nonetheless for the way it would enrich her life. Perhaps, instead of trying to keep relationships static, we could accept that people will come in and out of our lives. We may be together with someone for a time, learning from them and enjoying them, but we may drift apart or change in ways that mean we're no longer so valuable to each other.

Flexibility means being open to times when we have gone in different directions, and appreciating that that is okay: it doesn't have to take away from the time during which we had more in common. We might decide that it is acceptable both to become closer to people *and* to become more distant, rather than viewing the one as necessarily good and the other as necessarily bad. Of course, this involves being flexible enough with ourselves to accept that we change and not to feel that we should be some static thing for the people in our lives. This includes not berating ourselves if there is something that we are no longer able to offer. If we can accept becoming closer *and* more distant, we may find that relationships become more elastic, moving apart when our values are in different places, and becoming closer when they have reconverged again, perhaps several times over the course of our lives.

Compassion

If we expand the commitment of compassion out to ourselves and to everyone in our lives, then we might find it useful to do the compassion activity for other people beyond our partners. What is it like to imagine first a friend, then a stranger, and then someone we find difficult, through all the stages of their lives as we did for a partner before? Is compassion something that we can extend beyond those closest to us?

Compassion means putting ourselves in the shoes of others and imagining what things might be like from their perspective, rather than just seeing the world through our own lens (see Chapter 7). We can challenge ourselves to assume that, however other people are behaving, what they are doing is sensible for them, rather than saying that they are being problematic or irrational. Compassion might also involve affirming that the people in our lives are acceptable as they are, rather than pointing out their flaws and trying to change them. Perhaps this involves lowering our own masks occasionally to show that we also struggle, rather than presenting everyone with an unrealistic point of comparison against which to judge themselves (see Chapter 1).

Freedom

Finally, the commitment of freedom to ourselves and to others involves taking *mutual* responsibility in relationships: not assuming that it is the other person's responsibility to look after them and keep them going, nor assuming that they are *our* responsibility and disempowering the other person.

This is not always easy. What does it mean to acknowledge mutual responsibility in a relationship with someone who brought us up, for example, or who has taught us, or looked after us, or had power over us in some respect? Being open about such power dynamics and reflecting on how they impact on the relationship is important. Part of this is acknowledging the power inherent both in being the more obviously powerful one, *and* the less obviously powerful one. Those in positions of responsibility can feel crushed under its weight and vulnerable to criticism, just as those in less responsible positions can feel precarious and as if others have control over their lives.

There are likely multiple dimensions of power at play in any one relationship, for example in relation to who is older and younger, richer and poorer, more or less educated, more or less experienced in relationships, from different classes, cultures or genders, etc. Also, even on one dimension, power may be complexly felt by those involved. For example, some middle class people feel that they should defer to their working class partners, considering them to have more real life knowledge, and feeling guilty if they disagree with them. Similarly, while the older person in the relationship may have the power that comes with experience and being seen as more mature, the younger person has power that comes with youth (being seen as more desirable and more flexible, for example).

Power dynamics shift and change over time. Think about your parents. Perhaps there have been key moments in your relationship when you realized that they didn't have all the answers you might once have thought they had, when your level of wealth or education overtook theirs, or when they became more dependent on you than you were on them.

If we recognize that all relationships are co-constructed then conversations about these power dynamics become possible. We can embrace each other's freedom and find ways in which we might be mutually supportive of one another's projects (see Chapter 7).

Committing to freedom means valuing the freedom of others to make their own choices. This might mean demonstrating that we trust them without trying to interfere (unless we are explicitly asked for advice). We can recognize that they are the person best placed to make their decision; that how things are for us is not how things are for them; that what might not work for us might work for them; that what didn't work for them in the past might work now; and that, even if they choose something problematic, it might be a necessary and important mistake for them to make and to learn from. Committing to our own freedom means recognising that the same is true for ourselves, however much we might like to abdicate responsibility and ask other people to make our decisions for us. It means taking responsibility for the choices we do make: not expecting ourselves to find some perfect answer, but realising that what we do will impact on other people and not trying to pretend that we have no other options. Commitment to our own freedom means not offering more than we have to give, or letting go of ourselves completely in order to be something for other people. It means continuing to care for ourselves.

These are very different ways of understanding commitment to the rules with which we started this chapter.

These kinds of rules are not rules that we are given, but rules which we create for ourselves and perhaps rewrite over and over again. It is hard to know what to commit to when everything is uncertain and up for question. The examples I've given are only some suggestions, and they are by no means always easy to put into place.

Returning to that idea of being gentle and firm, it is important to hold commitments gently, rather than being tempted to cling on too tight, or to hurl them away immediately if they don't work well. It is also important to be firm. Rather than soothing ourselves by eliciting promises that no one can really make, we can commit to keep doing what we *can* offer, recognising that it will take strength and courage to stick to it.

So we return to where we started this book: the idea that loving others in our lives involves loving ourselves. When we monitor ourselves and our relationships, trying to ensure that we follow the rules and fit into what is normal, we are often completely taken up with that. We are so busy comparing ourselves, judging ourselves, and trying to improve ourselves that we don't look out beyond our own lives at all. We are so intent on making sure we're in the right relationship, that it conforms to the rules, and that other people approve of it, that we may not really see the other person we are with, either. Rewriting the rules involves finding ways of being with ourselves, and those close to us, that are less scrutinising and judging, and more open and compassionate. Practising that way of being in our intimate relationships means that we will be more tuned in to the rest of the world as well, instead of hiding away in our own little units, trapped by our own fears and desires.

In the concluding chapter of the book, we'll return to our relationship with ourselves in order to briefly explore how we might go about rewriting our own rules of relationships, in practice.

Chapter 10

Rewriting your rules

Now that we've reached the end of the book, I hope that it has been an interesting, and useful, journey through the rules of relationships. In each chapter, we've considered what the taken-for-granted rules are. We've explored reasons why we might want to question these rules. We've examined some of the alternative rules that groups and individuals have tried, and we've wondered what it would be like to go beyond rules and to embrace the idea that this aspect of relationships is uncertain: would we still want some guidelines, agreements or boundaries in place? How flexible and fluid would these be?

As I said at the start, my aim wasn't for you to follow each chapter through to the end and to agree with wherever we got to by the final paragraph. It would be a shame if that happened, because it would mean that the book wasn't open enough. Rather, I hope that you followed the path of each chapter as far as made sense for you, and picked the aspects that resonated with your experience.

It might be that you realized you were quite happy with the existing rules, but you were pleased to have had a dialogue about *why* that is the case by responding to my questions. Perhaps you're now following them in a more examined way, and understanding why they are not for everybody. It might be that one of the alternative rules put forward matched your own way of thinking perfectly, so you are now heading off to explore that in more depth, or that you already had your own alternative rules in place and it was valuable to see how other people were doing it, or to realize that you weren't alone.

One thing that I hope you will take away is that clinging to the common rules too rigidly often, paradoxically, ends up with us being less likely to get what we were aiming for in the first place. The rule that we should constantly monitor ourselves and compare ourselves to others in order to be successful actually often leaves us suffering and unfulfilled (Chapter 1). Striving towards a certain bodily appearance often leaves us less tuned in to our bodies, and may lead to a lifelong struggle with them (Chapter 2). Yearning to find The One means we are less likely to find a fulfilling relationship, as nobody can ever be totally 'perfect' or 'right' (Chapter 3). Trying to force ourselves to have 'great' and/or 'normal' sex means that we are less likely to enjoy sex as we're not tuned in to what we actually find enjoyable (Chapter 4). Striving to attract the 'opposite sex' through figuring out how their gender works and playing them gets in the way of mutually fulfilling relationships (Chapter 5). Many people find it difficult to match up to rigid rules of monogamy, and end up being non-consensually non-monogamous (Chapter 6). Attempting to avoid conflict often leads to conflict (Chapter 7). Finally, rigid rules around breaking up and staying together can put pressure on relationships, meaning that we either leave them too quickly or stay in them when we are miserable (Chapters 8 and 9).

If you have stuck with the book as far as this, I'm guessing that the idea of rewriting your rules has some relevance to you, and that you are now considering doing this yourself in relation to at least one of the aspects of relationships that we've covered. For that reason, this final chapter offers some practical suggestions for how to go about rewriting your rules from here. It includes some of the problems and pitfalls you may come across, as well as some ideas for how you might work rewriting your rules into your life on a more daily basis.

Why not rewrite your rules?

We have touched on the fact that many barriers are in place when we decide to rewrite our rules. It is important to be aware of these, because it is by no means an easy or pain-free path that you are taking.

In one of his Discworld novels, Terry Pratchett introduces the metaphor of the crab bucket. Someone explains to the main character, Glenda, that you don't need a lid on a bucket of crabs: if any of the crabs make it over the rim of the bucket, all the other crabs will pull it back in. Pratchett continues:

> Crab bucket, thought Glenda . . . That's how it works. People . . . disapproving when a girl takes the trolley bus. That's crab bucket. Practically everything my mum ever told me, that's crab bucket. Practically everything I've ever told Juliet, that's crab bucket, too . . . It's so nice and warm on the inside that you forget that there's an outside. The worst of it is, the crab that mostly keeps you down is you.[1]

Perhaps the main thing that prevents us from rewriting our rules is the crab bucket: both the other crabs pulling us back into the bucket if we show any sign of leaving, and the comfortable cosiness that we, ourselves, find in the bucket, mean that we are unlikely to go over the top on our own.

As Pratchett, and the philosopher Michel Foucault, both point out, these days the crab bucket is rarely policed with a mallet. In most arenas it is not that we will be hit over the head if we leave the bucket (as we would, for example, if we were bisexual, lesbian, or gay, in one of the countries which still considers homosexuality to be a crime). Rather, the crab bucket is policed by our own self-monitoring (see Chapter 1) as we compare ourselves against each other, and try hard to be normal like everyone else (the other crabs). It is policed by the disapproval which we fear so much because it will reinforce our belief that we're not really okay. It is policed by ridicule, and the fear of standing out from the crowd and being exposed as freakish, weird, or different.

To put it another way, a colleague saying 'Aren't those last season's shoes?' That's crab bucket. Looks of pity on the face of your relatives when they ask if you've found a nice boy or girl yet. That's crab bucket. Gossipy water cooler conversations about everyone else's sex life: crab bucket too. Jokey teasing about how your heterosexual mate is feminine or gay, that's crab bucket. The community writing a petition to try to close down the swingers' club in their neighbourhood: very much crab bucket. Neighbours' disapproving glances when they overhear you having an argument: also crab bucket. You saying 'He's a bastard' or 'She's a bitch' when your friend goes through a break-up: you're in the crab bucket. Everyone asking when you're going to tie the knot: crab bucket. That constant nagging fear in the back of your mind that you might not be normal. That is *definitely* crab bucket.

Even if you do rewrite the rules, you will not necessarily find yourself out of the crab bucket. As we've seen, those who step outside the mainstream rules often cling hard to any alternative rules they can find, because being on the outside is such a precarious place to be. That often means wanting everybody else in their group to reinforce those rules by following them too. There are queer crab buckets, alternative crab buckets, lesbian crab buckets, Buddhist crab buckets, swinger crab buckets, academic crab buckets, trans crab buckets, goth crab buckets, therapist crab buckets, kink crab buckets, anarchist crab buckets, and asexual crab buckets. There is a certain irony as people in these groups look over to the mainstream crab bucket and see what is going on there, perhaps laughing at the crabs being pulled back into the bucket, not realizing that they are doing exactly the same thing. In order to avoid this, it is important that we recognize that there are multiple ways of rewriting the rules, and that what works for us may not be what works for somebody else.

The point of all this is to emphasize that the rewriting of rules is by no means easy. We have seen throughout this book how those who rewrite the rules are often demonized, pathologized or ridiculed: viewed as being bad, sick, or foolish. Remember Rubin's charmed circle and outer limits of sex (Chapter 4), or the bullying and hate crimes against people who step too far outside the rules of gender (Chapter 5), or the lack of legal rights for people who have more than one partner (Chapter 6)?

Also, when we rewrite the rules we are often held to a much higher standard than everyone else. It's as if we have to be the poster child for the thing that we are doing differently. If we're the only gay couple on our street then we may well be viewed as representative of all gay people and feel under pressure never to have a public argument or loud sex. If we do ever mess up or fall over, and we are outside the rules, then we are likely to be criticized for it far more than anybody else would be. We saw in Chapter 6 that, when polyamorous people break up, their monogamous friends and family often take that as proof that polyamory cannot work, whereas monogamy is rarely blamed for the break-up of monogamous relationships. The comedian Eddie Izzard has a routine about how it is not considered okay if he falls over wearing high-heels, even thought it is considered endearing if a woman like Sandra Bullock falls over her heels in a movie. If a person who is into kinky sex is sexually assaulted, they are treated as more responsible for what happened than a person who is not into kinky sex. You can almost hear the condemnation – 'What did you expect if you stepped outside the crab bucket?' – and also the relief, because if you *had* 'succeeded' it would have meant that those inside the crab bucket might be better off outside it as well, and that is a terrifying prospect for them.

What can we do about this? If we are keen to rewrite our rules then it is worth keeping in mind that we are not on an easy path, and that there will be an almost gravitational pull back into the crab bucket, or into a new crab bucket. Awareness of that, and support from others who are also rewriting their rules, can help a great deal.

Rewriters of rules ourselves, or not, we *can* make a commitment to try not to be judgemental of people who are doing things differently. If we could stop stigmatizing anyone who steps outside the norm, and be more accepting of a diversity of ways of living and relating, then life would be a good deal better for everyone. Those who do rewrite the rules to some extent would also feel less of a desperate need to cling to new rules or to completely reject and dismiss people who follow the old ones. One thing that I have tried to do in my own work is to challenge the standard way of treating people who step outside the rules (as objects of fascination who we need to explain) and, instead, to treat them as a diverse group of people who probably have many reasons for doing what they are doing, and from whom we potentially have much to learn (about specific ways of rewriting rules, and about what that process is like).

The crab bucket situation, as we have seen, means that we are constantly drawn into 'them and us' thinking. Either 'they' are the freaks who have left the crab bucket and who threaten and endanger us and 'we' are the normal people who are doing things right, or 'they' are the blind idiots scuttling around in the bucket and 'we' are the wonderfully liberated rebels who can see just how stupid they are. Each of these 'them and us' ways of thinking reinforces the other. It is important to realize that we can't step outside of culture entirely. We are always in relation to it in some way, whether we are reproducing it or resisting it. If we resist it in this critical, ridiculing, judgemental, fashion, then we actually reinforce the beliefs that most people have about what those outside the crab bucket are like. Indeed, we may well make it even harder for other people to leave the crab bucket. Going back to Chapter 7, perhaps what is needed is compassionate listening on both sides, rather than dichotomizing the world into 'them and us' and demonizing and stigmatizing the other. Countless psychological and socio-historical studies have shown us that 'them and us' thinking is the first step on the path to cruelty and tyranny. Being on the outside of the crab bucket is no excuse for doing it.

These difficulties inherent in rewriting the rules point us back again and again to the importance of caring for ourselves when we embark upon such a project.

It is tempting, once we realize that we have been stuck in these rules for ages, to throw them all up in the air simultaneously and to try to live differently immediately. This is extraordinarily difficult: habits of a lifetime are rarely broken in a few hours, and the kind of shock and disapproval we will get from those around us will be hard to bear. Perhaps we can consider how we might rewrite our rules in ways that are gentle and compassionate with both ourselves and others, instead of demanding that we, and everyone around us, accept and celebrate a complete transformation overnight.

Related to this is the fact that embarking on a process of self-transformation can easily slip back into that hard way of being which we covered in Chapter 1. It can feed the idea that we are not okay the way we are and that we need to be better. That is not to say that we can't change, and that it isn't a good idea to rewrite our rules. However, we need to think carefully about why we are doing it, and take the process gently, rather than using it as a way of eradicating everything about ourselves that we don't like.

On a similar note, if we throw ourselves too blindly and completely into processes of change, we can end up becoming quite self-focused and not being there for the people around us, even as we demand *their* support for what we are doing. While others do need to respect that you are doing what is right for you, rather than trying to make you do things their way, it is important that you also respect their way of doing things. To be mutually supportive, we must care for the people in our lives through what they are doing, as well as for ourselves through what we are doing.

Perhaps the hardest thing about rewriting the rules is that it is likely (I would go so far as to say inevitable) that you and others will be hurt in the process. When you step outside of the taken-for-granted rules and start writing them yourself, you are very likely to stumble and fall over along the way, because there is much less to hang onto. For example, you might well find yourself grabbing a new rule too tightly, and insisting that other people in your life grab it too, even though it isn't good for them at all. Or you might become tense and uptight around people in your life, such as family, who are still following the old rules, and hurt their feelings. Or you might launch into some new community thinking that it is perfect, and end up feeling hurt and betrayed when you realize that the people you meet there are human and flawed too.

At such times, it is easy to become overwhelmed with guilt and self-recrimination, to feel a total fool, perhaps to sneak sheepishly back into the crab bucket. Alternatively, you might lash out with a bunch of self-justifications (see Chapter 7) and carry on regardless, convincing yourself that there is some perfect world around the corner if you just keep going. Either way, you are hurting, and people around you are probably hurting too.

To balance this, it is vital to remember that there is suffering within the rules at least as much as there is outside them. It is not that there would have been no pain, for yourself or others, if you had remained within the rules. It is painful to feel constrained by the rules, and it is cruel to others to keep on insisting that they follow them.

When we hurt ourselves and others through rewriting the rules, perhaps we can resist the urge to drown in guilt (which doesn't really make it better anyway) or to bolster ourselves with false self-justifications. Perhaps we can acknowledge that when we make choices in our lives they *will* impact on ourselves and on others, and take responsibility for that impact. Perhaps we can acknowledge that it was 'my bad' and sincerely apologize, letting ourselves really hear how the other person is hurting, taking their forgiveness if it is offered, not insisting upon it if it is not. Going back to Chapter 1, by facing the inevitable imperfections, flaws and potential in ourselves we can more easily own up to them when we do behave poorly, and also forgive others when they do the same, because we know that we share that capacity.

In relation to this, it is worth being prepared for the fact that some people who are close to us may well claim that they have been hurt when we rewrite our rules, saying, for example, that this means that what we are doing is wrong. For example, there is the parent who says 'How could you be gay? You're breaking my heart', the wife who tells her husband that he isn't allowed to wear a dress because it hurts her too much, or the friend who says they won't be friends with somebody who is kinky because they find it too disgusting to imagine. At such times, it is well worth remembering that we are not responsible for other people's emotions, and that it really *is* okay to rewrite the rules. We may want to be patient and give such people time to adjust, but it *is* down to them to change their attitude, rather than being down to us to drown in shame and guilt, or to stop what we're doing.

If we have made it clear to someone in our lives that we're not going to follow the mainstream rules, then it isn't fair for them to turn around later and say that it wasn't okay with them for us to do that. If we didn't know that we were going to rewrite the rules, but found that we wanted to later on, this is still fine, because people change over time. The only thing that isn't okay is when we know that we want to rewrite the rules in some way, but don't tell people around us because we think they would be displeased (for example, if we are non-monogamous without telling our partner, or keep an important part of our lives from those to whom we are closest). However, in this case, if they find out and are upset by it, it isn't rewriting the rules which was problematic, but rather the deception involved.

Finally, it is important to remember that, as we have seen, uncertainty can be a very difficult thing for humans to handle. We might rewrite our rules to such an extent that we recognize that we, and everyone around us, is plural and in process, and that there are no given rules to hold onto, and that we make our own meanings in life. However, this may leave us feeling untethered in a scary way, as if we are floating around with nothing to anchor us. We can feel that we are going crazy, especially when we are in a world in which most people around us do believe in the rules and follow them rigidly.

I think that an idea from Buddhism can be helpful here, and that is the notion of 'chop wood, carry water'. Buddhist monks are in a lifelong process of rewriting the rules: they are called upon to embrace uncertainty, to recognize that they have no coherent self, and to have compassion to all creatures, drawing no lines between them. To do this, they meditate for hours a day, days a week, and weeks a year.

What do they do to stop themselves floating away and disintegrating entirely? They chop wood and carry water. They ground themselves in the very practical and mundane tasks of everyday living: often those that remind them how much they are in the world, and the day to day rituals that care for their bodies and the bodies of others.

If you are keen to rewrite your rules, I would suggest that you also think carefully about how you will ground yourself on a daily basis. When we are drawn to different ways of living and relating, we can easily spend a lot of time thinking about it, writing about it, reading about it, and talking to like-minded people about it. We can find ourselves becoming tangled up and confused in the various threads of the ideas that we are spinning, maybe even to the point where we obsess that some mysterious answer is just out of our grip, or become paranoid that other people are trying to prevent us from finding it. Going outside the rules can be a frightening place to be.

Given that our daily lives are unlikely to involve chopping wood or carrying water, what might we do to ground ourselves? Think about what works for you.

Generally, the types of things which work well are those which ground us in the physical world, those which remind us of the fact that we inhabit our bodies (see Chapter 2), and those which involve gently bringing ourselves back to the present moment, rather than spinning off into thinking or talking about ideas (see Chapter 9). Some possibilities you might consider include:

- Going for a walk during which you focus on the sights and sounds around you and the feel of your body, rather than getting carried off on thoughts or plans (swimming, riding, driving, running, or other activities can also work in this way).
- Cooking meals for yourself (and/or others) where your focus is on the rhythm of chopping the food, putting it together, and enjoying the process.
- Enjoying a hot bath, a sauna, a massage, or anything that involves focus on physical sensations.
- Practising daily breathing or walking meditations which are all about being in the present moment, rather than reflection or analysis.[2]
- Focusing on a good book, movie, piece of music, or TV programme.
- Having conversations with the kinds of friends who help you to feel grounded and good about yourself in the world.
- Building in some daily rituals that ground you, such as taking 5 minutes to sit and enjoy the scenery when you walk the dog, leaving early so you have half an hour in a café before work, or practising being in the moment every time you wash your hands or wash the dishes.[3]
- Thinking about the structure of your day: the structure of regular work is a very grounding thing for many people. If you are unemployed, retired, or work from home, you can end up feeling quite untethered, so it is worth building some structure and contact with other people into your days and weeks, in ways which work for you.

Practical suggestions for rule rewriting

Thinking back to Chapter 1, the ideas which I just suggested here map very much onto gentleness. If you remember, I said that it is important to build both kind, and reflective, self-care into our lives. The reflective type of self-care maps more onto being firm with ourselves. If we are serious about rewriting the rules, we also need time to reflect on how we're going to do it, grounding this in kind self-care so that we are strong enough to do it, and aware of the limits on how far we are able to go.

The danger with reflective self-care is that it can turn us in on ourselves further, rather than out towards the world. In the Introduction, I called this book an 'anti-self-help book' because I didn't want it to be yet another book that tells you that there is something wrong with you that you need to put right by further self-monitoring and self-perfecting. The rules we have criticized in this book are out there in the world; they are not problems within individuals which need fixing. However, it is easy to slip back into that common way of thinking and to focus too much on ourselves and our relationships, berating ourselves for following the rules and trying to change ourselves and/or our relationships to make us better. We can end up spending much of our lives bound up in the drama of figuring out what is 'wrong' with us, or analysing our relationships, finding that we have less and less time and energy for anyone else in our lives or for doing anything more proactive about addressing the cultural rules which are the real root of the problem.

For this reason, it is worth considering both forms of personal reflective self-care which you might build into your life, and ways in which you might engage in more social change if you are convinced that some of the rules around us are not so useful. You will probably find that the two feed into each other

Here are some suggestions for personal reflection:

- Doing some of the activities suggested through this book and on the website (www.rewriting-the-rules.com).
- Keeping a journal or blog in which you write about your thoughts, reflections, and experiences as you engage in rewriting the rules. You might find it helpful to write dialogues between different aspects of yourself, or letters to future or past versions of yourself (see Chapter 1).[4]
- Finding ways of looking back over your life story and coming to love that (see Chapter 1). For example, writing memories which are sparked by particular objects, making montages with music or photographs, drawing comics strips of key moments, or creating story bracelets with different beads representing different events.
- Giving yourself thinking time in the day, during which you sit somewhere quiet and conducive to thought and allow yourself to mull over what is going on and how you might creatively engage with it.
- Building a thinking partnership with a friend.[5] You can meet regularly and each allow the other person 30 uninterrupted minutes to talk through their

thoughts, experiences, and reflections, and to be listened to by someone who will help them work it through.

- Practising more proactive forms of meditation, like the compassion meditation in Chapter 9.
- Reading other books and websites mentioned in the notes at the end of this book, on the website, or recommended by friends, which address these kinds of questions and speak to you.

Here are some possibilities for more social forms of activism:

- Joining a group of like-minded people locally or online where you can discuss the issues that interest you most and provide mutual support (for example, there are communities for different sexualities, or ways of doing relationships, or for certain political, philosophical, or spiritual beliefs which resonate with the ideas presented in this book. Putting these terms into an online search engine should allow you to find them).
- Finding and carrying out your own mini-activist strategies, like the stickers that my friend Trish put up about attractiveness (see Chapter 2).
- Getting involved in listening to and/or counselling other people who are struggling with these issues, for example through phone helplines or voluntary counselling organizations.
- Making art, music, poetry, or fiction about the rules you find problematic, or alternative ways of relating, which you can share.
- Contributing articles, or creating blogs, about these topics for other people to read.
- Writing letters to newspapers, TV companies, or advertising standards authorities about their representations.
- Writing and speaking to politicians and law-makers about relevant policies and laws which you think would be worth changing.
- Getting involved in training and education: for example, training medics or police about groups who are outside mainstream rules, or offering sex or relationship training to young people.
- Putting on events for like-minded people if nothing already exists.
- Making yourself visible as someone who is doing things differently and is happy with that, ensuring that you have the energy required to do this, that you have access to support if you do face criticism for it, and that others in your life are willing for you to do this if it means identifying them too.

With all of these lists, it is important to remember that different things work for different people at different times.[6] There is no one perfect way to practice kind or reflective self care, and we will all have different strengths and skills that we can bring to social engagement, rather than thinking that we *should* be able to do something that isn't for us.

Also, it is important to be realistic about self-care. Many people assume that they *ought* to meditate, keep a journal, do yoga, and everything else, and this becomes another stick with which to beat themselves when they are not doing these things. We need to consider which forms of self-care we'd actually like to do (otherwise we'll probably let them slip and feel bad about it), and which we can realistically build into our everyday lives. We also need to be careful about the reason for doing them, lest we fall back into self-perfecting and trying to fix ourselves.[7]

Another stumbling block about self-care is the idea that caring for ourselves is selfish. Most of my clients and friends have found it very difficult to build in daily kindnesses towards themselves, or to give themselves an hour in a café writing once a week, because they have a big message that this constitutes being self-absorbed, self-centred and spoiling themselves. In response to this, I would say that we are *not* good for the people around us if we don't care for ourselves. We might think that we are self-sacrificing if we spend every moment of the day on other people and never take a moment for ourselves, but this probably means that we are a negative influence on those around us in the following ways:

- If we haven't rested and been kind to ourselves, we are likely to be wrung out and tired and not to have much to offer the people in our lives when they want our support.
- If we never take time for reflection, then we are likely to respond to other people in a knee-jerk fashion, just repeating what we have heard or making assumptions about what may be helpful to them. If we have taken time to inform ourselves and reflect on these matters, then we may have much more useful, and nuanced, advice to offer.
- If we don't care for ourselves, we are more likely to respond to other people in ways that shore up our own sense of self, for example by trying to keep them in the crab bucket, or by encouraging them to be things for us, rather than for themselves.
- If we aren't used to looking after ourselves, then we are likely to have poor ideas about what we are, and are not, able to offer other people, perhaps offering too much and then resenting it, or having to admit that we can't actually offer it and pulling the rug out from under the people to whom we have offered it.
- If we don't care for ourselves, then we are poor role models for others in our lives, giving them the impression that self-care is only necessary if you are weak or selfish, for example.
- If we don't look after ourselves, we are not likely to be very good in conflict situations because we won't find it easy to put ourselves into others' shoes or to hear them (see Chapter 7).
- If we make our lives all about other people, we are likely, eventually, to resent that, or to become scared and threatened if those other people show signs of not needing us any more. If we don't embrace our own freedom, then it is hard to embrace the freedom of others, and we are likely to be drawn into fixing them (see Chapters 5 and 7).

I would like to conclude this chapter with a reminder that rewriting the rules is not a one-off event, but rather a continual process. Like a spiral, we will likely find ourselves going over the same ground again and again, but each time perhaps going a little deeper, so we shouldn't be concerned if we sometimes find ourselves right back where we started. If you read a chapter in this book more than once over the years, you may well find that it is still relevant, but that different aspects of it resonate with you the second, or third, time around.

So, rather than holding on to a new rule once we have it, perhaps we can remember to treat it lightly and be prepared to let it go, or at least to edit it, as situations change. For example, I remember a colleague who said that a major rule for her was to always trust friends over partners, because they were the ones who had her best interests at heart. Then she found herself in a situation where she had a kind and supportive partner, but some quite self-centred friends. She changed her rule to 'trust whoever has my best interests at heart, regardless of who they are'. Possibly, as her life goes on, that rule, too, will change. Similarly, when I was first writing about sex I rewrote the rule that people should have 'normal' sex to be that people should have whatever consensual sex was pleasurable to them. However, I still regarded sex as being a pretty fundamental thing in people's lives, and thought that lack of sexual desire probably meant that something was wrong. If you read Chapter 4, you will see that I have now rewritten that rule and believe that sex is something that can ebb and flow and that it is perfectly fine to have periods, or even a lifetime, of not being sexual (in the standard sense) if that's what works for us. Perhaps that is a rule that will change again for me, as time goes on.

I found an illustration of the need to keep rewriting the rules in an essay by the writer Mary Gaitskill. She says that 'Growing up in the 1960s, I had been taught only how to follow rules that were more important than I was'. For Gaitskill, the rule that 'good girls never had sex and bad girls did' was later supplanted by the rule that 'if you were cool you wanted to have sex as much as possible with as many people as possible'. She goes on to say that these rules encumbered her with an 'inability to speak (for myself) . . . because I had never been taught how'.[8] I hope that this book gives some practical suggestions for how you might speak for yourself and write your own rules, as well as elaborating some of the pitfalls and problems that are likely to come up.

I want to end this book by thanking you for your bravery and commitment in following me on this journey. I will finish with a quote from Vivien Burr and Trevor Butt, whose work we've met throughout this book.

> It is a brave person who tries to defy the categories, expectations and anticipations of others. Individual reconstruing is not necessarily echoed throughout the rest of society. But surely there can be no such change without it.[9]

Notes

Introduction

1 Plummer, K. (2003). *Intimate citizenship*. Seattle, WA: University of Washington Press.
2 Giddens, A. (1992). *The transformation of intimacy: Sexuality, love and eroticism in modern societies*. Cambridge: Polity Press.
3 Copping, J. (2009). 'Recession sees marriage rate rise'. Accessed from www.telegraph.co.uk/finance/recession/4409405/Recession-sees-marriage-rate-rise.html on 7 November 2011.
4 Bauman, Z. (2003). *Liquid love: On the frailty of human bonds*. Cambridge: Polity Press.
5 Thanks to Relate therapist Rose-Mary Owen for this analogy.
6 Detailed statistics for the US are available from www.divorcerate.org. The UK ONS statistics are summarized on www.ons.gov.uk/ons/rel/vsob1/divorces-in-england-and-wales/2009/index.html. Accessed on 1 November 2011.
7 Duncombe, J., Harrison, K., Allan, G., & Marsden, D. (Eds) (2004). *The state of affairs: Explorations in infidelity and commitment*. New Jersey: Lawrence Erlbaum Associates, Inc.
8 The UK ONS statistics on this are summarized on www.statistics.gov.uk/hub/people-places/housing-and-households/households. Accessed on 1 November 2011.
9 Beck, U., & Beck-Gernsheim, E. (1995). *The normal chaos of love* (p. 5). Cambridge: Polity Press.
10 Batchelor, M. (2001). *Meditation for life*. London: Frances Lincoln.
11 Warner, M. (1999). *The trouble with normal: Sex, politics, and the ethics of queer life*. Cambridge, MA: Harvard University Press.
12 Thanks to Cathy Aymer of Brunel University for this analogy.

1 Rewriting the rules of yourself

1 You can read more about this sense of lack in Majid, B. (2008). *Ending the pursuit of happiness*. Somerville, MA: Wisdom.
2 There are several recent books which explore these ideas in more depth. For example, de Botton, A. (2004). *Status anxiety*. London: Penguin; James, O. (2007). *Affluenza*. London: Vermilion; and Naish, J. (2008). *Enough*. London: Hodder and Stoughton.
3 The idea that people are encouraged to constantly monitor themselves comes from the French philosopher Michel Foucault. A good introduction to his work is Downing, L. (2008). *The Cambridge introduction to Foucault*. Cambridge: Cambridge University Press.

4 If you want to know more about anxiety and depression, the main current theories and therapies are covered in Barker, M., Vossler, A., & Langdridge, D. (Eds) (2010). *Understanding counselling and psychotherapy*. London: Sage.
5 You can read about this study in Butt, T. (2004). *Understanding people*. London: Palgrave Macmillan.
6 Rowan, J., & Cooper, M. (Eds) (1999). *The plural self: Multiplicity in everyday life*. London: Sage.
7 This activity comes from Neimeyer, R. A. (2006). *Lessons of loss: A guide to coping*. Memphis, TN: Center for the Study of Loss and Transition.
8 Spinelli, E. (2005). *The interpreted world: An introduction to phenomenological psychology*. London: Sage.
9 Gergen, K. J. (2000). *The saturated self*. New York, NY: Perseus Books.
10 Plummer, K. (1995). *Telling sexual stories: Power, change and social worlds*. London: Routledge.
11 Bazzano, M. (2009). Brave new worlding. *Existential Analysis*, *20*(1), 9–19.
12 Much of this chapter is informed by Stephen's book, Batchelor, S. (1997). *Buddhism without beliefs*. London: Bloomsbury.
13 Batchelor, M. (2007). *Let go: A Buddhist guide to breaking free of habits*. Somerville, MA: Wisdom.
14 Van Deurzen, E. (1998). *Paradox and passion in psychotherapy: An existential approach to therapy and counselling* (p. 13). London: Wiley.

2 Rewriting the rules of attraction

1 At the time of writing, you could find magazine lists of the top 'sexiest women' at http://www.fhm.com/girls/100–sexiest-women and men at www.glamourmagazine.co.uk/celebrity/sexiest-men. Accessed on 1 November 2011.
2 Much of this chapter is informed by Gill's work, which is nicely summarized in Gill, R. (2006). *Gender and the media*. London: Polity Press.
3 Gill, R., & Scharff, C. (Eds) (2011). *New femininities: Postfeminism, Neoliberalism and subjectivity*. Basingstoke, Palgrave Macmillan.
4 Gill, R. (2007). Supersexualize me: Advertising and the 'midriffs', in F. Attwood (Ed.), *Mainstreaming sex: The sexualization of culture* (pp. 93–110). London: I.B. Tauris.
5 One demonstration of this is the Dove Evolution video, which could be found here at the time of writing: www.youtube.com/watch?v=hibyAJOSW8U. Accessed on 1 November 2011.
6 British Medical Association (2000). *Eating disorders, body image and the media*. London: British Medical Association.
7 Becker, A. E. (1995). *Body, self and society: The view from Fiji*. Pennsylvania, PA: University of Pennsylvania Press.
8 Grigg, M., Bowman, J., & Redman, S. (1996). Disordered eating and unhealthy weight reduction practices among adolescent females. *Preventive Medicine*, *25*, 748–56.
9 Garner, D. M. (1997). Body image survey. *Psychology Today*, *30*, 30–85.
10 Harper, D., Wacker, D. P., & Cobb, L. S. (1986). Children's preferences toward peers with visible physical differences. *Journal of Pediatric Psychology*, *11*, 323–342.
11 Colles, L. (1998). *Fat: Exploding the myths*. London: Carlton Books Ltd.
12 Stainton-Rogers, W., & Stainton-Rogers, R. (2001). *The psychology of gender and sexuality*. Buckingham. Open University Press.
13 At the time of writing, you could still view the clip on: www.youtube.com/watch?v=RxPZh4AnWyk. Accessed on 1 November 2011. A similar moment happens in the short story *The Dance of the Happy Shades* by Alice Munro, in her edited collection of the same name.

14 Hardie, E., & Buzwell, S. (2006). Finding love online: The nature and frequency of Australian adults' internet relationships. *Australian Journal of Emerging Technologies and Society*, *4*(1), 1–14.

15 Jenkins, E. (1999). *Tongue first: Adventures in physical culture* (p. 7). New York, Virago.

16 Wolf, N. (1991). *The beauty myth*. London: Vintage.

17 Cooke, K. (1996). *Real gorgeous: The truth about body and beauty*. London: Bloomsbury.

18 Orbach, S. (2010). *Bodies*. London: Profile Books.

19 Matthews, E. (2006). *Merleau-Ponty: A Guide for the Perplexed*. London: Continuum.

20 Malson, H. (1998). *The thin woman*. London: Routledge.

21 Bordo, S. (1990). Reading the slender body. In M. Jacobus, E. Fox Keller, & S. Shuttleworth (Eds.), *Body/Politics: Women and the discourses of science* (pp. 83–112 at p. 89). London: Routledge.

22 del Busso, L., & Reavey, P. (2011). Moving beyond the surface: A poststructuralist phenomenology of young women's embodied experiences in everyday life. *Psychology & Sexuality*. Available online at DOI 10.1080/19419899.2011.589866. Accessed on 1 November 2011.

3 Rewriting the rules of love

1 Ussher, J. M. (1997). *Fantasies of femininity: Reframing the boundaries of sex*. London: Penguin.

2 Gauntlett, D. (2008). *Media, gender and identity: An introduction*. London: Routledge.

3 Zappa, F. (1990). *The real Frank Zappa book* (p. 89). London: Picador.

4 Johnson, K. R., & Holmes, B. M. (2009). Contradictory messages: A content analysis of Hollywood-produced romantic comedy feature films. *Communication Quarterly*, *57*, 352–373.

5 Holmes, B. M. (2007). In search for my 'one and only': Romance-oriented media and beliefs in romantic relationships destiny. *Electronic Journal of Communication, 17*(3).

6 Baucom, D., & Epstein, N. (1990). *Cognitive-behavioural marital therapy*. New York, NY: Brunner/Mazel.

7 E.g. Snyder, B. (2005). *Save the cat: The only book on screenwriting you'll ever need*. Studio City, CA: Michael Wiese Productions.

8 Hogg, M., & Vaughan, G. (2010). *Social psychology*. Upper Saddle River, NJ: Prentice Hall.

9 Coontz, S. (2005). *Marriage, a history*. New York, NY: Penguin.

10 Ibid., p. 10.

11 Gill, R. (2006). *Gender and the media*. London: Polity Press. See also DePaulo, B. (2006). *Singled out. How singles are stereotyped, stigmatised and ignored, and still live happily ever after*. New York, NY: St. Martin's Griffin.

12 A breakdown of the reasons why this statistic is untrue could be found on www.snopes.com/science/stats/terrorist.asp at the time of writing.

13 Hansen-Miller, D., & Gill, R. (2011). 'Lad flicks': Discursive reconstructions of masculinity in popular film. In H. Radner & E. Pullar (Eds.), *Feminism at the movies*. New York: Routledge.

14 Gerstel, N., & Sarkisian, N. (2006). Marriage: The good, the bad, and the greedy. *Contexts, 5*(4), 16–21.

15 You can find the original version in Hagan, S. (1997). *Buddhism plain and simple* (p. 42). London: Penguin.

16 Storr., A. (1997). *Solitude*. London: HarperCollins.

17 Johnstone, L. (2000). *Users and abusers of psychiatry*. London: Routledge.
18 Fullbrook, E., & Fullbrook, K. (2008). *Sex and philosophy: Rethinking de Beavoir and Sartre*. London: Continuum.
19 Knowles, R., & Moon, R. (2006). *Introducing metaphor*. London: Routledge. Thanks to Simon Harrison for introducing me to these ideas.
20 Burr, V., & Butt, T. (1992). *Invitation to personal construct psychology*. London: Whurr Publishers Ltd.
21 This idea is discussed in more depth in Welwood, J. (2006). *Perfect love, imperfect relationships*. Boston, MA: Trumpeter.

4 Rewriting the rules of sex

1 Plummer, K. (1995). *Telling sexual stories: Power, change and social worlds*. London: Routledge.
2 Sex therapist Pamela Stephenson-Connolly points out the same thing, and challenges this idea of 'normal' sex in useful ways in her book Stephenson-Connolly, P. (2011). *Sex life*. London: Vermillion.
3 Rubin, G. (1984). Thinking sex: Notes for a radical theory of the politics of sexuality. In G. Rubin (2012). *Deviations: A Gayle Rubin Reader* (pp. 137–181). Durham, NC: Duke University Press.
4 This diagram is from p. 152 of Rubin's paper. For an updated version which imagines what the circles look like now that people are trying to have sex which is both 'normal' and 'great', see Mulholland, M. (2011). When porno meets hetero: Sexpo, heteronormativity and the pornification of the mainstream. *Australian Feminist Studies*, *26*(67), 119–135.
5 Attwood, F. (Ed.) (2007). *Mainstreaming sex: The sexualization of culture* (pp. 93–110). London: I. B. Tauris.
6 Storr, M. (2003). *Latex and lingerie: Shopping for pleasure at Ann Summers*. Oxford: Berg.
7 Byers, E. S. (2005). Relationship satisfaction and sexual satisfaction: A longitudinal study of individuals in long-term relationships. *The Journal of Sex Research*, *42*, 113–118.
8 Miller, S. A., & Byers, E. S. (2004). Actual and desired duration of foreplay and intercourse: Discordance and misperceptions within heterosexual couples. *The Journal of Sex Research, 41*, 301–309.
9 Macdowall, W., Wellings, K., Nanchahal, K., Mercer, C. H., Erens, B., Fenton, K. A., & Johnson, A. M. (2002). Learning about sex: Results from Natsal 2000. *Journal of Epidemiology and Community Health*, *56* (supplement 2), A1–A26.
10 Barker, M. (2011). De Beauvoir, Bridget Jones's Pants and Vaginismus. *Existential Analysis*, *22*(2), 203–216.
11 Barker, M. (2011). Existential sex therapy. S*exual and Relationship Therapy*, *26*(1), 33–47.
12 Hite, S. (1976). *The Hite report on female sexuality*. New York, NY: Dell.
13 The clitoris extends back through the body which means that, for some, it *is* stimulated by vaginal or anal penetration. Also, some can orgasm purely through tensing the muscles in the pelvic region, some by stimulation of other body regions, and some from breathing in certain ways or fantasising. For more about different kinds of orgasms, see Carrellas, B. (2007). *Urban tantra*. Berkeley, CA: Celestial Arts.
14 Barker, M., Bowes-Catton, H., Iantaffi, A., Cassidy, A., & Brewer, L. (2008). British bisexuality: A snapshot of bisexual identities in the UK. *Journal of Bisexuality*, *8*, 141–162.
15 Clarke, V., Ellis, S. E., Peel, E., & Riggs, D. W. (2009). *Lesbian, gay, bisexual, transgender and queer psychology: An introduction*. Cambridge: Cambridge University Press.

16 Rochlin, M. (2003). The heterosexual questionnaire. In M. S. Kimmel & A. L. Ferber (Eds.), *Privilege: A reader* (pp.75–76). Boulder, CO: Westview Press. Available from http://www.pinkpractice.co.uk/quaire.htm at the time of writing.

17 Kitzinger, C. (2005). Heteronormativity in action: Reproducing the heterosexual nuclear family in after-hours medical calls. *Social Problems, 52*(4), 477–498.

18 Weeks, J. (2003). *Sexuality*. London: Routledge.

19 Reiner, P. B. (2009). Meditation on demand. *Scientific American*. Available from http://www.scientificamerican.com/article.cfm?id=meditation-on-demand at the time of writing.

20 For more detail on this, see Hird, M. (2005). *Sex, gender and science*. Basingstoke: Palgrave Macmillan.

21 This example comes from a presentation Leonore Tiefer gave to the 'sexualisation of culture' conference in late 2011, but you can read more about her ideas about sex in Tiefer, L. (2004). *Sex is not a natural act*. Boulder, CO: Westview Press.

22 Langdridge, D., & Barker, M. (Eds.) (2007). *Safe, sane and consensual: Contemporary perspectives on sadomasochism*. Basingstoke: Palgrave Macmillan.

23 Rubin, op cit, p. 283.

24 Denman, C. (2004). *Sexuality: A biopsychosocial approach*. London: Palgrave.

25 Whether it is most appropriately in the realm of psychiatry or of criminal law is up for debate.

26 Friday, N. (1980). *Men in Love*. New York, NY: Dell; Friday, N. (1991). *Women on top*. New York, NY: Simon and Schuster.

27 For suggestions about role-play versions of such fantasies, see Easton, D., & Hardy, J. W. (2004). *Radical ecstasy: SM journeys to transcendence*. California, CA: Greenary Press Ltd.

28 MacNeil, S., & Byers, E. S. (2005). Dyadic assessment of sexual self-disclosure and sexual satisfaction in heterosexual dating couples. *Journal of Social and Personal Relationships, 22*, 169–181.

29 Renaud, C., & Byers, E. S. (1999). Exploring the frequency, diversity and content of university students' positive and negative sexual cognitions. *Canadian Journal of Human Sexuality, 8*(1), 17–30.

30 10–15 per cent of people report being into kink: Janus, S. S., & Janus, C. L. (1994). *The Janus report on sexual behavior*. New York, NY: John Wiley & Sons, Inc.

31 E.g. O'Sullivan, L. F., & Allgeier, E. R. (1998). Feigning sexual desire: Consenting to unwanted sexual activity in heterosexual dating relationships. *The Journal of Sex Research, 35*(3), 234–243.

32 From http://www.hugoschwyzer.net/2008/06/15/the-opposite-of-rape-is-not-consent-the-opposite-of-rape-is-enthusiasm-a-revised-and-expanded-post.

33 Gathorne-Hardy, J. (2004). *Kinsey: Sex the measure of all things*. Indiana, IN: Indiana University Press.

34 Available from www.humansexmap.com at the time of writing.

35 Barker, M., Richards, C., Jones, R., Bowes-Catton, H., & Plowman, T. (2012). *The Bisexuality Report: Bisexual inclusion in LGBT equality and diversity*. Milton Keynes: The Open University, Centre for Citizenship, Identity and Governance.

36 Barker, M. (2002). Slashing the Slayer: A thematic analysis of homoerotic Buffy fan fiction. Presentation to the first annual conference on readings around Buffy the Vampire Slayer, Blood, Text and Fears, University of East Anglia, Norwich, 19–20 October 2002. Available from http://oro.open.ac.uk/23340 at the time of writing.

37 www.asexuality.org.

38 For examples, see Orbach, S. (1999). *The impossibility of sex*. London: Allen Lane.

39 Hall, M. (2001). Not tonight dear, I'm deconstructing a headache: Confessions of a lesbian sex therapist. In E. Kaschak, & L. Tiefer (Eds.), *A new view of women's sexual problems* (pp. 161–172). New York: Haworth.

40 Barker, M. (2011). Existential sex therapy. *Sexual and Relationship Therapy*, *26*(1), 33–47, 40.
41 Diamond, L. (2009). *Sexual fluidity*. Cambridge, MA: Harvard University Press.
42 See www.cosrt.org.uk for more detailed advice.
43 A version of this can be found at the scarleteen website at www.scarleteen.com.

5 Rewriting the rules of gender

1 This is adapted slightly from the diagrams on pp. 148 and 149 of Gauntlett, D. (2008). *Media, gender and identity: An introduction*. London: Routledge.
2 This advert could be viewed at www.youtube.com/watch?v=hq9stciOBTM at the time of writing.
3 Fein, E., & Schneider, S. (2000). *The complete book of the rules*. London: Thorsons.
4 Strauss, N. (2005) *The game*. New York, NY: Canongate.
5 From www.fhm.com/upgrade/sex-advice/relationships-how-honeys-think-78578.
6 From www.cosmopolitan.com/sex-love/dating-advice/first-time-thoughts?click=cos_ new.
7 For a review of the evidence against popular psychology depictions of gender differences in relationships, see Conley, T. D., Moors, A. C., Matsick, J. L., Ziegler, A., & Valentine, B. A. (2011). Women, men, and the bedroom: Methodological and conceptual insights that narrow, reframe, and eliminate gender differences in sexuality. *Current Directions in Psychological Science*, *20*, 296–300.
8 de Beauvoir, S. (1949/1997). *The second sex*. H. M. Parshley (Trans.). New York, NY: Vintage.
9 See http://en.wikipedia.org/wiki/Dykes_to_Watch_Out_For#Bechdel_test.
10 McRobbie, A. (2009). *The aftermath of feminism: Gender, culture and social change* (p. 67). London: Sage.
11 Johnstone, L. (2000). *Users and abusers of psychiatry*. London: Routledge.
12 Gough, B., & Edwards, G. (1998). The beer talking: four lads, a carry out and the reproduction of masculinities. *The Sociological Review*, *46*(3), 409–435.
13 Harrower, J. (1998). *Applying psychology to crime*. London: Hodder and Stoughton.
14 Mind (2007). Men's mental health. Accessed from http://www.mind.org.uk/help/ people_groups_and_communities/mens_mental_health on 14 November 2011.
15 Recent bromance movies at the time of writing include *Knocked Up*; *Superbad*; *I Love You, Man*; and *Hot Tub Time Machine*.
16 Strauss, op cit p.249.
17 Agnew, C. R., & Gephart, J. M. (2000). Testing The Rules of commitment enhancement: Separating fact from fiction. *Representative Research in Social Psychology*, *24*, 41–47.
18 Davidson, C. V., & Abramowitz, S. I. (2010). Sex bias in clinical judgment: Later empirical returns. *Psychology of Women Quarterly*, *34*(3), 377–395.
19 Hegarty, P., Lemieux, A., & McQueen, G. (2010). Graphing the order of the sexes: Constructing, recalling, interpreting, and putting the self in gender difference graphs. *Journal of Personality and Social Psychology*, *98*(3), 375–391.
20 Available from www.amptoons.com/blog/the-male-privilege-checklist at the time of writing.
21 Bem, S. L. (1975). Sex-role adaptability: One consequence of psychological androgyny. *Journal of Personality and Social Psychology*, *31*, 634–643.
22 Richards, C., & Barker, M. (Eds.) (forthcoming, 2012). *Sexuality and gender for counsellors, psychologists and health professionals: A practical guide*. London: Sage.
23 Eugenides, J. (2003). *Middlesex*. London: Bloomsbury.
24 Fausto-Sterling, A. (1999). *Sexing the body* (p. 31). New York, NY: Basic Books.

25 For more on all aspects of the neuroscience of gender, see Fine, C. (2010). *Delusions of gender: The real science behind sex differences*. London: Icon Books.
26 Wetherell, M., & Edley, N. (1999). Negotiating hegemonic masculinity: Imagery positions and psycho-discursive practices. *Feminism and Psychology, 9*(3), 335–356.
27 Day, K., Gough, B., & McFadden, M. (2003). Women who drink and fight: A discourse analysis of working-class women's talk. *Feminism and Psychology, 13*(2), 141–158.
28 Anderson, E. (2009). *Inclusive masculinity*. London: Routledge.
29 Vincent, N. (2006). *Self-made man*. London: Atlantic Books.
30 The original 'baby X' study was reported in Seavey, C. A., Katz, P. A., & Rosenberg Zalk, S. (1975). Baby X: the effect of gender labels on adult responses to infants. *Sex Roles, 1*(2), 103–109. It has been replicated several times since then.
31 See Wood, G. (2005). *Sex, lies and stereotypes*. London: New Holland Publishers; Cameron, D. (2007). *The myth of mars and venus*. Oxford: Oxford University Press.
32 Rivers, I. (2001). The bullying of sexual minorities at school: Its nature and long-term correlates. *Educational and Child Psychology, 18*(1), 33–46.
33 Wilchins, R. A. (1997). *Read my lips: Sexual subversion and the end of gender*. Ann Arbor, MI: Firebrand Books.
34 Interestingly, even this traditional pink and blue distinction has not always been attached to gender as it is currently. In the early 20 century, boys wore pink, advertised as 'a more decided colour', and girls wore blue, advertised as 'delicate and dainty': Goldacre, B. (2007). Bad Science: Pink, pink, pink, pink. Pink moan. *The Guardian*, 25 August 2007. Accessed from http://www.badscience.net/?p=518 on 2 January 2009.
35 For more activities for exploring your gender, see Bornstein, K. (1997). *My gender workbook*. New York, NY: Routledge.

6 Rewriting the rules of monogamy

1 See Van Deurzen-Smith, E. (1997). *Everyday mysteries: Existential dimensions of psychotherapy*. London: Routledge.
2 Bauman, Z. (2003). *Liquid love: On the frailty of human bonds* (p. viii). Cambridge: Polity Press.
3 For more on this tension, and how it can be addressed, see Perel, E. (2007). *Mating in captivity: sex, lies and domestic bliss*. London: Hodder & Stoughton.
4 Weatherall, A. (2002). *Gender, language and discourse*. London: Routledge.
5 Barash, D. P., & Lipton, J. E. (2001). *The myth of monogamy: Fidelity and infidelity in animals and people*. New York: W. H. Freeman & Co.
6 Rubin, R. H. (2001). Alternative family lifestyles revisited, or, whatever happened to swingers, group marriages and communes? *Journal of Family Issues, 7*(6), 711.
7 Goodwin, R. (1999). *Personal relationships across cultures*. London: Routledge.
8 Vangelisti, A. L., & Gerstenberger, M. (2004). Communication and marital infidelity. In J. Duncombe, K. Harrison, G. Allan, & D. Marsden (Eds.), *The state of affairs: Explorations in infidelity and commitment* (pp. 59–78). New Jersey: Lawrence Erlbaum Associates.
9 Warren, J. T., Harvey, S. M., & Agnew, C. R. (2011). One love: Explicit monogamy agreements among heterosexual young adult couples at increased risk of sexually transmitted infections. *Journal of Sex Research, 48*(1), 1–8.
10 Frank, K., & DeLamater, J. (2010). Deconstructing monogamy: Boundaries, identities, and fluidities across relationships. In M. Barker & D. Langdridge (Eds.), *Understanding non-monogamies* (pp. 9–22). New York: Routledge.
11 Nelson, T. (2010). *The New Monogamy*. Accessed from www.psychotherapynetworker.org/magazine/currentissue/926–the-new-monogamy on 30 March 2011.

12 Blumstein, P., & Schwartz, P. (1983). *American couples: Money–work–sex.* New York: William Morrow & Co.

13 Bonello, K. (2009). Gay monogamy and extra-dyadic sex: a critical review of the theoretical and empirical literature. *Counselling Psychology Review*, *24*(3) & (4), 51–65.

14 Barker, M., & Langdridge, D. (2010). Whatever happened to non-monogamies? Critical reflections on recent research and theory. *Sexualities*, *1*(6), *748–772.*

15 Heldman, C., & Wade, L. (2010). Hook-up culture: Setting a new research agenda. *Sexuality Research and Social Policy*, *7*(4), 323.

16 Sheff, E. (2010). Strategies in polyamorous parenting. In M. Barker & D. Langdridge (Eds.), *Understanding non-monogamies* (pp. 169–181). New York: Routledge.

17 Adam, B. D. (2006). Relationship innovation in male couples. *Sexualities*, *9*(1), 5–26; McDonald, D. (2010). Swinging: pushing the boundaries of non-monogamy? In M. Barker & D. Langdridge (Eds.), *Understanding non-monogamies* (pp. 70–81). New York: Routledge.

18 Wosick-Correa, K. (2010). Agreements, rules, and agentic fidelity in polyamorous relationships. *Psychology & Sexuality*, *1*(1)*,* 44–61.

19 Finn, M. (2010). Conditions of freedom in practices of non-monogamous commitment. In M. Barker & D. Langdridge (Eds.), *Understanding non-monogamies* (pp. 225–236). New York: Routledge.

20 Two books which give more practical advice about the kinds of agreements people put in place in relation to open non-monogamy are Easton, D., & Hardy, J. W. (2009). *The ethical slut: A practical guide to polyamory, open relationships and other adventures.* Berkeley, CA: Celestial Arts; and Taormino, T. (2008). *Opening up: A guide to creating and sustaining open relationships.* San Francisco: Cleis Press, Inc.

21 Heckert, J. (2010). Love without borders? Intimacy, identity and the state of compulsory monogamy. In M. Barker & D. Langdridge (Eds.), *Understanding non-monogamies* (pp. 255–266). New York: Routledge.

22 Wilkinson, E. (2010). What's queer about non-monogamy now? In M. Barker & D. Langdridge (Eds.), *Understanding non-monogamies* (pp. 243–254, 253). New York: Routledge.

23 Richards, C. (2010). Trans and non-monogamy. In M. Barker & D. Langdridge (Eds.), *Understanding non-monogamies* (pp. 121–133). New York: Routledge.

24 Burr, V., & Butt, T. (1992). *Invitation to personal construct psychology.* London: Whurr Publishers Ltd.

25 A notable exception to this is Rowe, D. (2001). *Friends and enemies: Our need to love and hate.* London: HarperCollins.

26 *About a Boy* and *I Love You, Man* are refreshing exceptions to this rule.

7 Rewriting the rules of conflict

1 Adapted from a version first published in Barker, M. (2010). Self-care and relationship conflict. *Sexual and Relationship Therapy*, *25*(1), 37–47.

2 For more on dynamics between people in couples and groups, see Vossler, A. (2010). Systemic approaches. In Barker, M., Vossler, A., & Langdridge, D. (Eds.) (2010). *Understanding counselling and psychotherapy.* London: Sage.

3 For further information on this topic see www.hiddenhurt.co.uk or www.thehotline.org.

4 Tavris, C., & Aronson, E. (2008). *Mistakes were made (but not by me).* London: Pinter & Martin.

5 Sartre, J-P. (1943/2005). *Being and nothingness.* H. E. Barnes (trans.). London: Verso.

6 Sartre, J-P. (19471989). *No exit.* S. Gilbert (trans.). New York: Vintage Books.

7 Pratchett, T. (1998). *Carpe jugulum* (p. 210). London: Doubleday.

8   Batchelor, S. (1997). *Buddhism without beliefs* (p. 68). London: Bloomsbury.
9   Leather, P., Lawrence, C., Barnard, C., & Cox, T. (1998). *Work-related violence: Assessment and intervention*. London: Routledge.
10 This process of interpretation and escalation is beautifully captured in Roger McGough's poem *You and I*, available if you search for it online, and from Henri, A., McGough R., & Patten, B. (1983). *After the Mersey Sound . . . New Volume*. London: Penguin.
11 Gergen, K. J. (1999). *An invitation to social constructionism*. London: Sage.
12 In Milne, A. A. (1926/1977). *Winnie-the-Pooh*. London: Methuen. See www.rewriting-the-rules.wordpress.com/2012/01/06/heffalumps-and-conflicts.
13 Chödrön, P. (1994). *Start where you are: How to accept yourself and others*. London: HarperCollins; Chödrön, P. (2001). *The places that scare you: A guide to fearlessness*. London: HarperCollins.
14 de Beauvoir, S. (1948/1976). *The ethics of ambiguity*. Bernard Frechtman (trans.). New York, NY: Citadel Press.
15 These ideas come from de Beauvoir's writing and from the philosopher Martin Buber: Buber, M. (1937/2004). *I and thou*. R. Gregor-Smith (trans.). London: Routledge.
16 See BBC2 (2001). *Five steps to tyranny*. Directed by E. McIntyre. Available, at the time of writing, from http://www.youtube.com/watch?v=68GzOJQ8NMw.
17 Strasser, F., & Randolph, P. (2004). *Mediation: A psychological insight into conflict resolution*. London: Continuum.
18 Rosenberg, M. B. (2003). *Nonviolent communication: A language of life*. Encinitas, CA: PuddleDancer Press.
19 Easton, D., & Hardy, J. W. (2009). *The ethical slut: A practical guide to polyamory, open relationships and other adventures*. Berkeley, CA: Celestial Arts.
20 Crowe, M., & Ridley, J. (2000). *Therapy with couples: A behavioural-systems approach to couple relationship and sexual problems*. Oxford: Blackwell.

8   Rewriting the rules of break-up

1   Edwards, D., & Potter, J. (1992). *Discursive psychology*. London: Sage.
2   Loftus, E. F., & Ketchum, K. (1994). *The myth of repressed memory*. New York: St. Martin's Press.
3   Tavris, C., & Aronson, E. (2008). *Mistakes were made (but not by me)*. London: Pinter & Martin.
4   Yalom, I. D. (2001). *The gift of therapy* (pp. 176–177). London: Piatkus.
5   Epstein, M. (1995). *Thoughts without a thinker* (pp. 80–81). New York, NY: Perseus Books.

9   Rewriting the rules of commitment

1   Copping, J. (2009). Recession sees marriage rate rise. Accessed from http://www.telegraph.co.uk/finance/recession/4409405/Recession-sees-marriage-rate-rise.html on 7 November 2011.
2   Heaphy, B., Smart, C., & Einarsdottir, A. (forthcoming, 2012). *Same sex marriages: New generations*. Basingstoke: Palgrave.
3   Barker, M., & Langdridge, D. (Eds.) (2010). *Understanding non-monogamies*. New York: Routledge.
4   For this I reviewed the popular marriage and civil partnership vows which are available online. The wikipedia page on this topic presents a pretty good overview: http://en.wikipedia.org/wiki/Marriage_vows. It should be noted that this refers to the colonising cultures of the US, Canada, Australia, and New Zealand, rather than to indigenous cultures who may well have quite different commitments.

5 If you are interested in the answer to this question, Kassia Wosick-Correa found that a third of her polyamorous participants had been together over 10 years. 10–20 percent had been together for 5–9 years, and similar proportions for 3–5 years, 1–3 years, and under a year. Thus, it certainly seems that openly non-monogamous relationships can last just as long as monogamous ones. However, the point here is to question why it is longevity of relationships that we define as the single marker of whether they are successful or not. Wosick-Correa, K. (2010). Agreements, rules, and agentic fidelity in polyamorous relationships. *Psychology & Sexuality*, *1*(1), 44–61.
6 Heckert, J. (2010). Listening, caring, becoming: Anarchism as an ethics of direct relationships. In B. Franks, & M. Wilson (Eds.), *Anarchism and moral philosophy*. Basingstoke: Palgrave.
7 Hanh, T. N. (1988). *Peace is every step*. Berkeley, CA: Parallax Press.
8 There is more about the practice of remaining present in Barker, M. (forthcoming 2013). *Mindful counselling and psychotherapy: Practising mindfully across approaches and issues*. London: Sage.
9 Batchelor, S. (1997). *Buddhism without beliefs* (pp. 84–86). London: Bloomsbury.
10 For more on how this might be achieved, see Perel, E. (2007). *Mating in captivity: Sex, lies and domestic bliss*. London: Hodder & Stoughton.
11 For an accessible introduction to this, see de Board, R. (1997). *Counselling for toads*. London: Routledge.
12 Samuels, A. (2001). *Politics on the couch: Citizenship and the internal life*. London: Karnac.

10 Rewriting your rules

1 Pratchett, T. (2009). *Unseen academicals* (p. 218). London: Doubleday.
2 See Batchelor, M. (2001). *Meditation for life*. London: Frances Lincoln.
3 Hanh, T. N. (1991). *The miracle of mindfulness*. London: Random House.
4 Adams, K. (1990). *Journal to the self*. New York, NY: Grand Central Publishing.
5 Kline, N. (1999). *Time to think*. London: Ward Lock.
6 Cooper, M., & McLeod, J. (2010). *Pluralistic counselling and psychotherapy*. London: Sage.
7 Chödrön, P. (2001). *The wisdom of no escape: How to love yourself and your world*. London: HarperCollins.
8 Gaitskill, M. (1994). On not being a victim. *Harper's*, March 1994, 35–44.
9 Burr, V., & Butt, T. (1992). *Invitation to personal construct psychology* (p. 30). London: Whurr Publishers Ltd.

Index